KNOWLEDGE MANAGEMENT
IN
LIBRARIES

KNOWLEDGE MANAGEMENT
IN
LIBRARIES

Piyush Kanti Mahapatra
Bhubaneswar Chakrabarti

Ess Ess Publications

4837/24, Ansari Road, Darya Ganj,
New Delhi-110002
✆ : 3260807, 3201533
Fax : 3274173
E-mail: essess@del3.vsnl.net.in
url:http://www.essessbooks.com

First Published 2002

ISBN : 81-7000-331-8

Price : Rs. 750/-

Published by:
Ess Ess Publications
4837/24, Ansari Road, Darya Ganj,
New Delhi - 110 002
Phone : 3260807
Fax : 3274173
E-mail : essess@del3.vsnl.net.in
url:http://www.essessbooks.com

Laser Typesetting:
Mukesh Graphics
L-2/8, Mangolepuri, New Delhi
Ph.:7924405

Printed at :
Print Line

Contents

Preface

The organisation of knowledge has a wide international perspective. The use of networks for online information retrieval, access to library catalogues and document delivery means that systems developed in a library are increasingly being accessed can be stored, in print or in a computer, independently of human being. Knowledge refers to a subsequent stage, in which information is absorbed and assimilated by new uses.

How is your home organised ? Is it a single space, or does it consist of various rooms or areas, each differentiated by particular contents ? As those contents are in complete disarray, or are they arranged systematically ? These activities illustrate the widespread, largely unconscious classification of objects in our surroundings for practical convenience.

The organisation of knowledge is concerned with establishing systems for organising documents and infromation so that they can be retrieved by the user as and when required. A cataloguer is a facilitator of the communication process. The neophyte cataloguer and classifier should be acquainted with the essential concepts underlying all cataloguing and classification. This book is written for anyone concerned with the organisation of knowledge, whether in traditional libraries or in any of the modern forms of information service.

To keep text as clear as possible, bibliography has been organised in one sequence at the end of the volume.

Our very first obligation is to Mrs. Sheel Sethi of Ess Ess Publication, who has so much confidence in us and such eagerness to see the continuation of Library and Information Science Series. We are also thankful to Mr Pulak Pattanayak of American Information Resource Centre, Calcutta for his sincere help and cooperation.

Authors

1

INTRODUCTION

There is difficulty in defining information. But information workers commonly draw a distinction between information and knowledge. The exact nature of the difference is open to discussion, but most of us would accept a definition of information that considered it as data ordered in a meaningful fashion. If it is to be meaningful, then there must have been human intervention of some sort in its creation. But the information, so created, can be stored, in print or in a computer, independently of human beings. Knowledge refers to a subsequent stage, in which the information is absorbed and understood by new users. Information became popular soon after the invention of printing in the fifteenth century, when the natural thing to do was to press a Latin tour into service to convey a new idea. The base of the term comes from formatio, and forma, both of which give the idea of shaping something or of forming a pattern. So much for classical etymology. According to Notbert Wiener, the founder of cybernetics " Information is the name for the content of the outer world when we adjust to it and make our adjustment felt upon it. To live effectively is to live with information."

Claude Shannon defines information as that which adds to a representation ... He suggests that we have received information when what we know has changed. Information is that which logically justifies alternation of, or reinforcement of a representation or state of affairs. Representations may be explicit as in a map or proposition or they may be implicit as in the recipient X state of goal-directed activity. The ebb and flow between information and knowledge is tackled the various members of the information profession. All *information has some kind of originator.*

For information in the book-form, this is the author. The material is made available to a wider audience by the publisher, a component in the information chain. Copies of the published book can be stored in a library for subsequent use. If all goes well, the final member of the information chain - the reader will obtain knowledge of some sort from the book. Thus we see that the information chain has put emphasis on the role of the originator and the *final viewer, or reader* as being central to the transmission of knowledge. The steps between seem to be concerned rather with information. Hence, it is customary to speak of publishers, librarians and other intermediaries as information - *handlers rather than* knowledge - handlers. A publisher does not need to understand physics in order to produce a physics book; nor does librarian need to know physics in order to make the book accessible to readers. However, all intermediaries do provide an input of knowledge : this special knowledge of how to handle information efficiently and effectively.

The organisation of knowledge is a process that has been recognised for thousands of years. With the expansion of knowledge the need to organise it becomes all the more necessary and pressing. A vast number of different means of organising knowledge have been devised and exploited since the earliest times. The objective of the organisation of knowledge is to permit that knowledge to be found again on a later occasion. It ensures the successful subsequent retrieval.

DOCUMENTS

Documents are physical artifacts in which information has been stored for use beyond the immediate moment. Documents contain both factual and non-factual information. They carry and convey the wisdom of sages and scholars, experiences of the professionals in diverse fields, invention and discoveries of scientists and technologists, speculatic thoughts of philosophers and imaginations of artists. Documents are memories of mankind. They are in effect, external memories. The creators of documents have recorded ideas, feelings, images, and concepts in order to share them with others. Traditionally libraries were large collections of books. Modern libraries have a wide variety of non-book materials. The inclusion of such materials in library collections help librarians to serve people in as many ways as possible. Today's multi-media libraries offer countless advantages. People interested in music can learn much by reading books in libraries. They can also listen to musical recording which help a great deal in their understanding and appreciation.

In organising collections in the library we need to keep extensive collections of documents in the form of records or files which may contain letters, invoices, leaflets, personnel documents and a host of other documents. Three fields having separate lines of development are moving closer together. We can profitably make use of many of the tools of the organisation of knowledge. It is worth to note the following fields :

1. Catalogues and bibliographies - used by librarians to list the documents in a collection or on a specified subject.
2. Indexing and abstracting services - used by information scientists to identify documents that meet requests in a specific subject.
3. Records management systems - the responsibility of records managers and architects to maintain an orderly collection of records.

The three fields as noted above share some common goals, but they have followed different development paths.

SEARCHING AND BROWSING

The objective of the organisation of Knowledge is subsequent retrieval. It is worth to note that different users would like to retrieve a document or unit of information for different reasons and thus may approach the retrieval process in different ways. A fundamental difference in searching strategy is between known item searching browsing.

Known-item searching is done by users when they know what they are looking for and usually possess certain characteristic feature of the information or clue by which they can identify the item such as author, title, colour.

Proving is done when the user has a less precise view of the information or documents that may be available. Here he may not be sure whether his requirements can be met or precisely how they can be met. Browsing may be general or purposive. When the user has a fairly specific requirement, purposive browsing occurs.

TOOLS FOR THE ORGANISATION OF KNOWLEDGE

In order to organise knowledge, librarians have created a variety of tools. Here we introduce some definitions of common terms concerned with the tools for the organisation of knowledge.

Bibliographies - Bibliographies basically are lists of information packages. *Bibliographies are essential to scholars* and to those involved professionally with books and other sources of information and are also useful sources of information for all serious readers. They bring together lists of sources based on subject matter, on authors, by time periods, and the like. Some bibliographies include annotations, that is brief notes indicating the subject matter or commenting on the usefulness of the information.

Bibliographies can be attached to a scholarly work and consist of the information packages that were consulted by the author of the work. Each *information package represented* has a short description (not to be confused with annotations). A typical description includes author, title, edition, publisher, place, and data of publication for a book. Bibliographies may be printed or computer databases.

Each bibliography has a particular focus or arrangement. The most common ones are :

Subject - bibliographies gathering together publications or other information packages that are all about a particular subject.

Author - bibliographies of all or some of the works of a particular author and sometimes including sources about the author.

Language - bibliographies of textual entities in which the text is a certain language.

Time period - bibliographies listing all works that came to light in a particular period.

Locate - bibliographies listing all information packages created in a particular location.

Publisher - bibliographies listing all of the products of a particular publisher.

Form - bibliographies listing information packages that appear in a certain form, format, or genre.

Catalogues - Catalogues provide access to individual items within collections of information packages (for example, physical entities such as books, video cassettes, and CDs in a library; artists, works in an art museum; web pages on the Internet; etc.). Each information package is represented by a description of the package that is somewhat longer than a bibliography description. The descriptions are assigned one or more access points. An access point is constructed in a certain order (e.g. surname followed by foremane or forenames) and it is maintained under authority control. Authority control is the process of pulling together into a single authority record all the forms of name that apply to a single name; all the variant titles that apply to a single work; and all the synonyms, related terms, broader terms, and narrower terms that apply to a particular subject heading.

Indexes - Indexes provide access to the analysed contents of "bibliographic entities". Although back-of-the-book indexes also provide access to analysed contents of one work, they are not retrieval tools in the sense defined here; they are prepared at the time of publication, not later in an effort to provide bibliographic control.

They do, however, aid with retrieval of the information found in the text at hand.

Indexes can be found in print form or in machine readable form - either CD-ROM or online. Some print versions are arranged in alphabetical dictionary fashion, with entries for authors, titles and subjects. Both CD-ROM and online indexes have interfaces that dictate how these will be searched and how display will appear. As with OPACs there is no standardization from index to index. Although OPACs at least often have the standardization that comes from using the Anglo-American Cataloguing Rules, 2nd ed. (AACR2), there is no standard commonly used by the various indexes.

A computer-held databases - A database is a set of records that are all constructed in the same way and connected by relationship links. In relational databases the records may be divided into parts with the parts linked to each other to form individual records, but with the parts also having other links such as author-to-author or subject-to-subject.

File - a file is a collection of letters or documents dealing with one organization, person, area or subject. Arrangement and display have evolved in the online world from shelving and fitting in the paper world.

FUNCTIONS OF TOOLS

Charles Ammi Cutter defined the purposes of a catalogue. These purposes apply to any tool for the organization of knowledge. Cutter defined the range of functions of a catalogue thus :

1. To enable person to find a document of which the author; or the title or the subject is known.
2. To show what the library has by a given author on a given subject (and related subjects) in a given kind (or form) of literature.
3. To help in the choice of a document as to its edition (bibliographically) as to its character (literary or topical).

Of course, not all catalogues or other tools for the organisation of knowledge can fulfil all the aforesaid functions.

The first function concerns with the identification and location of documents from the various pieces of information that a user might bring to the catalogue or index.

The second function concentrates on keeping a record of the library stock as well as helping library users to find documents of whose existence they are unaware. The function is attained by the description in an index catalogue or database. By supplying details in the form of the title, edition, publisher and pagination, the description can help the user decide how relevant and helpful to document by distinguishing it from other and by pointing its nature - subject or quality.

2

KNOWLEDGE : NATURE AND CHARACTERISTICS

The word "Knowledge" can mean three things by our use. First, we use it to refer to a state of knowing, by which we also mean to be acquainted or to be aware of, to recognise or approached facts, methods, principles and so on. The common usage corresponds to what is often referred to as "Know about". Second, we use the word " Knowledge" to refer to "the capacity for action", an understanding of facts, methods, in the course of making things happen. This corresponds to "Know how." Third, we use the term "Knowledge" to refer, to codified, captured and accumulated facts, methods, principles, techniques and so on. When we use the term this way, we are referring to a body of knowledge that has been articulated and captured in the form of books, papers, manuals, computer code and so on. Data and information fit within the third category above, that is, the notion of a body of knowledge that exists apart from people. Knowledge is broader, deeper and richer than data or information.

There are two basic kinds of knowledge : 1. The kind that is reflected in a person's internal state as well as that same person's capacity for action and 2. The kind that has been articulated and frequently recorded. This brings us to the concepts of explicit, implicit and tacit knowledge.

EXPLICIT KNOWLEDGE

Explicit Knowledge is knowledge that has been articulated and more often than not, captured in the form of texts, tables, diagrams, and so on. An example of explicit knowledge with which we are familiar is the formula for finding the area of a rectangle (that is, length times width)

IMPLICIT KNOWLEDGE

Knowledge that can be articulated but hasn't is implicit knowledge. Its existence is implied by or inferred from observable behaviour or performance. This is the kind of knowledge that can often be teased out of a competent performer by a task analyst, knowledge engineer or other person skilled in identifying the kind of knowledge that can be articulated but hasn't.

TACIT KNOWLEDGE

Tacit knowledge is knowledge that cannot be articulated. Although disagreement about the definition of knowledge persists, there is much greater agreement about the type or form of knowledge that yields the greatest potential business value. Tacit knowledge is strongly implicated in organizational innovation. People develop and use tacit knowledge before they are able to formalize or codify it.

The explicit, implicit, tacit categories of knowledge are not the only ones in use. Cognitive psychologists sort knowledge into two categories : declarative and procedural. Some add 'strategic' as a third category.

Declarative knowledge has much in common with explicit knowledge in that declarative knowledge consists of descriptions of facts and things or of methods and procedures. For practical purposes, declarative knowledge and explicit knowledge may be treated as synonyms. This is because all declarative knowledge is explicit knowledge, that is, it is knowledge that can be and has been articulated.

One view of procedural knowledge is that it is knowledge that manifests itself in the doing of something. As such it is reflected in motor or manual skills and in cognitive or mental skills. We think, we reason, we decide, we play the viotew, we ride bicycles, yet we cannot reduce to mere words that which we obviously know or know how to do. Attempts to do so are often recognised as title more than after - the - fact rationalizations.

Another view of procedural knowledge is that it is knowledge about how to do something. This view of procedural knowledge accepts a description of the steps of a task or procedure as procedural knowledge. The obvious shortcoming of this view is that it is no different from declarative knowledge except that tasks or methods are being described instead of facts or things.

Strategic knowledge is a tour used by some to what might be termed know-when and know-why. We can separate our strategic knowledge only in the describing, not the doing. Consequently, strategic knowledge is probably best thought of as a subset of declarative knowledge.

It is important to recognize that the acquisition of declarative and procedural knowledge occurs in different ways. Although tacit knowledge cannot be reduced entirely to words, it is quite possible to acquire tacit knowledge through means other than verbal descriptions. If "knowledge management" is to have any meaning and any credence at all, we must say what we mean by knowledge - in all its variations.

KNOWLEDGE TRANSFER AND KNOWLEDGE CREATION

I. Nonaka addresses in his article "The Knowledge Creating Company" (published in *Harvard Business Revised*, November - December, 1991, pp 96-104) some important issues of knowledge transfer. He cites four such transfers or creations:

1. **Tacit to tacit** : Acquiring someone else's tacit G through observation, imitation and practice. Nonaka uses an example of a product developer who apprentices herself to a hotel chief famous for the quality of his bread. She learns how to make bread his way, including an unusual kneading technique.

2. **Explicit to explicit :** Combining discrete pieces of explicit knowledge to form new explicit knowledge. For example, compiling data and preparing a report that analyses and synthesises these data. The report constitutes new explicit knowledge.
3. **Tacit to explicit :** Nonaka cites here the product developer's subsequent conversion of her acquired tacit knowledge into specifications for a bread-making machine.
4. **Explicit to tacit :** Internalizing explicit knowledge. Here Nonaka indicates that the product development team acquired new tacit knowledge; specifically, they came to understand in an intuitive way, that products like the home bread-making machine can provide quality, that is, they can produce bread as good as that made by a professional baker.

On our part, we shall focus on three aspects of knowledge capture, sharing and transfer :

1. The process of capturing explicit knowledge, that is, of making implicit knowledge explicit.
2. The development of procedural knowledge (in the sense that the knowing is in the doing)
3. The transfer of tacit knowledge from one person to another without resorting to verbalization.

In all three cases, we will be discussing about the not simply learning from experience.

MAKING IMPLICIT KNOWLEDGE EXPLICIT

This is a process of articulation, of making implicit knowledge explicit. Sometimes we are able to do this on our own and sometimes it requires the assistance of someone like a performance analyst or a knowledge engineer.

DEVELOPING PROCEDURAL KNOWLEDGE

Here it is the skill development, specifically, the acquisition of explicit, declarative knowledge as the basis of or skill development.

TRANSFERRING TACIT KNOWLEDGE

Tacit knowledge cannot be articulated but it can be communicated or transferred.

In conclusion we can say that knowledge management seeks to manage knowledge. Of course knowledge itself is a very slippery concept with many different variations and definitions. The nature of knowledge and what it means to know something are epistemological questions that have perplexed philosophers for centuries and no resolution looms on the horizon.

Although disagreement about the definition of knowledge persist, there is much greater agreement about the type or form of knowledge that yields the greatest business value. Thus, although many of the early forays into knowledge management centered on the use of information technology to broaden access to documents and databases, there is by now widespread agreement that much of the highest-value knowledge within organization is uncodified. Quite simply, lots of valuable knowledge falls through the cracks within organisations, never finding its way into databases, process diagrams or corporate libraries. As a consequence, much of what the institution "knows" remains unknown or inaccessible to those who need it. Such knowledge is present within the institution, but it remains hidden, unspoken, tacit. This hidden or tacit knowledge takes one of two forms : 1. Knowledge embodied in people and social networks, 2. Knowledge embedded in the processes and products that people create.

People know more than they can say. That is, they are guided by knowledge that they do not know they have or that they find difficult to articulate. The form of embodied knowledge - the knowledge that resides in groups, terms or communities - is a key source of under - leveraged know - how in most organisations.

Beyond the knowledge that resides in people, we need to consider knowledge that resides in the things that people have produced. Knowledge may be embedded in product or product prototypes, in processes, as well as in documents. Processes are also sources of embedded knowledge and can serve as boundary objects in knowledge transfer.

Knowledge has a special meaning for the philosopher. Indeed, the study of the nature and validity of knowledge is a special field of philosophy called epistemology. In this contentions field of intellectual activity philosophers debate such difficult questions as : what can we know ? What is certainty ? What are the conditions of valid knowledge ? Some frequently quoted sentences define knowledge as "familiarity gained by actual experience, practical skill and acquaintance", or "intellectual experience with perception of truth" or merely "acquaintance with fact,". Thus knowledge can be used as synonym to 'acquaintance', 'familiarity', 'fact' or simply "to know".

Something becomes knowledge when it is known to someone. It therefore, follows that knowledge concerns two entities : Knowee and Knower. The knowee is something that is known. The knower is someone who knows. The knowee is the object and the knower is the subject. When a contact is made between the two knowledge emerges. 'Knowledge' is a seminal word and implies a deeper meaning. Many disciplines endeavour to study knowledge from different points of views.

DIFFERING VIEWS

The edifice of interrelated themes and subthemes that compose Britannica 3 is supported by ten pillars :

1. Matter and energy
2. The earth
3. Life on earth
4. Human life
5. Human society
7. Technology
8. Religion
9. History of mankind
10. The branches of knowledge.

Mortimer Adler, the designer of the Propaedia or outline of knowledge is eager to indicate that themes 1 - 10 are not to be treated as though they were form of evolutionary order as some classification schemes have followed. The branches of knowledge are constructs or viewpoints by which one enquires into, or thinks about, or comes to have knowledge of the word in which one lives. The whole arrangement is to be perceived as circle - a circle in which no point is either beginning, a middle or an end. However, 'knowledge is a growing organism' and every new edition of Britannica will include new data, information and knowledge. All is change; Britannica 3 and other recorded thought of humanity seems to represent a word 'outside' us, a word with its own laws and systems.

Karl Popper justified a useful model to account for this ceaseless, change. Popper has put forward three distinct 'words' : 'word 1', is the word of maternal things; 'word 2' of our thinking, believing, feeling, imagining, willing, knowing, and 'word 3' is the results of the continuing interaction between word 1 and word 2. The first word is the word of physical reality, the second is the mental analogue of the first. It is an 'inner' world of images, sounds and unspoken thoughts. Word 3 is the word of ideas, art, science, language, ethics, institutions - the whole cultural heritage, in short - insofar as this is encoded and preserved in such word 1 as brains, books, machines, films, computers, pictures, records of any kind.

If knowledge is what somebody knows then, without a knower, knowledge is an absurdity. The knower, however, knowledgeable, is a contingent social exative related to, and influenced by other human beings - all knowledge of its very nature has a social and cultural basis looking backwards and forwards in time.

VIEWS OF LIBRARIANS AND BIBLIOGRAPHERS

Since the renaissance, there have been two main approaches which are worthy of note : those that are leased on philosophical scheme and those that aim at a practical arrangement of materials nose, tongue, and skin. Any object comes in contact with any of the organs, the concerned sense organ gets stimulated and knowledge is gained. The five senses are known as basic senses.

EPISTEMOLOGY

Epistemology studies theory of knowledge. The term 'epistemology' comes from two Greek words - *Episteme* meaning knowledge, and *Logos*, meaning theory or account. Epistemology and investigates the origin, nature, limitation are methods of acquiring knowledge and relation between knowledge and belief. Epistemology as described by Descartes and Lock is a body of knowledge about knowledge.

J.F, Ferrier used the term 'Epistemology' in 1854. for the first time. Ferrier denoted the term as theoretical and philosophical study of knowledge. Originally it was a branch of philosophy. It has now acquired the dimension of and has claimed the status of an independent subject. Descartes and Locke have described it as "a body of knowledge about knowledge" We can trace the seed of the philosophical aspect of knowledge in the Vedas and the Upanishads.

GROUPING THE DISCIPLINES

There are disciplines that share concepts and methods and those that do not; there are disciplines that help in making money and other that keep one poor. It depends n the purpose of grouping such disciplines. Textbooks on logic begin by informing the reader that logic was a format subject, not a maternal subject like geology. There is also the more familiar trilogy - Sciences, social sciences, humanities. Philip Phenix in 1966 distinguished subject disciplines by the kinds of meaning they yield. His 'realms of meaning' run thus :

1. **Symbolies** : those studies that make use of conventional expressive forms to objectify and communicate meaning.
2. **Empiries** : The science that deal with the physical word, and living things. They put importance matters of fact, not the modes of expression.

3. **Aesthetics :** include literature, music, the visual arts and the arts of movement.
4. **Synnoetics :** deal with personal knowledge, the direct awareness of oneself, other person and things.
5. **Ethics :** concerned with personal conduct based on free, deliberate decisions.
6. **Synoptics :** includes philosophy, religion and history these disciplines combine empirical, Aesthetics and synnoetic meanings into coherent wholes.

It is one viewpoint, and a plausible one - it is also illogical, in that he applies more than one principle of division : hence the overlap between symbolies and aesthetic. Aesthetics is a subjective tour; it includes empirics. Paul Hirst grouped disciplines according to the form of knowing. Neale H. Mucklow has the claim that disciplines may be analysed for overlapping concepts methods and central themes. Rudolph Carnap distinguished between formal and factual sciences. Factual sciences having empirical content include disciplines that deal with factual data, such as anthropology, physics, biology, history and geography. The formal sciences without any empirical content, are systems of thought. Thus the formal sciences are logic and mathematics which are based on the axial principles of relationship and member.

In fact mathematics and logic are the only pure sciences in the sense that they order structures. We label some subjects as 'academic', whilst withholding that designation from others. The term 'academic' can mean scholarly, abstract, theoretical, cold unpractical - or useless - depending on one's point of view. Subjects were academic in the truest sense of the term if they enhanced the human spirit by a rigorous enquiry into the causes of things, followed by a disinterested, but disciplined reflection. It was not productive knowledge. If we say that physics is an academic discipline, we are not likely to be challenged. If we accord the same designation to library science, we are surely to be challenged.

UNIVERSE OF KNOWLEDGE AND THE LIBRARY

Libraries owe a great deal to universe of knowledge for their existence. In ancient days, there was a tendency, as well as reason, to retain knowledge in memory (Smriti). Knowledge retained in memory was disseminated to a chosen few through listening (Shruti). In those days universe of knowledge was limited and small. Time came when the universe of knowledge developed to such a dimension as no longer it was possible to retain it in memory. As a result, alphabets were invented and the printing press came into being. All these gave birth to recorded knowledge should be preserved somewhere for the posterity. It was further realised that preserved knowledge should also retrieved in minimum possible time. Once man learnt to record, preserve, libraries became the natural development. The task of the librarian is put knowledge to work.

3

KNOWLEDGE : ORGANISATION

Knowledge is the sum of information conserved by civilization. In its common and everyday usage, information is associated with a human situation, with a communication medium, with something that can be added and accumulated, with something factual, valuable, useful, useless or with knowledge. The term 'knowledge' includes not only those disciplines that make statements about the world, such as science, philosophy and history, but also those that create such as arts, crafts and professions. It is dynamic. New units of knowledge are being added to the existing knowledge from time to time.

A discipline is a branch of knowledge. The fundamental disciplines are the primary divisions of knowledge. These are described as intellectual forms of presentation of knowledge. Some prefer the term 'Forms of knowledge' to 'Fundamental disciplines'. They are similar to forms of presentation in that they tell us what a book is rather what it is about. For example, 'A history of India' is history; it is written in the discipline of history, but it is about the events in the past life of Indian people. Subdivisions are areas of specialisation written knowledge for example, Zoology, Botany, Physics, Chemistry, etc. within natural sciences.

Classification is the act of organising the universe of knowledge into some systematic order. It has been considered the most fundamental activity of human mind. In constructing classification schemes for knowledge the details of relationships between the various forms of knowledge are to explored.

TYPES OF CLASSIFICATION

John Dewey claimed that knowledge is classification. If this comment is treated as a pointed expression rather than a definition, it does underline the central importance of classification in at least some forms of knowledge. In science, classification is coextensive with knowledge. Scientists are always specialists and each group is interested in a particular section of the world's phenomena. A phenomenon is anything that can be directly apprehended by the senses or an event that may be observed. In the natural sciences, we find classification at its most precise and systematic. Majority of the people would probably associate the classifying of knowledge primarily with the question of phenomena. However, the term refers to something quite different : the philosophic enquiry as to the forms that knowledge takes and their definition.

Both the classification of knowledge and the classification of phenomena are their theoretical matters. Librarians must take account of them since knowledge in all its forms is what they have to organise. Their ultimate concern, however, are practical. In addition to these pure knowledge questions, they must take into account the books and other media by which knowledge is conveyed, the uses to which it may be put, and the people for whom it is intended. To the librarian, then, classifying knowledge is a complex idea.

While scientists have simple the forms of nature to identify and the philosophers the forms of knowledge, librarians should take into consideration all significant aspects of knowledge as it is communicated. Their aim should be to present knowledge in such a way that it is easily accessible to users, and for this the overriding principle must be that of helpfulness.

Librarians should distinguish between helpful arrangement and accurate specification. The former is based and users' needs and interests; it is very much matter of judgement, particularity in general contexts where a great variety of users must be catered for. The latter is based on the nature of knowledge, and it is objective within agreed definitions. We can argue effectively about the most helpful arrangement in given circumstances, but not about the specification of documents : that is a matter of verification.

One major cause of confusion between a helpful arrangement and an accurate specification is the nature of main classes in general schemes. In a pure knowledge classification, such names as 'philosophy', 'science', 'history' and 'religion' would refer to the whole of those forms and nothing but those forms. In a bibliographic scheme, these classes contain the selection of material considered most useful, by the scheme's maker, to those whose primary interest in the form concerned. For example, philosophy will include only such major branches as metaphysics and epistemology, while more specialised studies, such as philosophy of law, education or religion, are considered more helpfully collocated with other forms of writing the history of philosophy, which is a branch of history, not of philosophy.

For the librarian, classifying knowledge implies two quite distinct activities. One is the making of systems, and the person who does this is known as a classificationist. The other is the specification of individual document and their allocation to appropriate places in the system. This is done by classifiers. The classificationist must have special competence in construction techniques.

SCIENTIFIC CLASSIFICATION

Stephen Korner, in the Encyclopaedia Britannica (15th ed) article on classification theory, states :

"Formulation of scientific laws presupposes classification, because to formulate a law of nature is to state relations between members of different classes."

C.F.A Pantin suggests that :

"One way of defining the objective of the natural sciences is to say that it is to determine the principles underlying the classification of objects and events...in all the sciences, the determination of the class to which a phenomenon belongs is one of the most important conclusions of a piece of scientific research. In this sense, all the natural sciences are classificatory".

Librarians need not concern themselves with the methods used by scientists to arrive at their classes of natural objects, which they can merely be taken as granted. Since classifications are not permanent, even in the natural sciences, they must be open to change. Furthermore, they should recognise that the sciences are a special case, and that strict logical methods do not apply elsewhere in defining classes. According to Wittgenstein the idea of resemblances between members of a family came nearer to describing the normal formation of classes than the logical criterion of necessary and sufficient conditions. This can be evident in the nature of literary genres, such as tragedy and comedy. There is no logical definition of tragedy : one can ask of a new work only whether it bears sufficient resemblance as a whole to those by Sophocles, Ibsen, Shakespeare and others accepted in the Canon.

Although classifiers should be aware of such matters, the main lander falls on the classificationists. They must know what there is to choose from and must judge what know what there is to choose from and must judge what is both desirable and practicable.

PHILOSOPHIC CLASSIFICATION

The nature of knowledge itself is a primary theme in philosophy. Librarians are not concerned with the epistemology which is meant for defining what qualifies for the title of knowledge. Librarians should rather concern themselves with everything in print. Insofar as philosophers attempt to define the divisions of knowledge proper, they have some relevance to the task of librarians. We cannot expect a consensus among philosophers as to whether the forms of knowledge represent the innate features of human mind. Philosophers of widely differing views have reached very similar conclusions as to the number and nature of these forms. Aristotle demonstrated the empirical approach. His criteria for distinguishing the forms of knowledge were aims, subject matter and mode of enquiry, which produced a primary division of theoretical knowledge, practical knowledge and productive knowledge. The divisions of these three primary forms in the modern context were natural sciences, mathematics and metaphysics for theoretical; ethics and social sciences for practical; and fine arts and useful arts for productive knowledge.

Francis Bacon was concerned with the state of knowledge in his day. In the *Advancement of learning*, he says, "it is my intention to make the circuit of knowledge, noticing what parts lie waste and uncultivated and abandoned by the industry of man; with a view to engage, by a faithful mapping of the deserted tracts, the energies of public and private persons in their improvement "

R.G. Collingwood proposed five innate forms of knowledge in philosophy, science, history, art and religion. Nowadays, philosophers of education are likely to show keen interest in the forms of knowledge in subject analyses of individual documents. The classification may be directly applicable in defining their essential nature. Some philosophers instead of discussing the criteria for defining the forms of knowledge have put forward the schemes for practical purposes apart from showing the existing and possible divisions of knowledge. The well known scheme that Frances Bacon used in the *Advancement of learning*, has no further implications. It is orderly, but the particular bears no significance. I know correctly means according to Bacon, "To know through reasons." Hobbes defines similarly, "Therefore knowledge through which we recognise the truth of a proposition is knowledge of an object form its causes and its origination through proper derivation in thinking".

According to Desecrates, knowledge is the "recognition of truth from its primary causes". Locke , although denying the function of principles - or axioms, as he calls them as a constitutive moment for acquiring knowledge, regards demonstrative, deductive in digits as being of fundamental importance in furnishing the basis for man's knowledge. This definition of knowledge as demonstrative, deductive insights whose methodic example is constituted by the demonstrative procedure in mathematics is of fundamental importance for the refection on order and method in the era between Renaissance and Enlightenment.

August Comte propounded a very distinctive theory of the way in which knowledge developed historically and of the relationship between its branches. He first set aside theology and metaphysics, as representing superseded, stages of human thought and practical disciplines as applications of the theoretical. Comte regarded philosophy as the coordination of all the sciences : mathematics, astronomy, physics, chemistry, biology and sociology. In Comte's classification we have a distinctive philosophical view point, known as positivism. Comte had a major influence on Henry Evelyn Bliss in the design of his Bibliographic Classification.

If salvation of the soul was the aim of all knowledge, theology became the queen of sciences. Medieval schemes reflect these conditions in their similarity to each other and in the way that they incorporate Aristotle's classification with religious outlook.

BIBLIOGRAPHIC CLASSIFICATION

The idea of classification as the detailed specification of individual works is essentially a twentieth century one. As late as 1874 W.S. Jevons described the classification of books as a logical absurdity and a practical impossibility. On the first point he was correct but on the second history proved him wrong. If we consider the unique combination of details in each document, then classification is a logical absurdity : There can be no mutually exclusive classes in those terms. If instead, we concentrate on the essential theme of each document, then there is no difficultly. Before the late 19th century, this idea did not have any impact on librarians. The typical arrangement of library would consist of some 20 or 30 classes with their appropriate books arranged in a fixed order on the shelves.

To judge the requirements of classification at any period it is necessary to examine the current social conditions. The number of books in existence, the rate of continuing publication, the size of librarians, the degree of literacy in the community, the number of library users, and their various reasons for reading are all relevant factors. These conditions began to change more rapidly during the 19th century and America was the first country to respond to the new demands. When Dewey published his classification in 1876, however, its thousand divisions were considered excessive.

The modern era began badly with Dewey's Decimal Classification which was an attempt to fit knowledge into a fixed and regular pattern. Dewey was quite open about his obsession with the usefulness of decimal numbers and, historically, his procedure is understandable, since a device for maintaining a relative order was a necessity for the new style of detailed classification.

The Universal Decimal Classification tried to turn the Dewey system into a more modern and flexible one. Poor foundations and lack of a coherent theory merely created a ramshackle structure. It is a pity that for so long these two schemes have been the standard offered for international cooperation. Standardisation is welcome, but only if there is an adequate standard available. The primary responsibility of any library is to its own users. One may question the judgement of Ernest Savage, but his intention was admirable when he chose the Library of Congress Classification for Edinburgh Public Library.

Among those who put intellectual considerations first, there is a school of thought which advocates beginning bibliographic classification with the classification of phenomena. This is, in effect, to treat knowledge as a homogeneous whole, which it is not. We are offered such theories as evolution and integrative levels as the model for a general scheme; but these theories refer to nature, and it is only in science that nature is the direct object of study. More generally, there has been a modern tendency to base the classification of knowledge on the example of science. Before the twentieth century the aim of bibliographic classification was clear and simple, but the complexities of modern life have led to differences of opinion as its application and uses.

AMERICAN ATTITUDES TO KNOWLEDGE

According to Daniel Boorstin, the Americans have established a new concept of knowledge. Where European culture depended on the monumental accomplishments of the few, the new American culture depended on the novel, accenting ways of the many. Much of the authentic knowledge of the New World was a by-product of travels with a practical purpose and knowledge seemed to come in miscellaneous parcels. Boorstin gives the example of one self-educated man who probably discovered more plants than any other American, although he was more collector than student and had little knowledge of botanical principles. This aptness for collecting new items, coupled with the indirectly to systematize there, he regards as symbolizing the tendencies in American thought. He further suggests that this atomizing influence of the American environment was contagious.

There also seems to be a political element in present - day American attitudes to knowledge and its classification. Mortimer recalls "That it is traditional in library literature to recognizes that Dewey was very much influenced by Harris, that Harris was an Hegelian and that Hegelians are a species of unscientific metaphysicians who believe that are reality is constituted by a hierarchy of reaching up to the Prussian state as the class of all classes".

If the idea of hierarchy creates such emotional response, the antipathy to classification scheme is not surprising. Classification, however, is not first a matter of systematic order. Subject headings and cross-references are a classification system presented in a different way.

FACETS OF INDIAN THOUGHT

India is traditionally imbued with the philosophy of eternity and assigns to transitory events only a relative and minor importance. India always seeks for the underlying unity within, before, and after all single things and events.

In such a culture, we should expect to find the 'monumental accomplishments of the few' and striving for a comprehensive system. Ranganathan's best known contribution, the fundamental categories, derives from Aristotle. There is no metaphysical claim that reality shows a five-fold division, but merely that the categories represent the broadest classes of phenomena that are useful in bibliographic classification.

According to Ranganathan there are five categories of phenomena. These categories are Personality, Matter, Energy, Space and Time.

Ranganathan did not attempt to apply these categories to knowledge as a whole, but looked for their manifestation in particular subject fields. Categories of phenomena took their place within the forms of knowledge and specialised disciplines, supplemented by such characteristics.

B.C. Vickery has suggested another set of categories - whole thing - kinds (of a thing) - Parts (of a thing) - Materials - Properties - Processes - Operations - Agents - Space - Time. This detailed set is particularly appropriate to the fields of science and technology.

FACET

When phenomena are studied in the context of a particular discipline they can be brought together into closely defined groups. In other words phenomena can be divided into groups or class on the basis of shared characteristics. *These groups or classes constitute the facets of that discipline.*

Example of phenomena with the subject area of Medicine are heart, lungs and liver. These phenomena are all parts of the body. They are called part of a body facet. Therefore, the facet of a subject field consists of number of phenomena within that subject. They share some characteristics in common.

Simply stated, a facet is the sum total of isolates formed by the division of a subject by one characteristic of division. In other words, in the literature of a given subject area, it is normally possible to identify a number of facets and, by applying several characteristics of subdivision, to divide isolates into facets. A characteristic of subdivision is an attribute of property which all concepts in a given facet have in common and by which isolates can be grouped.

CULTURAL ASPECTS OF KNOWLEDGE

If a particular religion is dominant in a particular culture, then it is accorded pride of place in the organisation of recorded knowledge. In a Eurocentric culture the dominance of Christianity can be explained historically. But this dominance in a classification scheme is difficult to justify to multi - cultural and multi - faith users. This problem has an acute practical side as publishing expands in the area of comparative and non - Christian religions. Yet cultural bias in Knowledge Classification is not a western preserve. Ranganathan describes the vedic system of knowledge thus :

1. Dharma

Concerned with the preservation of society as a coherent organisation. The minimum and primary knowledge for being a member of the community. It dealt with law, religion, philosophy and ethics.

2. Artha

The knowledge required by for its own sake - or joy in artistic creation. It covered linguistics, literature and five arts.

3. Karma

Knowledge pursued for its own sake - or joy in artistic creation. It covered linguistics literature and fine arts.

4. Moksha

The knowledge that only a small minority in any community find competence or leisure to develop or appreciate. It meant spiritualism and mysticism.

THE CLASSIFICATION RESEARCH GROUP (CRG)

The increasing output of science and technology during the 20th century, accelerated by the two World Wars, concentrated the attention of Americans and Europeans on the needs of special subjects. America tried to do without classification : the original Uniterm system of Mortimer Taube tried to make subject specification a purely clerical task in selecting key - words from a document.

In England, the more systematic European tradition is exemplified by the CRG. The CRG was formed in 1948 after a Royal Society Scientific Information Conference. The CRG has been a major force in the development of classification theory, contributing significantly towards work on a new general bibliographic classification scheme.

It is interesting to note that which classification is fundamental to the activity of librarians, the profession as a whole seems to unaware of its importance. If it were otherwise, the means for producing a new general scheme would have been provided long ago.

As it is, the profession falls back on the conviction and dedication of the few for this vital contribution to the smooth functioning of society, the classification of knowledge.

Human knowledge is partial and our varied approaches to the world around us are manifested in distinct forms of knowledge, or fundamental disciplines. The word 'discipline is used indeterminately for any systematic body of knowledge, so it is necessary to add 'fundamental' where referring to these major divisions. There is considerable degree of agreement among modern philosophers as to what they are. Agreement on the division of knowledge into disciplines does not mean agreement on the unity of knowledge. There is no guarantee that various bodies of knowledge fit together to form a comprehensive picture of reality.

According to J. H. Randall, the American Philosopher, a useful distinction exists between the *World for knowledge* (which is assumed to be one) and the *World of knowledge* (may remain many). At the extremes both mystic and scientist agreed to the unity of knowledge, but we continue to have quite distinct bodies of knowledge about the universe.

Those who are interested to construct classification schemes for knowledge should explore the details of relationship between the various forms of knowledge.

The purpose of bibliographic classification is to organise the knowledge produced by specialists so that it may be available for wherever requires it. This type of classification deals with knowledge after it has embodied in documents, but in doing so must make use of both of specialist findings and philosophical views. Here it is not objects as observed in the world with which we are concerned, but their reflection in subjects as treated in documents.

UNIVERSE OF SUBJECTS

Knowledge includes both those disciplines that make statements about the world and those that create. Librarians are not experts on the universe of knowledge. It is the province of philosophers, scientists and historians. Librarians are interested in their findings. They must base their work on areas of knowledge for bibliographical classification. To distinguish the work of librarians Ranganathan introduced the term 'Universe of Subjects'.

We need to be aware that knowledge is the product of ideas, and subjects are products of knowledge as will be evident from the following definitions.

"**Idea** : The product of thinking, reflecting, imagining, etc, got by the intellect integrating with the aid of logic, a selection from the appreciation mass, and or what is directly apprehended by the intuition, and deposited in the memory" [Prolegomena p. 95]

Knowledge : The totality of ideas conserved by the humans.

Subject : An organised or systematised body of ideas, whose extension and intention are likely to fall coherently within the field of interest and comfortably within the intellectual competence and the field of inevitable specialisation of a normal person.

[Prolegomena : p. 102]

Universe : Aggregate under consideration in a given context

[Prolegomena : p. 106]

In order to construct and maintain the schemes of classification along proper lines, it is essential to make a systematic study of the formation, structure and development of universe of subjects.

ATTRIBUTES

A critical examination and thorough analysis of the development of universe of subjects world reveal that owing to organised relay research, incentives population and other process the universe of subjects has been expanding its fold very rapidly. The attributes of the universe of subjects may be stated thus :

Dynamic continuum

The modern age is an age of problems and their situations. Due to social pressure scientists have been involved and engaged in continuous research (As a result, an unending spiral of ** research) has been created. Relay research may mean a fresh but continuous research at different stages. Research, as a matter of fact, is an unending process. It never ends. When any problem arises, research is undertaken to solve at and put into practice. But this is not the end. The solution may create some other problems. This puts pressure on researchers to undertake research afresh. This leads to relay research which is like a spiral movement. Spiral means unending curves - like threads of a screw. Relay research implies spiral of research.

According to Ranganathan, "at present organised relay research is producing a continuous cascade of new micro subjects, each stimulating another in succession in every area of subjects. This cascade makes the Universe of Subjects a growing and depending continuum".

Infiniteness

At a given moment a certain number of subjects are known, but many more new subjects may continue to come to light in future from time to time. There are infinite number of subjects hidden in the universe of knowledge which will continue to grow. In future many more subjects are likely to arrive and be recognised at proper time. Hence the number of main or basic subjects are infinite.

Proliferation

In various ways the universe of subjects going with a Basic subject can get proliferated.

Grafting

Grafting is a process in which a shoot of one tree when inserted in another tree becomes the other's part producing a different variety of the tree. As a result of grafting, we can grow more than one colour of rose flower on one tree. In universe of knowledge, some branch of certain subject gets attached to and accepted by another subject as if grafted into it. This process makes a subject multidimensional.

Exponential growth

Universe of subjects is turbulent ever growing dynamic continuum. Universe of subjects is growing with tremendous speed. Millions of documents containing advances in knowledge of various disciplines are being created each year in every field. The maximum number of divisions likely to be thrown forth by it in some array or other of its development seems unpredictable.

MODES OF FORMATION OF SUBJECTS

Different specialists have recognised different types of relations between the components of a subject or the modes of subject formation in the universe of subjects. Discussing the utility of studying modes of formation of subjects Ranganathan states "It will be an advantage to examine the modes of formation and the structure of the subjects in the universe of subjects and of the isolate ideas in the universe of isolate ideas, as a preliminary to the theory of Freely - Faceted Classification - that is, the Analytico - Synthetic Classification - guided by Postulates and Principles". In designing schemes for Classification of subjects get formulated. This resulted in his general enunciation of modes of formation of subjects. He had initially brought to light five modes of formation of subjects. : Loose Assemblage, Lamination, Dissection, Denudation and superimposition. Later his school of thought developed this view point. In 1975. M.A. Gopinath and S.Seetharama put forward the following modes of formation of subjects :

Loose Assemblage : It is the assembling together of two or more subjects (simple or compound) and isolates ideas. Assembling is done to express one or other possible relations between the components of the assembly. The result is a complex isolate kind 1 (Loose Assemblage 2) or complex isolate Kind 2 (Loose Assemblage 3). Each component in the assembly is called a 'Phase'. there are six kinds of Phase Relations :

1. General Relation
2. Bias Relation
3. Comparison Relation
4. Difference Relation
5. Influencing Relation
6. Tool Relation

Loose Assemblage Kind 1 : takes place when two or more basic subjects are studied in any of the six types of relation. It is based on 'Inter - subject Relation'

Examples :

General :	Relation between Psychology and Medicine
Bias :	Psychology for Doctors

Comparison :	Comparative study of Psychology and Medicine
Difference :	Difference between Psychological and Medical treatment
Tool :	Application of Psychology in Medical Science.
Influence :	Influence of Psychology on medical science.

Loose Assemblage Kind 2 : It occurs when two or more facets of the same schedule. It is based on Intra - facet Relation.

Examples :

General :	Relation between Morphology and Physiology
Bias :	Anatomy for Pathologists
Comparison :	Anatomy Psychology compared
Difference :	Difference between Psychological and
Tool :	German music through painting
Influence :	Influence of Hinduism on Buddhism.

Loose Assemblage Kind 3 : It is said to exist when two or more isolates of one and the same array are studied in any of the six types of relation. It is based on 'Intra - Array' Relation.

Examples :

General :	Relation between DDC and UDC
Bias :	The bias of UDC towards DDC
Comparison :	Psychology of man and woman compared
Difference :	Difference between Psychology of man and woman
Tool :	Bengali music through Hindusthani music
Influence :	Influence of Hariyana Buddhism on Malyalam.

LAMINATION

It means thin separable layer. Here lamination is a process

in which one or more isolate facet(s) or basic class are compounded over one another to form a thin separable layer. this may happen in two ways.

When the basic layer is a basic subject and other layers are isolate ideas, a compound subject is formed (Lamination Kind 1).

For example, Agriculture of Corn. This compound subject is formed by the lamination of Basic Subject (BS) 'Agriculture' and isolate idea 'corn'. Similarly, History of Indian Constitution - History (BS) India (isolate) Constitution (Isolate)

Lamination 2 : Here compound basic or compound isolates are formed. *Examples* :

Magnetism in Quantum Physics (Basic Subject Magnetism Combines with Quantum Physics)

'Urban Youth : Here one isolate idea 'Youth' has been compounded with the isolate idea 'Urban' from the same schedule.

FISSION

Fission is the process of division or splitting or breaking up into parts. This process has, until recently, been denoted by the term 'Dissection'. Dissection usually implies the splitting, breaking up, etc. of an entity into parts by an outside agency. But fission is an internal process of division without an involvement of an outside agency. Philosophy is a basic subject. it may spilt into logic, epistemology, metaphysics, ethics and aesthetics.

Isolate ideas may be fissioned in the following ways as array division : Asia - Iran, India, Nepal.

FUSION

Here two or more primary basic subjects are fused together in such a way that each of them loses its individuality. This mode makes a new primary basic subject.

Examples :

Astrophysics (Fusion of Astronomy and Physics)

Bio - Chemistry : It is a primary basic subject achieved by the fusion of Chemistry and Biology.

DISTILLATION

Through this process a pure discipline is evolved as a Primary Basic Subject. For example, Management Science. Consider the following subjects :

Management of Chemistry Laboratory

Management of School

Management of Industry

The component idea "Management" in each of these subjects is an isolate. The three subjects go respectively with the Primary Basic Subjects "Chemistry", "Education" and Industrial Economics." In this way, the idea "Management", denoting a practice - in - action, can occur in a variety of subjects going with different Primary Basic Subjects. On the basis of observations, experiments, and experiences of which taken together can constitute a theory of management may be distilled out. When this happened, persons began to specialise in the new emerging discipline. The ideas generated by the specialists in the new discipline could not be helpfully placed as an isolate idea. It was found necessary to deem the ideas to go with a new Primary Basic Subject.

In distillation of kind 2 the idea occurs in subjects going with of particular Basic Subject only and there may be a trend towards the formation of a new discipline with recognisable literary warrant. New Primary Basic Subjects formed by Distillation of Kind 2 are :

Statistical Calculus, Operations research, Nursing, Demography.

AGGLOMERATION

Agglomeration is the formation of a new subject by gathering together more than one subject in rounded manner, as if a ball is made by rolling different pieces of wool in one. Ranganathan earlier used the term 'partial comprehension' instead of agglomeration. In agglomeration kind several subjects are treated integrally or disjunctively in one and the same document. It covers subjects going with successive Primary Basic Subjects enumerated in the schedule

Example Natural Sciences

Social Sciences

Humanities

Agglomerate of kind 2 is an agglomerate comprehending subjects going with non-consecutive Primary Basic Subjects with respect to the schedules of a particular scheme for classification. For example, Psychology and Sociology, Political Science and History.

CLUSTER

It was formerly called 'Subject Bundle'. Sometime several specialists from different disciplines may study a particular phenomenon or an entity. This kind of study leads to interdisciplinary or multi-disciplinary research. There is a core entity of study. Inputs or viewpoints from different specialists are gathered together into a field of study. This is explained as clustering around a core entity. The core entity is the focus of cluster.

Let us consider documents each dealing with one of the following subjects.

Mathematics in India	Education in India
Chemistry in India	Geography of India
Medicine in India	History of India

The subjects will normally go respectively with the Primary Basic Subjects Mathematics, Chemistry, Medicine, Education, Geography, and History. A document on "Indology" (Indian Studies) may contain contributions on serval of the above-mentioned subjects as well as on other such as Science in India, Religion in India, Indian Philosophy, Economy of India, Indian Civilisation, etc.

collected together. Here, 'India' is the core entity of study in each of the contributions. The subject-field of the collection taken as a whole represents a clustering of subjects around the node "India". Similarly, Sinology. (Chinese study), Nipponology (Japanese study), African study or in general, subjects falling in the subject-field "Area study" is an example of this clustering phenomenon

STRUCTURE OF UNIVERSE OF SUBJECTS

The mode of formation of a subject leaves its impress on the structures of a subject. Here structure refers to division of the universe of subjects at idea and verbal planes. Universe of knowledge can be divided or classified in idea planes on the basis of the following:

1. Dichotomy
2. Decachotomy
3. Polychotomy

1. **Dichotomy :** Dichotomy means division into two. It is also known as 'Binary Classification'. The schematic representation of dichotomy is called "Tree of Porphyry". Tree of Porphyry attracted Bentham who appreciated 'The matchless beauty of the tree of porphyry' It must have surved well the purpose of the early man. But in present days the mushroom growth of universe of subjects makes the method of dichotomy redundant.

DECACHOTOMY

Decachotomy signifies division into ten. Many attempts have been made to classify universe of subjects into ten divisions at each stage. With the classification of universe of subjects by Melvil Dewey in 1876, Decachotomy method gained popularity. But from the point of view of turbulence of universe of subjects and of its growing in different directions and at different stages, decachotomy is unnatural and arbitrary. In this context Decachotomy is as arbitrary as dichotomy. The Decimal Bed is as much a Procrustean Bed as the Binary Bed of Kant, the Universe of Subjects transcends the capacity of the one as much as the other. For, it is the creation of the intellect. The intellect cannot be tied down with a decimal thong. The universe of subjects created by it cannot be folded up into neat layers of ten. Even the editors of DDC have accepted the limitation of Decachotomy by agreeing. "Theoretically the division of every subject into ten parts is absorbed".

POLYCHOTOMY

Polychotomy means division into many. It is a useful method to classify universe of subjects. It can be practised in two ways : limited polychotomy and unlimited polychotomy. In limited polychotomy the number of the base at each stage is fixed or pre-determined depending upon the requirement at the given time. For example, in 1893 C.A. Cutter in his 'Expansive Classification' introduced limited polychotomy by making the number of divisions at each stage 24. Within 50 years, the rate of growth of the universe of subjects found 24 divisions to be inadequate. This proves that the number of divisions should at no stage be pre-determined. This can be achieved only with the help of unlimited polychotomy.

PROLIFERATION

Ranganathan described various ways in which the universe of subjects going with a Basic Subject can get proliferated. For example, a complex subject in that universe of subjects may be formed by attaching some other basic subject as a phase. A compound subject may be formed by attaching one or more isolate ideas to the basic subject. Such isolate ideas can themselves proliferate by various ways.

DEVELOPMENT OF THE UNIVERSE OF SUBJECTS

In the past there was no incentive for organised and cooperative development of the universe of subjects. There was seldom cooperation among the men of genius scattered all over the glove. The development of applied subjects was slow and casual affair.

At the present time social pressure is leading to a conscious, organised and planned development of universe of subjects. Further research log isolated individuals is substituted by organising relay-research. As a result the research potential of the world is less exposed to wastage. The result of such an organisation of relay-research is considerable increase in the formation of new subjects. At present organised relay - research is creating a continuous cascade of new micro subjects, each stimulating another in succession in every area of subjects. This cascade makes the universe of subjects a growing and deepening continuum.

4

Knowledge Classification : Concept and Structure

The organisation of knowledge is a process that has been accepted as necessary for thousands of years. A vast number of different means of organising knowledge have been devised since the earliest times, although many of the systems in use today have evolved over the past 120 years or so years. Any attempt to organise knowledge, in order to justify the effort involved, should have an objective. In general, the objective is to permit that information or knowledge to be found again on a later occasion. The objective of organisation of knowledge is successful subsequent retrieval. Before studying various approaches to the organisation of knowledge, it is important to note that different people may have to retrieve documents or unit of information for different purposes, and therefore may approach the retrieval process in different ways. A fundamental difference in searching is known-item searching and unknown-item searching.

Known-item searching is performed by users when they know author's name or title of the document. When they look for material on a particular subject, it is known as subject approach. This approach is for the unknown items. One user might retrieve a document as or result of known-item searching, whereas another user might retrieve the same document as the outcome of unknown-item searching. The information retrieval system must be added to support both types of user in their searches.

DEFINITION

Classification, broadly defined, is the act of organising the universe of knowledge into some systematic order. Classification was initially described as a mental process of ordering the universe and we have taken our library practice and reduced it to a mere act of storing and locating documents in a collection of materials. Library Classification serves as organising bibliographic entries in printed catalogues, bibliographies, and indexes in a systematic order.

1. to help the user identify and locate a work through a call number, and
2. to group all, related works together.

In order to fulfill the first objective, any method of measuring would be sufficient so long as there is a correspondence between the work on the document and that n the cataloguing entry. The second objective, on the other hand, represents a collocating function and requires the grouping of like materials together, on the basis of certain characteristics. (for example, author, physical form, date of publication, subject). In modern systems, subject is the prominent characteristic for grouping.

Classification was initially described as a mental process of ordering the universe and we have taken our library practice and reduced it to a mere act of storing and identifying documents in a collection of materials. On one hand we can speak of classification in the highest sense- that which hierarchically orders the universe allowing us to proceed from concept experience to concept experience, revising our categories, but building up our knowledge as a consistent attempted representation of the universal order. On the other, we merely speak of our library classification as shuffling device, devoid of that presence which exists when two are combined, as in the original encounter of the Dewey Decimal Classification and Baconian philosophy. Yet our age has a new philosophy and its herald, the computer, allows for quick and efficient manipulation of ideas, facets and subjects.

CLASSIFICATION IN EVERYDAY LIFE

The term 'classification' has come into our language in its present use from the field of classical logic. In its simplest meaning it is merely the grouping of various things on the basis of likeness. Whether or not we realise it we have used classification all during our life. On our ability so group things together according to likeness rests our chance for survival in this chaotic world. Even infants crawling about on the floor learn to classify things with which they collide. They group together those things that will cause pain when they but their heads against those and place in another group the softer, more yielding things which can hit without damage to themselves.

Everyday life abounds in the use of classification, although it is not generally realised. Although the persons who use it never employ the word 'classification'. The process is used in almost every walk of life. Take, for example the bus conductor and the way he arranges or classifies his wads of tickets. They must be arranged so that he can find the one required as quickly as possible. For that purpose tickets are arranged by price into 125 paise, 150 paise, and so on. To facilitate their ready identification they may each be made of different colours.

In a shop of any kind the employment of some kind of classification is essential, so as to facilitate speedy access to goods required. Thus in a grocers shop one will find all dairy products together, all cereals together and so on. In turn, each of these may be divided into smaller divisions of line objects. Thus dairy products may be divided into butter, cheese, eggs, etc. and in turn each of the classes of commodities may be further subdivided, if such subdivisions facilitate the use and sale of the objects concerned. Thus butter can be divided into Amul, Trihut, Vijaja, etc.

Factory stores arrange machinery parts together according to how they are used. Garment shops arrange garments by the make as the customer asks for them in that way. Record shops group gramophone records on the basis of certain criteria. Cinema and theatre allocate seats and of course, libraries organise collections. Convenience governs classification. It is the question of convenience that dictates the particular way in which things are to be arranged.

PURPOSE OF CLASSIFICATION

Behind all classification, as we have seen in the above cited examples, there is always a purpose. The purpose is to arrange things in the convenient order. It is a method of science, it is a way of knowing things. Classification, as noted earlier, is primarily an intellectual activity, not a physical activity. The classification may be examplified or illustrated by the grouping of objects in a library, museum or in a shop. But the mere physical grouping is not the real, essential classification. The essence of classification lies in the fact that certain things are thought of as related in cèrtain ways to one another.

NATURAL AND ARTIFICIAL CLASSIFICATION

Classification is the act of arranging things in classes according to common characteristics. Things are either already grouped together according to their likeness in natural or they are grouped together by man in his mind or in outer maternal. Things arranged according to likeness without the aid of man are nature. The classification can be divided into natural and artificial. A natural classification is one which groups or separates a series of things according to some fundamental likeness or unlikeness. It exhibits properties of things classified. For example, grouping of person according to age, grouping of garments according to material.

An artificial classification may be defined as one which

groups or separates a series of things according to some external likeness or unlikeness. In other words artificial classification is based on some artificial characteristics. For example, grouping of garments according to size.

The natural classification is scientifically fruitful while the artificial classification is not. Scientists in pursuit of knowledge have looked for those classifications that are most fundamental. They favour classes in which members have the largest possible number of features in common. In fact the members of a class derived from natural classification display far more affinities than those of an artificial class. For example, the classification of humans as 'male' and 'female' rather than by their weight.

Zoologists classify animals according to structural similarities. By this method whales belong to the same class - mammals - as horses, cows and mice. The layman generally thinks of whales as belonging to the same class as fishes because they both live in water. But this proves to be more or less isolated characteristic, that is artificial. But the previous one is natural classification.

CONCEPT

"Concept" is the most fundamental term in all studies related to classification. Many concepts are class concepts. They are our idea of a particular group of objects. Understanding a class-concept can be demonstrated in two ways - by the ability to say whether or not a given object belongs to the class, or by the ability to describe the characteristic by virtue of which it does belong.

I take an example : suppose someone said, 'That's a good book' and we asked him, 'what do you mean a good book ? This is a perfectly reasonable question; and it is also a question of concept because what we want to know is what counts as a good book' with him. Yet it would be wrong to say that we use wrong for the meaning of the word 'good'. 'Good' is a very common word, which we use correctly every day; it means, roughly, "to be commended" or "to be approved" or 'desirable'. We know this already. Yet we still ask, 'what do you mean by a good book ?

The best way of looking at this point is to say that in questions of concept we are not concerned with the meaning of a word. Words do not have only one meaning; indeed, in a sense they do not have meaning in their own right at all but only in so far as people use them in different ways. It is better to say that we are concerned with actual and possible uses of words. That is why it is no use looking up the word in a dictionary; it will not help when we ask 'what do you mean, a good book ? what we are really saying is, 'what counts as good book with you ?' Sometimes we behave as if all we had to do was to find out the real meaning of a word and then the answer to our question would be obvious. But unfortunately it is not so simple as that, and a moment's thought will show us that word do not have 'real meanings'. They have different uses and different applications. Our job is to analyse the concepts and map out these uses and applications.

LOGICAL DIVISION : THE BASIC RULES

The correct procedures in reasoning are found in logic. Any discipline that attempts to reach conclusion through the examination of evidence should seek the support of logic. Thus logic includes the fundamental principles of classification. Logical division is the process by which classes are divided into sub-classes by the addition of attributes. A distinction is sometimes drawn between classification and logical division. But in fact they are really two aspects of one activity. The basic rules of logical division is as follows :

1. The characteristic or principle of division must produce at least two classes. For example, if we apply the characteristic of sex to the class 'persons in general' we get two classes 'male' and 'female'.
2. Each stage of division should be based on one principle of division. In other words, only one characteristic must be

used at a time to produce mutually exclusive classes. Each characteristic should be exhausted before another is introduced.

If more than one principle of division is used at one time the result is likely to be 'cross-classification'. For example, the question 'Is this animal herbivorous or is it aquatic' is unanswerable because the animal might be both. The animal can eat plant substances and it can live in water. Classes which are divided by the application of division are called 'simple classes'. Those derived by the application of more than one principle are called 'superimposed classes'. Thus if the class 'animals' is divided, the class 'herbivorous animals' is simple class. The class 'herbivorous aquatic animals' is superimposed.

3. The sub-classes must be completely exhaustive of their parent class. Each class should be divided as minutely as possible. The sum of all the divisions and sub-divisions should be as complete as possible.
4. The process of division should proceed step by step. No step of division should be omitted. Otherwise proper classification will be uncertain.

LOGICAL DIVISION IN LIBRARY CLASSIFICATION

Logical division is limited to only one kind of relationship - that of a thing and its kinds. This relationship is also called 'genus species relationship'. It should be noted that the terms 'genus' and 'species' are here used in a logical sense. They have no necessary relationships to the 'genera' and 'species' of zoological and botanical Classification.

If we divide countries into those with a hot climate and those with a cold climate we are doing a logical division and showing genus/species relationship. Similarly Landscape painting is a kind of painting.

A serious confusion that crops up in a logical division is about partition - division of a whole into its parts. A leaf is a kind of plant substance. it is not however a kind of plant. The relationship between leaves and plants is not a genus/species relationship but a thing/part relationship.

Other examples of partitive relationship include spatial and time relationships. For example, India/Calcutta, Eighteenth Century/1775. These two relationships in common with the types exemplified by plant/leaf are essential partitive relationship. Calcutta cannot be a kind of India. Similarly 1775 cannot be a part of eighteenth century.

FIVE PREDICABLES

W.H. Phillips points out that "The principles laid down in the Predicables govern all classification, for all divisions proceed by the addition of differences to the genera". The terms genus, species and difference belong to a group of logical terms known as the Five Predicables. The five predicables point out all possible relations a predicate may express concerning a subject. These were advanced by the Greek logician, Porphyry. The five predicables may be explained thus :

1. Genus

A class of objects or ideas which is capable of division into two or more sub-groups, which are called species.

2. Species

Groups into which genus may be divided. Each group may itself become genus subject to further division.

3. Difference

A quality, which is added to genus forms species. We can illustrate three terms. The class of objects called 'military' aeroplanes is the genus. By the application of the characteristic 'purpose' we may derive the difference 'fighting'. Thus we have 'military' aeroplanes plus 'fighting' which gives species 'fighters'. The species can become a genus which can be divided by applying characteristic.

4. Property

A quality common to every member of the genus but which is not confined to that genus. Though not essential to the definition of that genus the possession of a property is inherent in the nature of a species.

5. Accident

A quality which may or may not be possessed by any member of the genus. It is not necessary for the definition of a species and its existence cannot be inferred by the definition. However, it may be used in practice as a difference. A property of the class aircraft might be their being subject to the effect of drag. This attribute is possessed by all members of the class. But this is not peculiar to it. Members of other class may have this attribute. For example, birds also have this property. Examples of accidents from this class are 'armed', 'unarmed', 'serviceable', 'unserviceable'.

TREE OF PORPHYRY

According to Porphyry classification should start with knowledge in its totality. In the well-known Ramean tree he illustrated the first three predicables. In the Tree of Porphyry a species is derived from a genus by the discovery of a difference. In other words division proceeds by the addition of difference to the genera. The genus is shown to divide into two species, one of which possesses the difference and the other does not. This sort of division; known as dichotomous division.

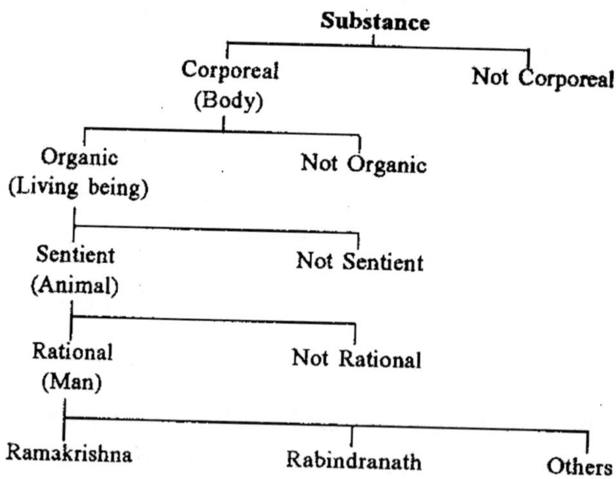

Substance, the single all embracing class from which the division commences, is called the summam genus. The intermediate classes - Body, Living, Being and animal are Subaltern genera. The class or classes with which the division ends are the infima species. The term 'substance' has great extension and small intension whereas Ramakrishna has great intension and small extension. The Tree of Porphyry is a simple example of hierarchy and a clear illustrative of method of subdivision, known as dichotomy or bifurcation.

CLASS MEMBERSHIP AND CLASS INCLUSION

The two aspects of a class-concept give rise to the terms 'class membership' and 'class inclusion'. Members of a class are the individual objects of which it is composed. For example, Ramakrishna, Rabindranath are members of the class 'Man'. The term 'class inclusion', on the other hand, is restricted to narrower classes included in a broader class. Narrower classes are also called sub-classes. For example, the sub-classes of the class 'Man' are rich men, poor men, beggar men, thieves.

CONNOTATION AND DENOTATION

Extension is often used as synonymous with denotation but sometime more usually, to mean all the species of a genus. Extension of a term is the aggregate of objects covered by that term.

Intension is often used as synonymous with connotation. Connotation means the set of properties (Characteristics) which define the term for class. The intension of a term is the aggregate of qualities implied by that term. In intension we consider the term from the point of view of its meaning or qualities.

We can illustrate the use of these terms in relation to the class 'library.

Denotation : Each and every library that exists, did exist or will exist.

Extension : Every kind of library - public library, academic library, special library.

Connotation (Intension) : The small number of qualities that constitute the definition of a library that is, a place where books and other library materials are kept, where they may be read, used and borrowed.

COORDINATE CLASSES

It is a series of coordinate classes derived from one principle of division. The coordinate elements on each level or stage of division form an array. For example, when 'Literature is divided according to characteristic of language we get English literature, French literature, German literature. The term 'Chain' refer to a string of subject, each of which represents a different level in the classification. Literature can be divided first by language and than by form and finally by period. For example :

Literature

(Language) Bengali | English | French | Other

(Form) Poetry | Drama | Fiction | Essay | Others

(Period) Early | Pre-Elizabethan | Elizabethan | Post-Elizabethan

THE KNOWLEDGE CLASSIFICATION

The term 'knowledge' includes not only those disciplines that make statements about the world, such as science, philosophy and history, but also those that create such as arts, crafts and professions. It is dynamic. New units of knowledge are being added to the existing knowledge from time to time. A discipline is a branch of knowledge. The fundamental disciplines are the primary divisions of knowledge. The fundamental disciplines are described as intellectual forms of presentation of knowledge. Some prefer the 'Forms of Knowledge' to 'fundamental disciplines'. They are similar to forms of presentation in that they tell us what book is rather what it is about. For example, 'A history of India' is history; it is written in the discipline of history, but it is about the events in the past life of Indian people. Subdivisions are areas of specialisation within knowledge, for example, zoology, botany, physics, chemistry, etc. within natural sciences. In constructing classification schemes for knowledge the details of relationship between various forms of knowledge are to be explained.

According to John Dewey Knowledge is classification. In science classification is coextensive with knowledge. Scientists are always specialists and each group concerns itself with a particular section of the world's phenomena. A phenomenon is anything that can be directly apprehended by the senses or an event that may be observed. The scientist is concerned with the classification of natural phenomena as perceived. He is not interested with classification of knowledge built up from investigating those phenomena.

Unlike scientists, philosophers are concerned with the general and fundamental nature of knowledge. They are interested in the universe of knowledge. Philosophers use various principles for dividing knowledge. It may be divided according to the knower (three fold division of animal knowledge, human knowledge and divine knowledge). It may be divided according to means of knowing (faculties of sense, reason, memory and intuition). It may be divided according to purposes (practical, intellectual, intertainment and spiritual)

The Twentieth Century has given both to the idea of classification as the detailed specification of individual works. The purpose of bibliographic classification is to organise knowledge provided by specialists. Both scientific and philosophic classification are primary forms. Bibliographic classification deals with knowledge after it has been enshrined in documents. Here it is not objects as observed in the world but their reflection in subjects as treated in documents. The bibliographic classifier looks for the theme of document - a process known as subject analysis.

GROUPING OF PHENOMENA

A category is a grouping of phenomena applicable to the whole or a large part of knowledge. In other words, categories are the most general classes of phenomena. According to Ranganathan there are five categories of phenomena. These categories are Personality, Matter, Energy, Space and Time. These five categories are applicable to all areas of knowledge. For general applicability they are known as fundamental categories. Ranganathan's best-known contribution the fundamental categories derives from Aristotle. There is no metaphysical claim that reality shows a five-fold division, but merely that categories represent the broadest classes of phenomena that are useful in bibliographic classification. Ranganathan did not attempt to apply these categories to knowledge as a whole, but looked for their manifestation in particular subject fields. Categories of phenomena took their place within the forms of knowledge and specialised disciplines, supplemented by such characteristics as point of view, intended audience and bibliographic form.

B.C Vickery has suggested another set of categories : Whole Thing - Kinds (of a thing) - Parts (of a thing) - Materials - Properties - Processes - Operations - Agents - Space - Time. This detailed set is particularly applicable to the fields of Science and Technology.

A distinction is drawn between disciplines and phenomena. Phenomena or things are studied by disciplines. For example, there are two concepts in the 'Psychology of Child', psychology is the discipline concept and 'child' is the phenomenon being studied by the discipline. This phenomenon can be studied by other disciplines such as Education, Medicine, etc. Thus the same phenomenon can be studied by different disciplines. In fact phenomena studied by disciplines play the role of subject concept. It tells what a document is about.

GROUPING OF PHENOMENA

When phenomena are studied in the context of - particular discipline they can be brought together into closely defined groups. In other words, phenomena can be divided into groups or classes on the basis of shared characteristics. These groups or classes constitute the facets of that discipline. Examples of phenomena with the subject area of Medicine are heart, lungs, liver, and kidney. They are called part of a body facet. Therefore, the facet of a subject field consists of a number of phenomena within that subject. They share some characteristics in common.

Simply stated the facet is the whole group of subclasses produced when a subject is divided according to a single characteristic. For example, the class Literature can be divided by the characteristic of form such as poetry, drama, fiction, etc. Within a facet, an individual member or isolate is called a focus. Poetry is the focus in the Form facet of the class Literature. From the whole facet 'Form' we focus our attention on a particular isolate. In plural it will be 'Foci'.

SUBJECTS

The subject of documents may contain any number of facets. If it contains, one facet it must be a basic subject such as Physics, Chemistry. They may be called simple subjects. They imply that documents deal with the whole field named does not not identify any particular phenomenon for attention.

The compound subject is composed of basic subject and isolates drawn from two or more facets of that subject. For example, the Curriculum of Primary School. Here Education is the basic subject and isolates 'Primary' and 'Curriculum' are drawn from two facets of that subject area Education. Compound subjects do not occur in scientific or philosophical classification.

Complex subjects are formed by coupling two or more distinct subjects on the basis of some relation between them. For example, Mathematics for Engineers.

SUBJECTS ANALYSIS

It is the analysis of subjects as they are expressed in documents. In subjects analysis we do not analyse the areas of knowledge in the broad sense. The subject content of a document comprises a number of concepts. In the subject analysis the classifier selects those concepts. The analysis describes the overall theme of the document. For example, 'Geography of India in the 18th Century'. If we analyse the subject we can get concepts : Geography/India/18th Century. Subject analysis may also be called conceptual analysis.

FACET ANALYSIS

Facet analysis is the analysis of a subject into facets according to certain principles enunciated for the purpose. According to Ranganathan it is an 'enumeration of the possible trains of characteristics by which a main class is divided'. The term 'main class' usually means the fundamental disciplines (which are few in numbers) and their major subdivisions, such as Physics, Chemistry, Literature. Ranganathan uses the term 'Basic Subject' to mean any area of knowledge in which a person can specialise. In the process of facet analysis the first postulate is : "Every subject has a Basic Subject". The second postulate is : "There are five and only five Fundamental Categories - namely, Time, Space, Energy, Matter and Personality.

CLASSIFICATION SYSTEMS

Classification systems for knowledge may themselves be classified according to purpose. A complete map of any area of knowledge, displaying all its concepts and their relationships, is known as a classification scheme or system. Such schemes may be designed for different purposes. E.C. Richardson gave a useful classification of these purposes. He divided systems first into theoretical and practical. He arranged theoretical system into three classes :

1. The philosophical or scientific, concerned with the order of sciences or the order of things.

2. The pedagogic, organised with reference to courses of education.
3. The encyclopaedic, area to pedagogic but included some material as well as outline.

It may be noted in passing that the earlier general encyclopaedias were arranged systematically by classification of knowledge. Modern encyclopaedias have been suffering from the disintegrating effect of alphabetical arrangement.

Richardson divided practical systems into the bibliothetic and the bibliographic. The bibliothetic is meant for arranging books on the shelves of library. The bibliographic is suitable for arrangement of titles in a bibliography. The later is more flexible than the former. Nowadays it is more useful to use the term 'bibliographic' to cover both these functions.

LIBRARY CLASSIFICATION

The main objective of a library is obviously to provide information and knowledge to those who need them through a collection of documents. Documents in libraries are physically collected and stored. They may be classified as physical objects. Documents include copies in print, in braille, or film, in sound and videotape. An article from a periodical is a document A report, thesis, a patent, a conference proceeding, an atlas - are all documents. It should not be thought that in any library the physical arrangement of documents will follow one basic principle consistently throughout. Different factors determine the arrangement of documents in a large library. Jack Mills in his book "Modern Outline of Library Classification" has noted the following factors :

(i) **The age of the reader :** Children's books are distinguished from adult's.

(ii) **The conditions attaching to use of material :** books for lending are distinguished from those which may only be referred to on the premises (reference books).

(iii) **The frequency of use of a book :** Current stock is openly accessible whereas reserve stock may be shelved in a stack.

(iv) **The size of the material** : books of unusual size are shelved separately.

(v) **Other physical characteristics** : gramophone records, tapes, slides, audio-visual materials are shelved separately.

(vi) **The thought content of the material** : factual literature is arranged by subject, imaginative literature by language, or author or literary form.

(vii) **The language of the material** : foreign works in their original languages may be separately arranged.

(viii) **The value of the material** : rare books are separately shelved.

(ix) **Peculiarities of forms of presentation** : files of bound periodicals are separately shelved.

(x) **Date of printing** : early printed nooks are shelved separately.

However, the thought content or the subject arrangement is still the document factor for deciding the sequence of documents.

All other factors as noted in the above list are in fact functional. In view of the functional factors a library has to adopt more than one sequence. This gives rise to parallel sequences in various collections in libraries.

DIFFERENT APPROACHES

A reader may demand a document by a particular author or of a particular title or on a particular subject. Let us examine to what extent each of these is helpful to readers :

1. Author Approach

If the arrangement by author is adopted documents of the same writer will stand together irrespective of the subject. This is a good arrangement for those authors whose works belong to belles - lettres. These works have more literary value than subject value. These are frequently grouped by language, form and by the name of the author. By this method all Bengali poetry, for example, is brought together and individual works within that group are arranged alphabetically by author. Such documents belong to what is called in library parlance the Literature Class. Author arrangement within this class will be useful to readers.

On the other hand, if documents having decided subject value are arranged by their authors, the reader who wants to see what the library has on Indian Architecture for example, will not find these documents together on the shelves. Author arrangement usually answers one of two questions :

(i) Has the library a work by a certain author whose name the reader knows ?

(ii) What works have been written by a certain author whose name the reader knows ?

But arrangement of documents on the basis of author is not always helpful to readers. Such an arrangement would not bring together documents on the same subject. In other words author arrangement fails to bring documents having the same specific subjects at one place.

2. Title Approach

Sometimes readers are likely to go to a library for a document having a certain title. If documents are arranged by title, it will satisfy the requirement of the reader who knows the title. But this arrangement will not finally helpful to readers. The title of a book is much less stable than the author's name. Titles may change from edition to edition. In books on science titles are often expressed under the heading 'Study', 'Examination', etc., and since titles are arranged by the accident of the first word this method has the least claim of three criteria to consideration. Moreover, title arrangement, like author arrangement, fails to bring together documents having the same specific subject at one place.

3. Subject Approach

A reader may not know many things about the documents

he wants, but he can approximately know what it is about. This is the subject approach. Majority of readers approach a specific document or documents on the basis of their subject. In looking for likeness in subjects of books a basis can be found for arrangement which will bring together large group of books. This arrangement will best answer the majority of demands made on the collection of the library. Therefore, in well organised libraries, documents are arranged on the basis of subject matter. Contents of books are to be classified in order to bring together information contributing to one and the same subject. Books on art, birds, history, philosophy, religion or science are wanted for the subject matter they contain, regardless of size, colour, title, publisher or even author. It is therefore most helpful to arrange books by subject. The subject approach is for the unknown items and only classification can meet this approach.

When we use the term subject we must always mean specific subject. The specific subject of a book is that division of knowledge, which exactly comprehends all the major factors that go to its creation. When we have decided upon the subject with which a book deals how are we to arrange it in relation to the subjects of other books ? Let us consider the following subjects : Sun, Moon, Planets, Earth, Solar System. On examination it will reveal that they are parts of the larger subject Astronomy. Sc they should be placed together on the principle that a reader interested in one subject is likely to be interested in another.

ALPHABETIC ARRANGEMENT

Everybody can work on alphabetical arrangement if it is not too elaborate. However, alphabetical arrangement is illogical and a unsystematic, everywhere dispersing related subjects. In fact the alphabetical arrangement defeats the very purpose of classification. The problems in the alphabetical arrangement will be evident from the following points :

1. The names of the subjects are not always unique..
2. Synonyms often pose problems on alphabetic sequence.

3. There are problems of homonyms.
4. The names of a subject may consist of two or more words, for example, Geography of India (under G), Indian Geography (under I). Is it to be under G or I?
5. It badly scatters related topics. The linking *see also* references are not as effective a guide to the related topics as a map of logical classification. If there is a request on wheat and if there is no item specifically on this, information may be found on Cereals, food crops, etc. How will these connections be shown in alphabetical arrangement ? Its use as the basic arrangement on shelves is therefore rarely attempted.

On the other the systematic arrangement is an economy to readers and librarians. It is suitable for the following reasons :

1. It brings like books together.
2. It saves time in finding them.
3. It reveals the strength and weakness of the collection.
4. It results in a more consistent collocation of closely related subject for convenience of reference and research.
5. It ensures easy insertion and replacement of individual books.
6. Along with the classified catalogue, it affords the readers a more comprehensive survey of the resources of the library.
7. It facilitates brousing in an open access system.
8. It helps in making of classified entries in catalogues.

HELPFUL SEQUENCE

Subject matter is the primary concern in library classification. The classification should ensure collocation of related subjects. This can be achieved if shelf arrangement follows a helpful sequence. Helpful sequence displays subjects on the shelves in such a way that a reader approaching a group of subjects at any point is led by the order itself to the specified subject he wants.

APUPA

According to Ranganathan, helpful sequence will not be achieved unless the APUPA pattern is observed. There are three types of document. Umbral document implies the totally relevant documents. This type of material is central to the subject interest of the reader. Penumbral document is partially relevant and is in some way related to the umbral document. It can satisfy the marginal interest of the reader. Alien documents is totally non-relevant and can be arranged as Alien - Penumbral - Umbral - Penumbral - Alien (APUPA). This sequence puts the most relevant documents in the centre with the shades of penumbral documents on both sides of the umbral documents and the alien documents at the out-skirt or as much away from the umbral documents. This is a powerful concept for maintaining filiatory sequence that is , placement of all the entities of a universe of knowledge in a definite sequence in one line according to the degree of their mutual affinities. The helpful sequence, therefore, is said to be the one which follows the APUPA pattern.

Knowledge Classification VS. Library Classification

In knowledge classification we arrange knowledge itself. But in library classification we arrange the expression of knowledge in written or other forms. A knowledge classification is abstract, for ideas only are arranged, whereas a book classification is concrete and concerned with ideas in their written representation a much more complex form. It is said that classification of books is the classification of knowledge conditioned by special features of the book. Can we assume that, apart from providing for forms a library classification is identical to classification of knowledge ?

The answer would be yes, with some minor adjustments. In order to make adjustments we have to allow for the way in which subjects are brought together in books. Books are actual indivisible objects. Their forms and purpose demand special treatment in an attempt to arrange them systematically on the shelves of a library. Library classification is therefore concerned with concrete objects. It has to be one dimensional from left to right along the shelves. But a knowledge classification is abstract. It is multi-dimentional. Library classification therefore, sets a limit by reference to knowledge as published. This practical check is known as literary warrant. Here the term 'literary' is used in its broad sense of writings.

LITERARY WARRANT

E.W. Hulme, the librarian of the Patent Office Library, London, published his 'Principles of Book Classification' in 1911-12 in *Library Association Record.* Hulme thought that all classifications could be arranged into two groups :

1. Mechanical,
2. Philosophical.

Book classification is mechanical. Hulme's principles of book classification are the following :

1. Book classification is the plotting of areas pre-existing in literature and coincidence with a philosophical order is no guarantee of accuracy.
2. Book classification is mechanical assembly of material into classes.
3. The division and coordination of classes in literature is determined mainly upon formal and non-philosophical lines.
4. Classification should be based on literary warrant. Hulme used the term 'literary warrant' with somewhat different meaning. We did not believe that library classification should be based on pure knowledge classification. He suggested that a library classification should be built up gradually from observation of the use made of books, rather than following a pre-conceived map of knowledge. He thought that aggregation of subjects in books was so peculiar that it was impossible to fit them into the divisions

of knowledge conceived by the philosophers. Hulme thought 'literary warrant' as a classification system of the subjects of books. This system is quite different from philosophical or scientific classification of knowledge. According to modern experts, Hulme's point indicated that some adjustments were necessary to make knowledge classification suitable for books.

Ranganathan also made use of this principle, but not in the sense Hulme made use of it. He suggested, when the literature on a particular subject grows in size, there may arise a need for providing a separate class for it in the scheme. Ranganathan's principle of literary warrant also requires that the various aspects of such a new subject should be tested as to bring these aspects first on which more literature has been brought out. He described the literary warrant thus, "The subjects in an array of subjects or the isolates in an array of isolates may be arranged in the sequence of the decreasing quantity of the documents published or anticipated to be published on them, except when any other overwhelming consideration rules it out".

FORMATION OF SUBJECTS

In taking about a subject we generally refer to a given area of knowledge. A subject might be considered to be defined by : an area of interest; an area in which an individual researches or professional works; an area in which an individual writes; and an area of knowledge which is studied.

As defined to Neelameghan "A subject is an organised or systematic account of an idea or body of ideas whose extension and intension are likely to fall within the intellectual competence and field of inevitable specialisation of a normal person." For example, "Cultural practices among Christians", "Social pathology" and "Sociology" is each a subject. But, not all that is embodied in the International Encyclopedia of Social Sciences, taken as a whole can be a subject, in the manner defined above.

The subject of documents may contain any number of

facets. If it contains one facet it must be a basic subject such as Physics, Chemistry. They may be called simple subjects. They imply that documents deal with the whole field named and does not identify any particular phenomenon for attention. The compound subject is composed of basic subject and isolates drawn from two or more facets of that subject. For example, "Development of Chemistry in the Twentieth Century" - basic subject component "Chemistry" and the isolate components "Development" and "Twentieth Century" attached to it; "The curriculum of Primary school" - Here, Education is the basic subject and isolates "Primary" and "Curriculum" are drawn from two facets of that subject area Education. Complex subjects are formed by coupling two or more distinct subjects on the basis of some relation between them. For example, Music for plant growth.

Different specialists have recognised different types of relation between the components of a subject or the modes of subjects formation in the universe of subjects. According to Ranganathan subjects in the universe of knowledge could be five methods : Loose Assemblage, Lamination, Dissection, Denudation and Superimposition. Later, his school of thought developed this view point and put forward the following modes of formation of subjects : Loose Assemblage, Lamination, Fission, Fusion, Distillation, Agglomeration, and Cluster.

Loose Assemblage

It is the assembling together of two or more subjects (simple or compound) and isolate ideas. Assembling is done to express one or other possible relations between the components of the assembly. The result is complex subject (Loose Assemblage 1), Complex isolate kind 1 (Loose Assemblage 2) or complex isolate kind 2 (Loose Assemblage 3). Each component in the assembly is called a 'phase'. There are six kinds of phase relations as noted earlier.

Lamination

It is constructed by overlaying facet on facet. When, the basic layer is a basic subject and other layers are isolate ideas, a compound subject is formed (lamination 1). For example, Agriculture of rice. This compound subject in formed by the lamination of Basic Subject (BS) 'Agriculture' and isolate idea 'rice'. Lamination 2 : Here compound basic or compound isolates are formed. For example, Magnetism in Quantum Physics - Basic Subject 'Magnetism' combines with 'Quantum Physics'. Rural Youths - Isolate idea 'Youth' combines with isolate 'Rural'.

Fission

Fission is the process of division or splitting or breaking up into, parts. This process has, until recently, been denoted by the term 'Dissection'. Dissection usually implies the splitting, breaking up, of an entity into parts by an outside agency. But Fission is an internal process of division without an involvement of an outside agency. Philosophy is a basic subject. It may split into logic, epistemology, metaphysics, ethics and aesthetics.

Fusion

Here two or more primary basic subjects are fused together in such a way that each of them loses its individuality. This mode makes a new primary basic subjects. For example, Bio-Chemistry: it is a primary basic subject achieved by the fusion of Chemistry and Biology. some other fused primary basic subjects are : Astrochemistry, Econometrics, Medical jurisprudence, Biolinguistics.

Distillation

Through this process a pure discipline is evolved as a primary basic subject. For example, management Science. New primary basic subjects formed by distillation of kind 2 are Statistical Calculus, Operations research, Demography.

	Loose Assemblage 1 *Inter - subject*	*Loose Assemblage 2* *Intra - facet*	*Loose Assemblage 3* *Intra - array*
General	Relation between political science and Economics	Relation between Morphology and Physiology	Relation between DDC and UDC
Bias	Mathematics for Physicists	Anatomy for Pathologists	The bias of UDC towards DDC
Comparison	Plants and Animals compared	Anatomy and Physiology compared	Psychology of man and woman compared towards DDC
Difference Comparison	Difference between Plants Plants and Animals compared	Difference between Anatomy and Physiology compared	Psychology of man and woman compared
Difference	Difference between Plants and Animals	Difference between Jainism and Buddhism	Difference between Psychology of man and women
Tool	Literature through art, a new approach to French literature	French music through painting	Bengali music through Hindustani music
Influence	The influence of Physics on Chemistry	Influence of Anatomy on Physiology	Influence of Hinayana Buddhism on Mahayana

Agglomeration

Several subjects are sometimes treated integrally or disjunctively in a book. An Agglomerate of kind 1 (earlier called Partial Comprehension) consists of subjects treated integrally or disjunctively in one and the same document. Examples of Agglomerate of kind 1 are : natural Sciences, Humanities, Social Sciences, Biological Sciences, Physical Sciences. Agglomerate of kind 2 is an agglomerate comprehending subject, going with non-consecutive primary basic subjects with respect to the schedules of a particular scheme for classification. For example, Psychology and Education, Political Science and History.

Cluster

Sometimes several specialists from different disciplines may study a particular phenomenon or an entity . This kind of study leads to interdisciplinary or multidisciplinary research. There is a core entity of study. Inputs or viewpoints for different specialists are gathered together into a field of study. This is explained as clustering around a core entity. This core entity is the focus of cluster. For example, Indology (Indian Studies) - India is the core entity of study. Similarly, Sinology (Chinese study), African studies.

STRUCTURE OF SUBJECTS

The mode of formation of a subject leaves its impress on the structure of a subject. Ranganathan enumerated the following kinds of structure :

Dichotomy

It is also known as 'Binary classification',. Here two divisions are formed in the first stage. In the second stage two divisions of each of these divisions are formed and so on. "Tree of Porphyry" is an example of binary classification.

Decachotomy

It signifies division into ten. Melvil Dewey divided the

field of knowledge into 9 main classes and the tenth class was formed of general documents. Each is again separated into 9 special divisions and a tenth division forming general work. A third division is then made by separating each of these divisions into 10 sections. This decimal subdivision is continued till it secures as many subsections as may be required in any topic.

Polychotomy

It means division into many. In 1893 C.A. Cutter in his "Expansive Classification" introduced limited polychotomy by making the number of divisions of each stage 24. Within 50 years, the rate of growth of the universe of that the number of division should at no stage be pre-determined.

Proliferation

Ranganathan suggested various ways in which the universe of subjects going with a Basic Subject can get proliferated. For example, a complex subject in that universe of subjects may be formed by attaching some other Basic Subject as a Phase.

CONSTRUCTION OF CLASSIFICATION SCHEMES

On the physical arrangement of materials, a classification scheme tries to indicate relationships between subjects by grouping them in particular order. This grouping process allows users to see the strength of relationships between particular concepts and should allow users to identify a 'map' of all the various relationships within a particular broad subject area. This idea of a conceptual map of a subject has a number of advantages. It obviously reduces the need to know exactly what a specific subject is actually called for, if the user identify the various relationships that each subject has, it should be possible to find the required subject area by browsing through either a physical arrangement of material or through some catalogue or index.

A classification scheme is defined as an orderly arrangement of terms of classes. The application of such a scheme is to a set of classes according to their subject content. In doing so the classifier should group documents on the same subject together into one class, and arrange classes of documents in a helpful order with respect to one another. It may be noted in passing that the creator of a scheme is called a classificationist while the person who applies such a scheme is referred to as a classifier.

Classification schemes may be general or special. A general classification scheme provides for the whole universe of knowledge. It deals with all subject areas. General schemes are used in public libraries, academic libraries and national libraries. Special schemes deal with restricted areas of knowledge such as education, law, chemistry, library science, soil science. A special scheme covers both a core subject and fringe subjects. The core subject is the named specialisation. The fringe subjects constitute the related subjects with varying degrees of importance to the specialisation. In library science the core subject is 'Libraries and their activities'. Fringe subjects are 'Bibliography' and a variety of social subjects. Special schemes are meant for special libraries, bibliographies, indexing and abstracting services.

APPROACHES

Classification schemes have been constructed by one or two different approaches. The first approach is enumerative. It is the result of the traditional ideas and theories that emerged from the makers of the scientific and philosophical classification schemes reaching right back to the Greeks. Traditional library classification schemes tend to enumerate or list all subjects and their subdivisions and provide ready-made symbols for them. An alternative model for constructing a classification scheme is to use in 'analytic - synthetic' or 'faceted' approach. It places emphasis on facet analysis and synthesis. It analyses and breaks up a subject into its component parts and reassembles those parts as required by the document to be represented.

COMPONENTS

A classification scheme comprises four components :

The schedules, in which subjects are listed systematically showing their relationships;

The notation which is the code for use in the index or catalogue, and has a self-evident order which helps in signalling the arrangement;

The alphabetical index which provides an entry vocabulary, or a list of terms for consultation, and identification of the place of a subject within the scheme;

And finally there must be rules for using the schedule.

In order to ensure that schemes are updated it is important to have some organisation which takes responsibility for revision and publication.

ENUMERATIVE CLASSIFICATION SCHEME

Enumerative classification schemes aim to enumerate or list all subjects present in the literature which the scheme is intended to classify. Thus, all simple, compound and complex subjects are listed in the schedules. Inevitably all subjects present in the literature cannot be listed for this would generate very lengthy schedules, and therefore listing of subjects must be selective. Enumerative schemes are produced by postulating a universe of knowledge (all knowledge in case of a general scheme, some part of it, for example, education, library science in case of a special scheme) and by dividing this into successively narrower classes. A steady process of division will result in very specific detailed concepts which will be listed in the schedules. Let us take a simple example from the field of education. First of all we have to divide the subject field into a number of groups, using a particular characteristic such as 'Level of education'. By using this characteristic we can divide the whole field of education into a first array of subjects. We can list the following :

Primary

Secondary

Higher

etc.

The first grouping of subjects should be done exhaustively, because if we omit a particular concept at this stage there will be problems in the scheme at a later date. The first grouping is then subdivided by a second characteristic 'Curriculum' that is , subjects taught. All subjects taught must subdivide each of the 'Levels of education' produced in the first grouping thus :

Primary
- Language
- Geography
- History
- etc.

Secondary
- Language
- Geography
- History
- etc.

Higher
- Language
- Geography
- History
- etc.

If third characteristic of education is 'Teaching method, 'This will create an array of concepts which include lecture, seminar, tutorial, and so on. This third characteristic will divide each of the subjects taught. Thus the schedule will be constructed as follows :

Primary	Secondary	Higher
Language	Language	Language
Lecture	Lecture	Lecture
Seminar	Seminar	Seminar
Tutorial	Tutorial	Tutorial
etc	etc	etc
Geography	Geography	Geography
Lecture	Lecture	Lecture
Seminar	Seminar	Seminar
Tutorial	Tutorial	Tutorial
etc.	etc.	etc.
History	History	History
Lecture	Lecture	Lecture
Seminar	Seminar	Seminar
Tutorial	Tutorial	Tutorial
etc.	etc.	etc.

In constructing a schedule, a number of decisions have to be taken. Some of these decisions are noted below :

1. The choice of characteristics to be used in dividing the subjects.
2. The order of characteristics to be applied in the process of division.
3. The order of concepts in each of the resulting arrays to be followed.

If the "curriculum" had been the characteristic used in the initial process of division than each 'Level of education' would have been subarranged under all the various subjects taught.

A classification scheme will therefore group together subjects that are the result of the first characteristic of division, while they will scatter subjects produced by subsequent characteristics. In the above examples the various subjects taught are scattered amongst all levels of education, while teaching by lecture method in particular is scattered amongst all subjects which are in turn scattered amongst all the various levels of education. The process of collocation and its corollary of separation is always evident in the process of classification. The decision over which the sequence of characteristics is chosen is therefore crucial to whole user orientation of a particular scheme. It is a problem of the citation order. The citation order will be discused in the next section.

However, we can see how the traditional enumerative classification schemes evolved from this process. Once the schedule has been produced then a notation is assigned to it. The particular problem of this enumerative approach is that emergence of new concepts creates major difficulties. Within this enumerative approach there are always certain overriding generalist concepts such as time and place which recur continuously throughout any subject. Theoretically such time and place subdivisions should be added on as a final characteristic and used to subdivide every single concept that exists in the schedules. A near solution to the problem would be to have certain numbers always meaning a particular time or a particular place which can then be added on to any other number in the schedule.

FACETED CLASSIFICATION SCHEME

Faceted classification relies not on the breakdown of a universe of subjects but on building up from the subject statements of particular documents. Faceted classification rests on the definition of a facet. By this method subject statements are analysed into their component elemental concepts, called isolates. These isolates are listed in the schedules we usually refer to such schemes as 'faceted' because isolates are arranged in groups, called facets, but an alternative name, 'analytico-synthetic', is more revealing of their nature. A facet, then, is the sum total of isolates formed by the division of a subject by one characteristic of division. Ranganathan was the originator of this technique. He demonstrated this technique in his 'Colon

Classification'. The Classification Research Group (CRG) founded in 1952 was responsible for spreading the ideas in the West. In fact, facet analysis - analysing the subject contents of documents into their facets -has now become a well established technique and tool for the construction of faceted classification schemes. let us demonstrate this technique.

ANALYSIS

Within subject field this requires the analysis of the subject into its elementary constituent terms or isolates. Before we start to arrange subjects systematically we have to establish what exactly are the subjects we wish to arrange. In subject analysis we do not analyse the areas of knowledge in the broad sense. The subject content of a document comprises a number of concepts. The analysis describes the overall theme of the document. For example, 'Teaching history in secondary schools by lecture method'. if we analyse the subject we get concepts : Secondary school/history/lecture method. Subject analysis may also be called concept analyses.

CREATION OF FACETS

We assemble isolates into homogeneous facets. Within facets the isolates become foci. The order of foci within facets should be helpful. Thus from our 'education' example we can cite facets in the following ways :

Level of education	Curriculum	Teaching method
1 Primary	A Language	a lecture
2 Secondary	B Geography	b Seminar
3 Higher	C History	c Tutorial

Here we have three facets : Level of education, Curriculum and Teaching method. If we indicate each focus by a notational symbol then the individual foci can be gathered from the relevant facets and the notational symbols joined together to form class mark. If we assign number 1, 2, 3, to the foci of the level of education facet, *Capital letters to the foci of the* *curriculum facet*, and the lower case letters a, b, c to the foci of the Teaching method facet, we can synthesise a class mark for 'Teaching history in secondary schools by lecture method' to give a notation say 2 cB or 2 Bc or Bc2 and so on. Thus in the faceted scheme we can synthesise the symbols by bringing the various foci together from different facets. In the enumerative scheme the concept for 'Teaching history in secondary school by lecture method' will be listed in the schedule. When a new concept arises we can easily insert it into the relevant facet in a faceted scheme. In an enumerative scheme this scope is absent.

In both systems certain key decisions are taken but in a different manner. In an enumerative scheme we need to be cautious about the application and order of characteristics to divide the subject. In a faceted scheme we must make sure that we have all the relevant facets for every subject. The decision over the order of division by characteristic is replaced by an identical decision over the order of precedence of facets. This we call citation order or combination order of facets. Thus we may have :

1. Level of education	2. Curriculum	3. Teaching method
Primary	Language	Lectures
Secondary	Geography	Seminars
Higher	History	Tutorials

If citation order is 1-2-3, a subject such as 'Teaching History in secondary school by means of lectures' would have its combination sequence of foci - Secondary School - History - Lectures. The effect of this citation order is to group all related documents as far as the first facet to be cited is concerned to provide much collocation but some scattering in the second facet and to offer a considerable separation in the facet cited last. Thus 'Lectures in Secondary School' would be subordinate to 'Secondary School', while 'lectures in higher education' would go under 'Higher education'. Thus the citation order or combination order of facets or facet order is a fairly fundamental decision to be taken in a faceted classification scheme.

ORDER OF FOCI WITHIN FACETS

Decisions are also necessary to determine the order of the foci within each facet. Ranganathan has prescribed some principles for arranging foci in a helpful sequence (Canon of helpful sequence).

1. Evolutionary order

It means later in evolution. Living things can be arranged in this way. In Zoology the evolutionary sequence from Protozoa to Mammalia can be observed.

2. Increasing complexity

When classes in an array show different degrees of complexity, they can be arranged in the sequence of increasing complexity. In Geometry, curves and surfaces can be arranged according to their degree of complexity.

3. Increasing quantity

Classes should be arranged in ascending sequence of the measure in which they share the characteristics, Musical composition can be arranged in the order of Solos, Duets, Trios, etc and Chorus.

4. Spatial contiguity

When classes of an array occur contiguously in space they may be arranged in a parallel sequence. In Asia we can arrange adjoining countries (contiguous) thus : China, Japan, South East Asia, India, Persia and so on.

5. Chronological or later-in-time

Classes in an array, if originated in different times should be arranged in a parallel progressive time sequence. Writers in literature can be arranged according to their date of birth. This order may be followed in cases where operations are considered sequentially.

6. Canonical order

This order implies a traditional order. It will be reflected in literary warrant (as warranted by the actual publication). For example, in text books of physics we often find the sequence - Heat, Light Sound, etc. It will be convenient to conform to this conventional order.

7. Favoured category

This is the limited sense of literary warrant. It means the volume of writings an a subject. The order would give precedence to the subjects in the array about which most are being published. Often we need to bring the most wanted item at the beginning of the sequence. For example, in Linguistics or Literature, we begin with the mother tongue.

8. Alphabetical order

Where none of the preceding methods is adequate, we may adopt alphabetical order. Examples are found in Biography, where individual topics are people, and Literature where 'authors' names' need to be arranged.

The designers of both types of schemes need to refer back to various subject disciplines and the needs of the users in order to find out sensible solutions.

COMBINATION ORDER OF FACETS

The scheme lists simple or single concepts which will have to be combined in order to accommodate complex subjects as they are encountered in documents. It should be noted that citation order determines the main categories for shelf arrangement, and determines the nature of collocation. Classification Scatters as it collocates. It can only group primarily by the features listed in one of the facets applied in classifying a document. For example, a document on history in secondary school could be classified first by the level of education facet or first by the subject facet. It is necessary to decide upon a citation order so that such documents are classified in a consistent manner.

Various principles for choice of citation order have been suggested. For determining the facet sequence Ranganathan enunciated three postulates :

1 (i) **Postulate of concreteness :** We should cite more concrete before the more abstract as in the order of PMEST from the initial letters of Ranganathn's fundamental categories - Personality, Matter, Energy, Space and Time.

(ii) **Postulate of Round :** "If the Fundamental Category Energy manifests itself more than once in one and the same specific subject the sequence of two Energy isolates is to be fixed on a general principle, referred to as Wall-Picture Principle".

Wall-Picture Principle : This principle may be stated as follows : "if two facets A and B of a subject, going with a basic subject, are such that the concept behind B will not be operative unless the concept behind A is conceded, even as mural is not possible unless the wall exists to draw upon, then the facet A should precede the facet B".

Let us consider the subject - 'Treatment of disease of children'. Here the concept of treatment depends on the concept of diseases. Unless we first recognise the existence of disease there is nothing to treat. Similarly the concept of disease depends on children. Diseases can exists only in the body. Therefore the citation order of the subject cited above would be : Children - Diseases - Treatment. The order is one of successively dependent concepts.

(iii) **Postulate of Level :** "Any of the Fundamental Categories Personality and Matter may manifest itself among the facets of a specific subject more than once in any one and the same round". For example, Criticism of Shakespeare's

Hamlet. In this title English, Drama, Shakespeare and Hamlet are deemed to be manifestations of Ps. The sequencing of the Personality isolates is to be on the basis of Wall-Picture Principle. The sequence of facets would be Language - Form - Author - Work.

2. Whole Organ Principle

If in a subject, facet B is an organ of facet A, then A should precede B. For example, Bicycle - wheel, Automobile - engine.

3. Purpose/Product

In many basic classes we find subjects in which the objective is to produce some particular product or achieve some particular purpose. In such cases the end -product or purpose should be treated as primary facet. For example, crop in agriculture. The purpose of agriculture is to produce crops.

FILLING ORDER

This is also known as schedule order. We need to study the way in which we should write out the schedule which will show the whereabouts in the sequence any given subjects-simple, compound - will be found. the most elementary principle of schedule order is the general - before - special. That is to say, the general subject would precede the specific subject. For example, a book on music in general would precede one on Rabindrasangeet.

Principle of inversion

Let us consider the following three titles within the basic subject Education:

Teaching by lectures

Teaching history by lectures

Teaching history in secondary - schools by lectures.

We can analyse the subjects thus :

Lectures

History : Lectures

Secondary Schools : History : lectures.

Using the citation order :

Level of education - Curriculum - Teaching method - We can arrange the subjects thus :

Secondary Schools : History : Lectures ...(1)

History : lectures ...(2)

Lectures ...(3)

In the first example level of education is specified, in the second no level is specified but we have subject taught and in the third only method is specified. If we are to follow the general - before - specific principle we need to bring title with teaching method first and the title with level of education last. Thus filing order would be in the order 3 - 2 - 1. That is to say, the schedule order is the reverse of the citation order. Unless it is followed there will be places in the schedule where fundamental principle of general - before - specific will be broken.

NOTATION

Classification schemes adopt a system of symbols as class marks which represent the classes and divisions. The purpose of using such a device, called notation is to represent the subjects and sometimes their relationships. The purpose of using notation is to provide a sequential order for a logical arrangement. In other words, order in classification system is shown by notation. We, therefore, need to choose a set of symbols with a conventional order. It is important to note that notation is not classification. Classifications are concerned with concepts. Notations are added to schedules.

Notations do not make the classification. They should be treated as subsidiary. A good notation cannot turn a bad schedule into a good one. But a bad notation can prevent an effective use of a good schedule.

The notation is usually in the form of numbers or letters or both. If only one type of symbol is used (For example, 0-9, a-z, A-Z). The notation has the quality of purity. A system that employs more than one type of symbol is called a mixed notation.

FUNCTIONS OF NOTATION

The notation must perform at least two functions :

1. The notation must show the desired order. This can be achieved by selecting a set of symbols with their own conventional order. Only a pure notation can give the self-evident order.
2. The notation frequently acts as a link between the catalogue and the shelf.

Qualities of notation

Qualities of notation fall into two groups : those which affect the case of use and those which ensure the inclusion of any new subject in its correct place in the scheme. The qualities represented by the first group are called psychological and the qualities represented by the second group may be called technical. After all notation must be acceptable to users. The psychological qualities of notation are summed up by the term simplicity.

A notation should be easy to read, write and remember. The qualities in the first group are : Purity, Brevity, Hierarchical, Mnemonic and Flexible. Purity is both psychological and a technical quality since the users must be able to follow the order of the notation.

The second group represents the essential function of a notation. That is to say the notation must provide a conventional order. The notation must be able to add new subjects as they arise in the correct place in the overall order. The quality required for this aspect of function is known as hospitality.

Pure Vs. Mixed Notation

In pure notation the users need not have to learn the filling value. Mixed notation does not have any accepted filing value.

But it provides more symbols for use than does pure notation. In other words, mixed notation gives a longer base than does a pure notation. The base means the number of symbols available in the system. For example, if we use numbers in system (0 - 9) the base is ten. If we use letters (A - Z) the base is twenty six. With a longer base the system can provide shorter notation for classes. Mixed notation increases the capacity of the scheme to house topics. E.C. Richardson, Henery Evelyn Bliss, S.R. Ranganathan and others advocated the use of mixed notation. In fact the use of mixed notation has become a necessity due to dynamic growth in the field of knowledge and its complex formation in documents.

Brevity

Bliss argued that a notation should be 'as short as is feasible'. The notation requires to be written on many records such as the spine of the book, the catalogue cards. Therefore the brevity in notation is desirable. Two factors determine the brevity:

1. The number of symbols available in the notation is known as the length of base. The longer the base the shorter the notation tends to be. If we use numbers we can represent ten subjects with one digit, six hundred and seventy six (26 × 26) with two letters and so on.

   There is a conflict between brevity and purity. A pure notation is simple, but it gives longer notation for subjects than does a mixed notation. If we use mixed notation the brevity is assured. But we get brevity by losing purity.

2. The allocation of spaces of symbols to subjects. Some subjects are static, some are dynamic. A poor allocation of spaces of symbols to dynamic subjects cause long notation For example, in DDC a static subject logic is allocated the span of numbers from 160-169. The scheme has only seven classes in Logic and each of them has notation of three digits. For dynamic subject Electrical Engineering is a good example. In DDC it has been allowed only 621.3. But the scheme has over 300 sub-classes in Electrical Engineering. As a result, most of them have

notations more than twice as long as those in Logic. Therefore, dynamic subjects should be allocated a large share of spaces of symbols.

Synthesis

The synthesis of notation affects brevity. In synthetic classification schemes only single concepts are listed. Each single concept must have its own individual piece of notation. In order to specify any composite subject the classifier has to combine these individual pieces of notation according to the specified citation order. A synthesised class number is, therefore longer than the one for its enumerative counterpart. To shorten the synthesised class number a device known as retroactive notation is used. It is interesting to note that an embryonic form of this device exists in DDC - the special use of the zero to introduce standard subdivisions. Here we have achieved synthesis with a pure notation by reserving the symbol O to act as a facet indicator. Because the elements must be combined in order, beginning at the end and working backwards, it is known as retroactive notation. Assuming an alphabetical notation is used, primary facets can be accommodated towards the end of the alphabet and each facet can be qualified by any facet preceding it. No special facet indicators are required, since each change of facet can be shown by a reversion to an earlier letter. Examples of such notation are found in the British Catalogue of Music Classification and Bliss Bibliographic Classification, 2nd ed.

Structural Notation

The structural notation displays or reflects the structure of the scheme. Such a notation is known as a hierarchical kind, as well as expressive. Structural notation tends to be longer than non-structural notation. For example,

Structural		*Non - Structural*
B	Mathematics	B
B_2	Algebra	B_2
B_{25}	Higher Algebra	B_3
B_{252}	Binary Algebra	B_4

The hierarchical notation displays relationship of subordination by adding a new symbol for each successively subordinate class.

It displays generic structure. Expressive notation displays syntactical structure. In other words it expresses the relationships among the subjects. An Expressive notation helps the user understand the systematic order. The hierarchical notation tends to be longer than non-hierarchical notation. But it helps the user to broaden or narrow down searches easily.

Hospitality

As stated earlier, schedule lists subjects or concepts in a helpful way and notation is added to the schedules to show its order. Since knowledge is dynamic, schedules need to accommodate new concepts in the correct place in the overall order. The notation should be able to accommodate insertions at any point where it will be necessary. This ability to accommodate new concepts in the correct placc is known as hospitality.

The notation must therefore, be hospitable. It should be noted that expressiveness and hospitality are mutually exclusive. Sooner or later one or other breaks down. In fact Expressive notation limits hospitality. If we insist on hospitality we have to sacrifice expressiveness. If we insist on expressiveness we are likely to find ourselves abandoning hospitality. There are two kinds of hospitality : hospitality in array and hospitality in chain.

Hospitality in array

This is hospitality to new co-ordinate concepts. Sometimes we need to interpolate new coordinate concepts into an existing array. Extrapolation means addition of concepts at the beginning and at the end of arrays. Ranganathan tried to provide means for the extrapolation of an array by what he called the Sector Device (originally named Octave Device). The first and the last symbols in each array may be reserved for the purpose of extending that array. In a numerical notation, the digit 9 would never stand alone, it would be used to introduce more coordinate concepts. Similarly letters Z, z can be used for the same purpose. For example,

1 2 3 4 5 6 7 8 91 92 ... 98 991 992 so on.

A B C D Y ZA ZB ZC ... ZY ZZA ZZB so on.

a b c d y za zb zc ... zy zza zzb so on.

Hospitality in Chain

This is hospitality to new subordinate concepts. A decimal fraction notation has infinite hospitality in chain.

Interpolations will be discussed in the section on Colon Classification.

Flexibility

The ability to accommodate new concepts is hospitality. The ability to accommodate alternative to suit certain needs is flexibility. In other words a notation may be hospitable to alternative locations and treatment.

Alternative locations

Life of a chemist may be classed either at Biography or at Chemistry to suit the needs of the library. We find such examples in DDC.

Alternative treatment

We can alter the filing order to suit our needs and in that case we need to alter the citation order also. UDC has a very flexible notation. The scheme has suggested filing order for the facet indicators but that is not mandatory.

Mnemonics

Mnemonics in notation are aids to memory. The term means that when a certain concept recurs in the scheme it is represented by the same symbol. Ranganathan suggested four kinds of mnemonics : Alphabetical, Scheduled, Systematic and Seminal.

Alphabetical mnemonics

The initial letter of a subject can be an aid to memory. They are often called literary mnemonics. For example, in Bibliographic Classification of Bliss 'C' stands for Chemistry, 'U' stands for Useful Arts. It can be applied to brands of cycles, motor cars, aeroplanes, etc.

Scheduled mnemonics

A scheme for classification should use one and the same symbol, as the case may be, to represent an isolate idea, array isolate idea, in whatever subject it may occur. Colon Classification conforms to the canon of scheduled·mnemonics. The repetition of schedules has been reduced to a great extent. It is economic. In Ranganathan's terminology the scheduled mnemonics satisfy the law of parsimony.

Systematic mnemonics

The arrangement of isolates in an array is effected by way of systematic enumeration in Colon Classification. In systematic mnemonics the following types of sequences are achieved : Time sequence, Evolutionary sequence, Spatial sequence, Quantity sequence, Complexity sequence, Canonical sequence, Literary warrant sequence. In fact the faceted scheme is fraught with mnemonic possibility, as each basic concept listed within a class will be continually represented by the same symbols.

Seminal mnemonics

Here the same concept is represented by the same number in all places of its occurrence but with different terms. The same digit should denote seminally - equivalent concepts in whatever subject they may occur. For example,

1. Wholeness, unity, God, one dimension.
2. Two dimensions, plane, anatomy, morphology.
3. Three dimensions, space, analysis, function.
4. Pathology disease, physiology, synthesis.

5. Energy, light, liquid, water, women, organic substance, ecology.
6. Mysticism, money, phylogeny, evolution, genetics.
7. Personality, ontogeny, public finance.
8. Travel, organisation, development.
9. Manipulation.

The idea behind seminal mnemonics is to provide classifiers with the power to anticipate revision correctly. Ranganathan applied the concept of seminal mnemonics intuitively in developing the schedules of Colon Classification. It is worth to note that notations are always written down and so memorability of notation is of minor importance. Still if it can be achieved it will be one more advantage. In fine all we can say with certainty is that two vital qualities of notation are ability to convey order clearly and the power to accommodate new subjects in their correct place in the existing classified arrangement.

ALPHABETICAL INDEX

In schedules we arrange subjects or concepts in systematic order. But systematic order is not self-evident. We add notation to schedules to show whereabouts of the subjects in the sequence. But the resulting class numbers lack meaning. User need entry vocabulary. They use words in their approaches to the system. They need alphabetical index. The index lists all the words that users will need to search under and translates them into the notation of the classification scheme. A good index should carry out two definite functions. It must :

(a) locate topics within systematically organised classification.

(b) show related aspects of a subject which the classification itself has scattered.

A distinction is sometimes drawn between the 'relative index' and a 'specific index'. The 'specific index', a name given by Berwick Sayers to the index to the Subject Classification (SC) of J.D. Brown, gives only one entry per term. The relative index, a name given by Dewey display relationships by bringing together under the name of a concept all the relations under which it is scattered in the schedules.

There are a number of problems to be solved before we can claim that we have provided a good index. The first problem is synonyms. In the schedules we normally use only one term for a particular concept, but there may be others. For example, Birds/ Ornithology - both these terms must be provided in the index. The second problem is homonym. It means the same word with different meanings. For example, 'Order'. The term 'order' may mean command, indent, arrangement. All these meanings should be specified within brackets. Otherwise confusion may crop up.

REVISIONS

The rapid advancement of knowledge requires that schemes undergo frequent revisions and updating. Revisions will be necessary but will take the form of extensions. In view of this, it is imperative that librarians become "independent classifiers". This means that librarians should have complete understanding of the principle, theories, and concepts of classification so that they are in a position to amend, modify or revise any classification scheme within the normal limits of human error.

DEWEY DECIMAL CLASSIFICATION

The bibliographic classification scheme designed by Melville Louis Kassuth Dewey (1851 - 1931) is one of the traditional classification schemes. The publication of a 42 - page pamphlet entitled, *A classification and subject index for cataloguing and arranging the books and pamphlets of a library*, in 1876 marked the beginning of both DDC and library classification. Today in its twenty first edition the Dewey Decimal classification has become the most widely - used library classification system. It has been adopted in all five continents of the world. Dewey was an assistant librarian at Amherst College in America when he developed the scheme. Apart from the classification scheme he became the first editor of the library journal in 1876 and the first Secretary of the American Library Association in 1876. Dewey was not the first to introduce subject arrangement of books in libraries. He was, however the first to introduce four innovative features in subject arrangement : relative location, decimal notation, detailed specification and relative index.

Prior to Dewey books were numbered according to their locations on the shelves. In other words, each book had a fixed location. Dewey introduced the idea of using notation to books themselves not the shelves. Notations are assigned to books in terms of their relationship to one another without regard to their locations. New books on a given subject could be inserted anywhere in the existing sequence. The decimal notation refers to the principle of dividing each class into ten subdivisions and each of these ten subdivisions into another ten subdivisions and so on. The relative location along with decimal notation made it easier to specify detailed subdivisions. In the relative index Dewey brings together under one term the locations in the schedules of a subject which in many cases, falls in several fields of study.

MAIN CLASSES

The division of main classes was based on a classification system devised by W.T. Harris in 1870. Harris based his scheme on an inverted order of Francis Bacon's classification of knowledge. Bacon's principle of division was based on the idea that there are three distinct mental faculties or foundations of knowledge : Memory, Imagination, and Reason. From these three fountains sprang three fields : History, Poesy and Philosophy. Dewey divided the whole of knowledge into ten main classes, and than divided each of these into ten subdivisions and then each of the subdivisions into ten sections. The main classes are :

000 Generalities

100 Philosophy and related discipline

200 Religion

300	Social Sciences
400	Language
500	Pure Sciences
600	Technology (applied Science)
700	The arts
800	Literature (Belles - lettres)
900	General Geography and History.

DDC is discipline -oriented scheme. The division of main classes and sub-classes is based on academic disciplines or fields of study rather than the subjects. As a result, the same subject may be classed in more than one place in the scheme. For example, the subject copper may be classed in Chemistry, Metallurgy, Mineralogy, Chemical technology and others depending on the author's approach. This approach is known as classification by discipline.

In general, arrangement is first by discipline, then by subject, with various levels of subject subdivisions, then by geographic and period specification, then by form of presentation. Literature (800) and Generalia (000) classes are deviated from this pattern. In the literature class the arrangement is first by the discipline (literature), then by language, then by literary form, then by period of composition. In the Generalia class certain categories of materials such as general encyclopedias (030), periodicals (050), newspapers (071-079), collections (080) and general publications of general organisations (061-068) are arranged by form, then by language or place as provided by the schedules. It is worth to note that these general materials do not deal with any specific subject and therefore do not belong to any specific disciplines. The literature class and these portions of the Generalities class are sometimes referred to as Form Classes.

It may be mentioned in passing that in DDC, Philosophy, Religion Languages, Literature, etc. have been established as coordinate subjects with social sciences, Pure Sciences and Applied Sciences. The fact that six out of nine main classes belong to the area of Humanities reflects the state of learning in the 19th century. Since Dewey's time advancement of knowledge in all fields has not been uniform in terms of either quality or velocity. This phenomenon has resulted in the unevenness in the scheme as it stands today. Classes such as Philosophy and Religion have remained fairly stable throughout successive editions, while others such as Sociology (later Social Sciences) and useful arts (later Technology/Applied Sciences) have undergone tremendous development and expansion.

NOTATION

The notation of DDC is beautifully simple and pure. The notational base 0-9, which is rather short and will therefore result in long numbers. A base of ten has become the major characteristic of DDC. In application a three-digit number is used by employing zeros to fill out the base number to three digits. For example, 500 for Pure Sciences, 510 for Mathematics. For numbers containing more than three digits, a point is placed after three digit. For example, 331.11 Labour force.

Another major characteristic of the notation is its hierarchical structure. The notation expressed the relationship between each unit of knowledge and its subordinate elements. Each main class is divided into ten divisions. The second position in the notation represents the division. Each division in turn is divided into ten sections. The third position of the notation represents the section. The following example illustrates the hierarchical structure present in both the notation and the classificatory categories :

500	Pure Sciences
510	Mathematics
516	Geometry
516.3	Analytic geometries
516.37	Metric differential geometries
516.372	Euclidian

As the classification progresses from the general to the specific, each level of division is indicated by the addition of one new digit.

In DDC there are several mnemonics which fall into systematic category, but in a limited way. For example, in literature within a particular language 'poetry' is always represented by 1. Thus 811 American poetry, 821 English poetry, etc. However, I does not by any means always mean poetry even within literature. Italy is represented by the notation 5 which recurs in numbers related to that country : 945 History of Italy; 914.5 Geography of Italy; 450 Italian language; 554.5 Geology of Italy; 195 Italian philosophy; 075 a newspaper in Italian language, DDC has become increasing in later editions. It provides for combination of notation in several ways.

NOTATIONAL SYNTHESIS : 19TH EDITION

The base number should always be taken from the schedules. The other elements may come from either the schedules or the auxiliary tables, or both. The order of the elements in each case is to be determined by instruction in the schedules or tables.

ADDING AN ENTIRE NUMBER TO A BASE NUMBER

A bibliography of physics **016.53**

1. The index provides a number for subject bibliographies 016
2. Turning to the schedules, the fixed under 016.1 - 016.9 a note is given "Add 100-900 to base number 016" which means that any number within that range can be added to 016 to get the number for bibliographies of that subject.
3. The number for physics .530
4. This number is added to the base number .016530
5. A point is inserted after the third digit and terminal 0 is removed 016.53

ADDING FROM PART OF THE CLASSIFICATION AS INSTRUCTED

Photographs of scientific subjects 779.95

1. Base number for photographs with instruction, "Add to base number 779 the numbers following
   704.94 in 704.942 - 704.949"
2. Find the most appropriate number in the sequence;
   Iconography of other specific subjects, with instruction; "Add 001-999 to base number 704.949
3. The number for science 500
4. Add 3 to 2 704.949500
5. Add the number following 704.9490 to (1) 779.9500
6. Insert point and remove terminal 0s 779.95

ADDING A NOTATION FROM THE AUXILIARY TABLES TO A BASE NUMBER

Table 1 may be used anywhere in the schedules entirely at the discretion of the classifier. Tables 2, 5, 6, 7 however, may only be applied by the classifier where instructed. It should also be noted that notations from Table 2, 5 and 7 may be added, according to instructions, to - 09, - 89, and - 88 respectively, in Table 1 and the results are then used as 'standard subdivisions'. Table 3 is intended solely for use in the 800 literature mainclass and Table 4 is used in the 400 language main class. All notations from auxiliary tables are preceded by a dash indicating that those are not, complete class but must be used in conjunction with number from the schedules.

TABLE 1 : STANDARD SUBDIVISIONS

All notations for standard subdivisions begin with a 0, for example; - 01 philosophy and theory; - 02 Miscellany; - 03 dictionaries, Encyclopaedias, Concordance; - 04 General Special; and so on. There is a schedule for time but still inflexible. With the exception of - 04, the classifier does not need any specific instruction in order to add the notations for standard subdivisions. The standard subdivision - 04 is reserved for special concepts which have general application throughout the regular subdivisions of certain specific subjects. Therefore, it varies from subject to subject and is to be used only when the special concepts are spelled out in the schedules. For example,

540 Chemistry

- 09 History

History of Chemistry 540.9 [not 540.09]

Before adding a standard subdivision to base number the classifier should remove all the zeros which are used fillers.

Restrictions on the use of standard Subdivisions

In addition to individual restrictions appearing in the schedules relating to specific numbers (for example, does not use 362.09, class in 362.9) certain general restrictions are set forth in the editor's introduction :

Unless there are instructions in the schedules permitting their use, the classifier should be cautions about adding a standard subdivisions to the number chosen for a work that deals with a subject more specific than the content of the number that is, when the subject represented in the work does not have its own specific number. For example, *a history of classification system* is classed in 025.4309, but *a history of BBK* (Russian scheme) which does not have its own number, is classed in 025.43, instead of 025.4309.

2. The classifier should not add standard subdivisions when they are redundant. For *a history of India* we need not add - 09 to 954, which already means history. Likewise, we need not add - 03 to 423 which already means *Dictionary of English language*.
3. "The editor recommends that the classifier should not add one standard subdivision to another standard subdivision unless there are specific instructions to do so".

When more than one standard subdivision is applicable to a work, the classifier should choose one. In choosing a standard subdivision, *the table of precedence* given at the beginning of Table 1 should be consulted. For example, 020.7 for *Journal of Education for Librarianship* rather than 020.5 or 020.705.

At notation 611 (Human Anatomy, Cytology, etc) instruction is given for the use of standard subdivision. Use 001 - 009 standard subdivisions for Human Anatomy. Example,

A dictionary of human anatomy	611.003
A Journal of human anatomy	611.005

At notation 350 *Public administration* instruction is given - Use 350.0001 - 350.0009 for standard subdivisions. Hence *a history of public administration* 350.0009. Such type of notes should be honoured before using standard subdivisions.

In the 20th edition, the following kinds of instructions indicate when a different number of zeros must be used :

1. Notation in the number column, for example, 620.009 for *history of engineering.*
2. The instruction at 324.241 to use 324.241001-241009 for standard subdivision gives us 324.241009 for *history of political parties in the United Kingdom.*
3. Footnotes leading to an add table in which, the subdivisions are supplied. For example, the add table under 616.1 - .9 indicates that 001 - 009 is to be used for standard subdivisions. At 616.1 the heading Diseases of the Cardiovascular system is governed by a note that says add as instructed under 616.1 - .9. For *the history of diagnosis and treatment of cardiovascular diseases* we get 616.1009.
4. Footnotes directly under an add instruction the use of extra zeros. For example, the footnote to the add note under 327.3 - .9 gives us 327.41009 for *the history of foreign policy of the United Kingdom.*

TABLE : AREAS

Areas notation specifies the geographic subdivision of a subject and may be used with numbers throughout the schedules as instructed.

Music Festivals 780.79. We are invited to subdivide further if need be, via the area table.

Music Festivals in India 780.7945[- 54 India form Table 2]

Foreign relations between Japan and India 327.52054

1. Base number for foreign relations between specific nations as listed 327 under 327.3 - 327.9
2. Areas notation for Japan - 52
3. Areas notation for India - 54
4. As instructed, add areas notation for one nation to the base number, add 0 and to the result add area notation for other nation. The order of areas notation is determined by the emphasis of the work.
5. If Japan is emphasised 327.52054
6. If India is emphasised 327.54052
7. If emphasis is equal, give priority to the nation coming first in the sequence of notations 327.52054. If no instruction is given and the classifier wishes to divide a subject by a geographical region, he must introduce the regional number by 09. For example, Railroad transportation in Japan 385.0952

To obtain numbers for geography of a specific location, area notations we added to 91. For example,

Geography of Japan 915.2 [- 52 Japan]

TABLE 3 : SUBDIVISIONS OF INDIVIDUAL LITERATURES

Notations from table 3 are used when applicable with the base numbers for individual literature identified by * under 810 - 890 in the schedules.

In the 20th edition we have basic number building facilities for works in an individual language by or about individual authors (with the use of Table 3-A) and by or about more than one author (with the use of Table 3-B). The following elements are used to build the numbers : base number; form period; kind, scope or medium; notation 08. Collection or notation 09 criticism (plus additional 0s in some cases); subform; additional notation from Table 3-C and the tables. For example,

An anthology of American Literature	810.8
1. Base number for American Literature	81
2. Subdivision for collection from table 3-B	- 08

Works by or about an individual author : restricted to a specific form and period (Table 3-A).

Spencer's Fairie Queene	.821.3
Base numbers for English literature	82
Form number	- 1
Period number	- 3

Literature for and by persons resident in specific continents, countries, localities (use Table 3-C)

A collection of French poetry by Swiss authors of the later 19 the century : 841.80809494

TABLE 4 : SUBDIVISIONS OF INDIVIDUAL LANGUAGES

Notations from Table 4 are used with the base numbers for individual languages marked in* 420 - 490 in the schedules.

French phonology 441.5

[- 15 Phonology from Table 4 to base number 44]

Bilingual dictionaries (- 32 - 39 from Table 4)

Class the bilingual dictionary first with more foreign language and secondly with the language clear to the user. If classification with either language is equally useful, class with language coming later in the sequence .420-490. In the 20th edition the instruction reads "The Decimal Classification's Division classes a bilingual dictionary with entry words in both languages with the language coming later in the sequence 420-490".

	Sanskrit - English dictionaries	491.2321
	[For English speaking regions]	
1.	Sanskrit dictionaries	491.23
2.	English language - 21 from Table 6	- 21
	Add to 2 to 1	
	Polyglot dictionaries are assigned to	413

TABLE 5 : RACIAL, ETHNIC, NATIONAL GROUPS

The notation from this table may be used with those numbers from the schedules and other tables to which the classifier is instructed to add "Racial, Ethnic, National groups notation".

	Chinese non-dominant aggregates	301.451951
1.	Social position of non-dominant aggregates	301.45
2.	Aggregates of other origins	301.4512 - .4519
3.	Add notation 2-9 from Table 5 to base number 301.451	
4.	Notation for Chinese - 951 from Table 5	
5.	Add 4 to 301.451	

Except where the schedules instruct otherwise, for a group outside the country of origin add 0 to the number from this table and to the result add areas notation from Table 2.

For example, Social position of Chinese in South Africa.

[- 68 South Africa from Table 2] 301.451951068

TABLE 6 : LANGUAGES

Notation from this table may be used with base numbers from the schedules and other tables to which the classifier is instructed.

An English translation of the Koran 297.122521

297	Islam and religions derived from it
.1	Sources, relationships, attitudes of Islam

.12	Sacred books of scriptures
.122	Koran
.1225	Translation

Translation of the Bible in German language 220.531

Translation of the Bible 220.5

German language - 31 from Table 6.

TABLE 7 : PERSONS

Notations from this table may be used with those numbers from the schedule and other tables to which the classifier is instructed.

Mathematics for engineers 510.2462

From Table 1 : 024 works for specific types of users

Mathematics 510.24. Engineers 62 from Table 7.

REVISION

The main method of revision has been by the publication of new editions. Revisions usually take the following forms : Expansion, Relocation, Reduction and Phoenix schedules. The last form is the most drastic form of revision. However, 'DC & Decimal Classification : additions, notes and decisions' is a useful means by which modifications can be announced in advance of a new edition.

ORGANISATION

Dewey set up the Lake Placid Club Education Foundation to carry on his work. In 1923, the Editorial Office was moved to the Library of Congress. The Forest Press publishes and markets the DDC. Consultation with user is achieved via the Decimal Classification Editorial Policy Committee, The British Liaison Committee and Australian Liaison committee. The OCLC (Online Computer Library Centre) has acquired the Forest Press, the publisher of the DDC.

DDC 21 : AN OVERVIEW

Changes in some areas have been found to be complex.

Table 2 Geographic areas, historical periods, persons - 47 Eastern Europe - Russia (completely revised) schedules 000 - 999

350 - 354Public administration (completely revised). the subdivisions and citation order have been changed. In DDC 20, topics of public administration were arranged under the jurisdictions Central government, Local government, United States federal government and specific central government. DDC 21 puts the topic first and then builds the number to bring out the jurisdiction, specific department or agency. The U.S. bias in wording and structure has been reduced. For example,

352.094	Public admin - Local govt. - Australia (now 351.094)
354.94	Public admin - Central govt. - Australia (now 351.94)

370 Education

Extensively revised in that some subdivisions have been reworked and expansions provided for new topics, e.g.

370.19	Educational sociology (now 306.43)
370.19342	Policy - Educational opportunity (now 379.26)
560 - 590	Life Sciences

Extensively revised

574	Biology. Number is no longer used. Biological processes have now been classed in the span 571 - 575

SELECTED REVISIONS

Schedules

004 - 006	Data Processing - Computer Science
004.678	Internet now has its own number (was 004.67 Wide - area networks)
230	Christianity Comprehensive works have been relocated from 200 (The Bible remains in 220)

398.209	Folk literature treated by specific continent, country, locality
508.2	Seasons (Now has its own number, was 508 Natural history)
781.64	Western popular music new Subdivisions added for ragtime, reggae and rap
796.22	Skateboarding (Now has its own number, was 796.21)
810 - 890	Literature Literary periods updated and expanded.

USES OF DDC

DDC was adopted by libraries widely both at home and abroad. Prominent users are *Booklist* (American Library Association), *Publisher's Weekly* (R.R. Bowker), *Book Review Digest*, *British Book News* (British Council) and *The annual Indian Books in Print*. National Bibliographies such as *British National Bibliography*, *Indian National Bibliography*, *Australian National Bibliography*, *Sri Lankan National Bibliography* and the *Canadiana* use the DDC.

It is used in all Commonwealth countries, Latin America, Norway, Italy, Greece, Israel, the Arab Countries, Southeast Asia and the Far East. Its use in international bibliographic records including MARC (Machine Readable Cataloguing) tapes are other factors contributing to its popularity and durability.

Electronic Dewey was published in 1993 in CD ROM (Compact Disc - Read Only Memory) form by Forest Press / OCLC. It heralds the electronic age of classification providing greater flexibility to access the data. After the demise of Dr. Comaromi, Joan S. Mitchell has been appointed Editor of the DDC.

DDC 21st edition was published in 1996 by OCLC Forest Press. DDC 21 includes three major revisions : 350-354 Public administration (a complete revision); 370 Education; and 560-

570 Life Sciences. Only two parts of 560-590 are completely revised : 570 (Biology in general), 583 Dicotyledons. Other notable revisions include 296 Judaism; 297 Islam; 368 Insurance and Table 2 area umbers - 47 for the former Soviet Union and - 499 for Bulgaria. Many new topics that have gained literary warrant since the publication of Edition 20 are now mentioned in the classification. For example, rap music, virtual reality, in-line skating and snow boarding.

The Abridged DDC 13 Edition was scheduled to be published in 1997.

RELATIVE INDEX

The final and significant part of the scheme is the relative index. Dewey said that his relative index was the most important part of the DDC. The name is derived from the fact that this sort of index displays relationships by bringing together under the name of a concept all the notations under which it is scattered in the schedules. In the schedules the different aspects of a subject are scattered according to discipline. In the relative index they are brought together under the name of a subject with their various location in the schedule indicated.

Here is an example from DDC 19

Iron

Age archaeology 933.16

alloys

Technology 669.141

Other aspects See Ferrous metals

Chemistry 546.621

Organic547.05621

EVALUATION

Being a pioneer scheme it is widely used because of this time factor rather than intrinsic merit. The scheme attracts those who are conventional to the point of timidity, receiving comfort and assurance from its long history and heroic resistance to change. One of the major objectives of DDC has been practicability. Dewey developed actual classifications and evolved theory round the practical schemes. Despite its drawbacks, this method has a great deal to concern it. It has survived many storms in the part several decades and is still the most popular scheme in the world today. A great deal has been written about the advantages and disadvantages of using the system. It is worth to highlight some of the opinions.

ADVANTAGES

1. It has a simple, pure notation. The pure notation of Indo-Arabic numerals is universally recognised. People from different cultures and language backgrounds can adapt to the system easily.
2. The self-evident numerical sequence facilitates filing and showing the class numbers are easy to read, write and remember.
3. The scheme is hierarchical, like a family tree. It can show the relationship of specific subject to the parent subject. The hierarchical nature of the notation can express relationships between and among the class numbers.
4. The scheme uses the decimal system which allows for expansion and subdivision so that new subject can be accommodated.
5. The scheme has an excellent relative index which brings together the different aspects of the same subject scattered throughout the schedules.
6. Alternative locations are allowed for many subjects so that differing libraries can cater to the needs of their own clientele.
7. The periodic revision at regular intervals makes the scheme up-to-date.
8. Finally, it is there. This means user can procure it easily and quickly.

DISADVANTAGES

1. The separation of related disciplines has been criticised, for example, Social Sciences from History; Languages from Literature; Psychology form Medicine.
2. The base of ten results in lengthy classification numbers. It also limits the hospitality of the notational system by restricting to nine divisions the capacity for accommodating subject on the same level of hierarchy.
3. No new subjects can be inserted between coordinate numbers. In many cases a new subject has been included as a subdivision under an existing subject. For example, 621.3 Electrical engineering.
4. The different rate of growth has resulted in an uneven structure. Some classes have become overcrowded. For example, Sciences and Technology.
5. The scheme reflects an Anglo-American bias in culture, language, literature, religion and elsewhere. Efforts have been made to internationalise the scheme by providing necessary options.
6. Relocations and phoenix schedules often create practical problems in reclassification.
7. The improper placements of certain subjects have been criticised. For example, Psychology as a subdivision under Philosophy, Sports and Amusements in Fine Arts.
8. In Literature class, literary works by the same author are scattered according to literary form. But most scholars would prefer to have them grouped together.

CALL NUMBER

To distinguish books on the same subject, an author notation is added to the classification number to form a call number. The name probably came from the fact that in the earlier days of closed stocks, a library user "called" for a book by means of its unique number. There are various kinds of author notation depending on the classification scheme used and the size of the collection. With the DDC several kinds of author notation are employed. The simplest form is the initial of the author's last name. Most libraries use Cutter numbers named after its designer Charles Ammi Cutter. He is the author of the Expansive Classification scheme. There are now three Cutter Tables. Two-Figure Author Table, There-Figure Author Table, and the Cutter - Sanlorn Table. Kate E Sanborn revised an early edition of Cutter Marks but the finished result is more of an independent table than an arrangement of the original scheme.

UNIVERSAL DECIMAL CLASSIFICATION (UDC)

In 1894 two Belgian lawyers, Paul Otlet and Henri La Fontaine became interested in the idea of 'Universal Index to Recorded knowledge' to be available to the world. This project was initiated in 1895 by the Institut Internationale de Bibliographie located in Brussels which later became the Federation Internationale pour Information et Documentation (FID). The projected compilation with which the two Belgians were busy was called Universal bibliographic repertory, a comprehensive classified index to all published information. The international nature of this endeavour meant that two men were attracted to the idea of retrieval system that overcame the language barrier. Seen from this aspect it will be plain from what points of view Otlet and La Fontaine developed Dewey's Decimal Classification into the UDC, a tool for classifying documents. They approached Dewey for permission to expand and modify DDC, then in its fifth edition, to suit the purpose of bibliography. The permission was given and the precious copy had to be brought all the way from the USA. The development of the scheme went ahead and in 1905 it was published as the *Manual Du Repertoire Universal bibliographie* in French. The record French edition was published over the years 1927 to 1933. The second edition had the title *Classification decimal Universelle* (UDC) which it has been known ever since.

As its origin suggests, UDC, was designed for detailed indexing of documents and not for shelf arrangement. Another person who became involved in the development of the scheme was Frits Donker Duyvis of the Dutch Patent Office. In fact UDC owes a great deal to the tireless efforts of this man who become the Secretary of the IIB in 1929. The IIB changed its name to IID (Institut Internationale De Dccumentation) in 1931 and again in 1937 to FID (Federation Internationale de Documentation). In 1986, FID has added the word *information* to its name.

The credit for introducing and popularising UDC in the United Kingdom goes to S.C. Bradford. The responsibility for publishing a full edition in English was initially taken by the British Society for International Bibliography and Aslib together. They published several parts. The full English edition has now been completed, published in separate parts for all the various divisions and subdivisions of the main classes. This is published by the British Standard Institution (BSI). BSI published an abridged edition. The BSI has also published BS 1000 M : 1985 - UDC. International medium edition. The index to this edition was published in 1988. The latest in the series of publications is BS 1000 M : 1993. International medium edition. Parts 1 and 2. London : British Standard Institution, 1993.

BASIC PRINCIPLES

UDC is an adaptation of DDC. It therefore, follows the basic outline of DDC in the main classes and major subdivisions. Both are general classification schemes. The degree of detail in UDC through common and special auxiliaries makes it suitable for bibliographic use. It is because of this reason UDC is known as bibliographic classification as against DDC which is called library classification. Both are basically enumerative classifications. UDC is nevertheless a faceted scheme because of its auxiliaries. These auxiliary tables give the analytico - synthetic character to the scheme. The main class structure is as follows :

0 Generalities, Science and Knowledge, Organisation, Information, etc.

1 Philosophy, Psychology, Morals

2 Religion, Theology

3 Social Sciences, Law, Government, Education, Commerce

4 Vacant

5 Mathematics and Natural Sciences

6 Applied Sciences, Medicine, Technology, Agriculture

7 Arts, Recreation, Entertainment, Sport

8 Language, Linguistics, Literature

9 Geography, Biography, History

This cutline shows class 4 to be vacant, linguistics have been moved from 4 to 8 in 1963 to make room for future development.

NOTATION

The notation is similar to that of UDC. Dewey's three - figure minimum is not required for main classes and their subclasses. In other words, UDC does not use the zero as a filler. For example, Literature is represented by 8 instead of 800. A point as in DDC is inserted after the third digit. For example, 591.185 animals. The UDC notation consists of the following sets of symbols :

1. Ten Indo-Arabic numerals 0, 1 to 9.
2. Roman alphabet, with capital and lower case.
3. Punctuation marks : Point, semi-colon, colon and inverted commas.
4. Mathematical signs : the plus and the equals.
5. Some other symbols like parenthesis, square brackets, stroke and apostrophe.

UDC has considerately more opportunity for synthesis, providing the facility for combining notations, not only by use of a set of auxiliary tables of common concepts, but by the use of a special symbol. Because the notation is like DDC, numeral and decimal, UDC can accommodate new concepts, where appropriate, and infinitum. The notation is thus hospitable and capable of reaching the required level of detail and specification.

AUXILIARY TABLES

The UDC has developed two kinds of auxiliaries - common and special. They permit much more scope for synthesis than can be achieved with DDC. The auxiliaries are a set of facets indicators which enable the classifier to synthesise freely. Common auxiliaries affect the whole scheme and special only specified parts of the scheme. These are located under the *Tables of auxiliaries* beginning on page 10 (3rd Abridged Edition, 1961) common Auxiliaries. The common auxiliaries denote generally recurrent characteristics, meaning features common to all subjects. They may be divided into two groups. Those that are simply signs that join other notational elements together and those that are signs that introduce explicit tables of subdivisions. The first auxiliaries are essentially signs which permit the combination of two or more numbers from the main schedules. These are the plus, the stroke, the colon, the square brackets and the double colon. These signs are :

(a) The addition sign + (plus) is used to join together two subjects not adjacent in the schedules. For example,

    54 + 66   Chemistry and Chemical technology

    The stroke / sign is used to join the first and the last of a series of consecutive UDC numbers to indicate a broader subject for which no single number exists. For example,

    23/28   Christianity

    Both plus and stroke would be filed before the single number.

(b) The relation sign : (Colon) is used to link two or more UDC numbers. For example,

    51 : 62   Mathematics for engineers.

It may be used for phase relations. here colon means reversible relation. For example,

17:7 Relation of ethics to art or

7:17 Relation of art to ethics.

[ ] Square brackets mean Algebraic subgrouping. For example, 31 : [622 + 669] (485) Statistics of mining and metallurgy in Sweden.

: : (double colon) Irreversible relation, especially in computerised systems.

For example, 061.2 (100) : : 002 FID International Federation for information and documentation. The use of : : (double colon) was recommended in 1974 and has now been incorporated in UDC (International Medium Edition).

(c) Equals = sign is used for languages. For examples,

A book on zoology in English languages 599 = 20

(d) The common auxiliaries of form are identified in a class number by their own facet indicator (0...) brackets - nought. For example, thesis in physics 53 (043.2)

(e) The common auxiliaries of place (1/9) brackets one-to-nine). For example, French Railway System 385 (44)

(f) The common auxiliaries of race and nationality allow particular races and nationalities to be identified in texts. They are shown by (=) brackets equal. For example, French folklore 39 (= 40)

(g) Time auxiliary is shown by " " (Quotation marks). For example, Twentieth century medicine 61 "19"

Dates are expressed in UDC a numerical statements

(h) Sometimes occasions may arise when it will be useful to name individuals or to list items denoted by a number. This can be done by alphabetical and (non-decimal) numerical subdivisions. For example,

Twenty first edition of Dewey 025.45 DDC 21

Individual members of a class are identified thus :

Philosophy of Kant	1 (Kant)
Life of Wells	92 (Wells)

(i) The point of view facet is indicated by .00 (point-nought-nought). It indicates the broader aspect of a particular subject. For example,

Mining personnel	622.007

A modification to the point-of-view facet is the ability to indicate the author's point of view. This is .000 followed by number. For example,

Social welfare from the Marxist point of view
362.000.335.5

SPECIAL AUXILIARIES

Unlike common auxiliaries, special auxiliaries are not listed in one place in the schedule. They denote locally recurrent characteristics. They are in fact subdivisions that deal with limited range of subjects only.

They are 'special' in the sense that their use is restricted to those classes of which they form an integral part. Special auxiliaries are identified by the facet indicators, - 1/- 9 hyphen series, .0 point-nought series and apostrophe series. Examples :

Safety Devices	621-77
Art aesthetics	7.01

'(Apostrophe) is synthetic, not analytical in function. Its use in Abridged edition is closely seen in parts of the Chemistry class :

Sodium	546.33
Chlorine	546.13
Sodium Chloride	546.33'13

The apostrophe series are at places fully listed, but elsewhere are derived through the device of parallel division. Example from International medium edition is given below :

329.12 13'23	Liberal-Progressive-Republican Parties
Synthesis of	
[329.12	Liberal attitude
329.13	Programic attitude
329.23	Republican attitude]

INTERNATIONAL MEDIUM EDITION

UDC International medium edition (BS 1000M) is issued by arrangement with the FID. It consists of two parts :

Part 1 Systematic tables (published in 1985)

Part 2 Alphabetical Subject Index (published in 1988).

The UDC (M) has been thoroughly revised, enlarged and reorganised. The following principal developments may be noted:

UDC Abridged edition had nine common auxiliary tables and three types of special auxiliaries. In the UDC (M) we have eleven common auxiliary tables with the addition of Table 1 (K) - 03 Common auxiliaries of materials and Table 1 (K) - 05 Common auxiliaries of persons and personal characteristics. It may be noted that - 05 divisions are used in some classes of the Abridged edition as special auxiliary numbers.

The common auxiliary subdivisions fall into two groups. The independent and dependent auxiliary tables. The independent auxiliaries are Tables 1 (C) to 1 (G) - the auxiliaries of language, form, place, race and time. The independent auxiliary subdivisions may additionally be used on their own to form the class number for document. the dependent auxiliary tables have always to be fixed to a UDC number : these are tables 1 (C) to 1 (K) - the auxiliaries of point of view, materials and persons. For example,

Persons	- 05
Buddhism	294.3
Buddhists	294.3 - 05.

INTERCALATION

It is a device that facilitates infixing. Infix is an element or a number that interrupts another number. Intercalation is the use of an auxiliary as an infix rather than a prefix or suffix. Certain auxiliaries may interrupt a main number creating a compound. For example,

Iron ore mining in India	622.341.1 (540)
Mining - India - Iron ore	622. (540).341.1

So creating an order such as

622

622 (540)

622 (540).341.1

The intercalation device changes the citation order of facets with a view to creating more helpful sequence.

FILING ORDER

The filling order is based on an approximately general-before-special sequence. A common auxiliary used as an independent number is filed before the main number. This is followed by a compound number having the plus sign or the stroke in it. Next the simple numbers are filed in the order of increasing length. It suggests a filing order in the introduction to English Abridged Edition (BS 1000 A : 1961, page 9). The International medium edition - English Text (BS 1000 M : 1985) contains the filing order on page xi.

ALPHABETICAL INDEX

The UDC index is relative. The index to the abridged edition is satisfactory. It includes synonyms and cross-references. UDC International medium edition has a computer - generated index. The alphabetical arrangement is by word - by- word.

MAINTENANCE AND REVISION

Before the end of 1991 the responsibility and updating of UDC was lying with the FID. The FID used to work in conjunction with national organisations having consultative arrangements with uses of the UDC.

In was the Central Classification Committee of the FID that maintained the master version of the scheme incorporating all approved amendments. The amendments proposed by users through subject committees were circulated as P-notes (Provisional or proposed alterations) to subscribers. After they became acceptable they were published in UDC's annual periodical Extensions and Corrections to the UDC.

From the end of 1991, responsibility and updating was assumed by a new organisation, the UDC consortium (UDCC). The UDCC published Extensions and Corrections to the UDC vol 17 in November 1995. The contents of this volume are as follows : includes a "Report of the UDC Editor -in Chief by I.C. McWaine" and the " Restructuring of class 61 - Medical Sciences" by I.C. McWaine and N.J. Williamson.

EVALUATION

Although UDC has inherited an unscientific structure from the DDC, it has evolved an extensive synthetic apparatus on an enumerative base, It certainly has more merits to its credit. It has consciously aimed at classifying microthought- the world of specialised packages of literature is periodical articles, reports, standard and the like.

UDC is a general scheme covering the whole field of human knowledge. The required degree of detail is achieved with the help of auxiliaries. The notation of UDC consists of Indo-Arabic numerals and sign which are understood internationally. Because of the use of auxiliary tables the UDC is an analytico - synthetic scheme. UDC has extremely flexible citation order. UDC is specially suited to special libraries.

'Universal' in title refers to the subject coverage. But it has never said down rules for international usage. As a result, there are as many interpretations of UDC as there are users of it. The notation often tends to be long and appears clumsy - its use on the shelves becomes difficult. Despite its many defects the UDC in still the most widely used system of classification.

COLON CLASSIFICATION

Shiyali Ramamrita Ranganathan is considered to be the foremost theorist in the field of classification. Colon Classification (CC) is a manifestation of his theory. Although Ranganathan's scheme of classification has not been widely used his theory has influenced in one or another, all currently used classification schemes. The Colon Classification received its name from the colon " " sign that Ranganathan used in his constructed facet formulas. In the first edition of CC this colon was the only sign used.

Ranganathan's philosophy of free combination of subjects was born when he came in contact with a 'Meccano' set in a toy shop in London. If a child can put together the same pieces in different objects, then this principle could be equally applied for the formation of subjects what was needed were the framing of rules for the construction of formulas for concept combination in the most versatile way. Inspired by the books of H.E. Bliss, Ranganathan wrote his Prolegomena to Library Classification in 1937 (3rd edition, 1967) in which he presented the theoretical basis for his classification. Over the years Ranganathan refined and redefined his thinking about classification. The first edition was published in 1933. The sixth edition came out in 1960 and the seventh appeared in 1987. Each edition reflected the progress of his thinking. Sometimes drastic changes took place between editions. The stability was sacrificed for the sake of keeping up with knowledge.

BASIC PRINCIPLES

Like many other schemes, the Colon Classification starts with a set of main classes. Each class is broken down into its basic concepts according to different trains of characteristics, called facet. All facets are regarded as manifestations of five fundamental categories. The sequence of these facets are determined by the principle of facet sequence. Each facet is further divided into elements, called isolates, according to certain principles. These are known as principles of helpful sequence. Since knowledge is dynamic the process of division continues.

Colon Classification has been developed as a freely faceted scheme. Unlike enumerative classification schemes it does not give complete readymade numbers in its schedules. The scheme is not subject to a pre-determined facet formula for compound subject going with a basic subject. The compound subjects are analysed into facets.

The facet term is translated into facet number. The facet numbers are synthesised with the help of appropriate connecting symbols. A combination or synthesis of notation is tailored for each word being classified. Ranganathan developed canons, principles and postulates for guidance.

BASIC LAWS

Ranganathan's five laws of library science are called fundamental laws. These laws govern the process of thinking and are involved when two or more canons or principles of classification lead to conflicting or equally valid alternate decisions. In fact they can resolve any problem in the fields of library science, library practice and library service. Basic laws are used at the level of basic process of thinking. Ranganathan has identified six basic laws :

1. **Law of interpretation :** 1008 principles of interpretation of the Nyaya - Kosa to be used to interpret schemes of classification.
2. **Law of impartiality :** preference should be given on sufficient grounds, not arbitrarily.
3. **Law of symmetry :** symmetrical counterparts should be given due weightage.
4. **Law of parsimony :** Overall economy of manpower, material, money and time should be considered.

5. **Law of local variation** : provisions should be kept for local use.
6. **Law of osmosis** : re-classification and re- cataloguing of newly accessioned material should be carried out according to new scheme or code.

These basic laws govern the process of thinking in general and that of classification in particular.

THREE PLANES OF WORK

The formulation of dynamic theory of classification was marked by the recognition and separation of three planes of work - idea place, verbal plane and the notational plane. The scheme of library classification passes through three planes of work. In the idea plane the scheme first enumerates the universe of subjects, states their interrelations and fixes their order. The findings of the idea plane are represented in terms in verbal plane. Finally these terms are transformed into notation in the notational plane. The idea plane is supreme, other planes are subordinate to it. They should carry out the findings of the idea plane.

CANONS

Canons are used in the context of divisions of the first order of the discipline of library science such as book selection, classification, cataloguing and so on. Ranganathan formulated 43 canons and put them into three groups according to the planes of classification :

1. Canons of idea of plane — 15 Canons
2. Canons of verbal plane — 4 Canons
3. Canons of notational plane — 24 Canons.

These canons are normally involved in the design of library canons. In Colon Classification they lay down the rhythm of the system.

FACET

Ranganathan considered the denotation of the term to be different depending on the context. At least there are two such denotations. Firstly, in the context of a scheme for classification, "the totality of the divisions of a Basic Class based on a single train of characteristics is said to constitute one of its facets". Secondly, "in a class number, the part of it corresponding to a single train of characteristics is said to constitute one of its facets". A facet has been taken to be the totality of one division of a Basic Class based on a single train of characteristics as well as one component of a class number or of a compound subject corresponding to such a division. In the class Literature, all enumerated languages, after which the national literatures are known, constitute the language facet of that class. In the same class, all literary forms (poetry, drama, etc.) constitute form facet. Within a facet an individual member is called a focus. Bengali literature, for example, is a focus in the language facet of the class Literature.

FUNDAMENTAL CATEGORIES

Fundamental Categories is a generic term. It denotes Time, Space, Energy, Matter and Personality. The concept of facet analysis led Ranganathan to devise the postulates of fundamental categories. These are only postulated categories without any metaphysical significance. A postulate is an assumption which is never put to test. It is a basis for argument and hence we cannot question. The veracity of the assumption. According to Ranganathan, in any given subject, there are maximum five fundamental categories. There can be less, but in no case, more than five these are commonly referred to by their initial letters PMEST, according to their decreasing concreteness.

Time and Space have the usual meaning. The usual time isolate ideas such as century, decade, years and so on are its manifestations. Another kind is day, night, seasons, etc. If the subject is stated as *economic conditions of India in the with century*, we can identify the time element in it.

Space isolate ideas such as the surface of the earth, the space inside it and the space outside it are its manifestations. Continents, countries, seas, deserts, etc. are taken to be manifestations of space. In the above title, we can easily find the space facet, India.

'Energy' is action of one kind or another. The action may be among and by all kinds of entities inanimate, animate, conceptual, intellectual, and intuitive. In the subject Library Science - Cataloguing, Classification, etc. are examples of energy. Similarly, in agriculture, ploughing, in education, teaching is energy.

The manifestations of 'Matter' are of three kinds - according to the 7th edition - Matter Material, Matter Property and Matter Method. Upto the sixth edition, matter was present in a few main classes. Matter Material usually implies material used for construction. In the subject, Sculpture, stone, marble, are considered. Matter Material. In Library Science books periodicals, maps, etc. are considered Matter Material. In sixth edition, in few cases, what was considered energy now forms part of matter facet. In Medicine, anatomy, physiology, diseases are now viewed as Matter Property. Similarly, in Agriculture, soil, manure, propagation are treated as manifestations of Matter Property. Magnetic method, Chemical method are matter method isolates to be found in Analytical Chemistry.

Personality has evaded definition. It is elusive and ineffable. It can only be said to be that which is not time, space, matter, energy. The residue may be regarded as Personality. Whole, part, portion of a concrete entity, organ of a concrete entity are all personality isolates. In Library Science, types of libraries are personality isolates.

BASIC FACET

The different fundamental categories are to be attached to a basic facet in the order of PMEST. Traditionally a basic facet stands for a main class, for example, Physics, Chemistry, Mathematics, etc. Let us analyse the following subjects into strings of key words denoting basic subject and its facets, manifesting one or the other of the fundamental categories :

1. Cataloguing of maps in college libraries in West Bengal in 1997

   Library Science (BS)

   Cataloguing (Action) |E|

   Maps (Material) /MMt

   College libraries (Core idea) |P|

   West bengal (country) |S|

   1997 (year) |T|

ROUNDS AND LEVELS

The fundamental categories may manifest themselves more than once in subjects of great intension. It is obvious that a subject area may well have more than just five facets. It might possess more than one personality facet or more than one energy facet, etc. This led to the postulates of Rounds and Levels.

POSTULATE OF ROUNDS

The first appearance of 'Energy' can be followed by a second round of 'Energy' facet. The second round may be followed by a third round and so on. The first manifestation is taken to end round 1 of the manifestation of the three fundamental categories. 'Personality', 'Matter' and 'Energy', the second is taken to end round 2 and so on. The first round is written as [1E], the second as [2E], the third as [3E] and so on.

Each of the fundamental categories 'Matter', 'Personality' manifests itself in round 1, round 2 and so on. They are written as [M], [2M], [3M]; [P], [2P], [3P] and so on. It should be noted that ordinarily any of the fundamental categories 'Space' and 'Time' may manifest itself only in the last round. Energy can start a new round. The chief problem in the theory of rounds concerns the round to which a P or M should be assigned. The postulate of Actand - Action - Actor principle, Wall - Picture principle, Cow - Calf principle, etc. help in determining the sequence.

POSTULATE OF LEVELS

It is quite common for a subject to possess more than one level of Personality or Matter. In some subjects we come across even fourth level of Personality. For example, O Literature. Literature (BF), Language [$_1P_1$]

Form [$_1P_2$]. Author [$_1P_3$]. Work [$_1P_4$]. All these isolates fall under the fundamental category personality. These occurrences are referred to as Levels of personality and they fall in the first round.

It is sufficient to represent 'Space' and 'Time' by [S] [T] respectively since they appear only in the last round.

POSTULATES OF FACET SEQUENCE

1. Postulate of first facet

In any compound subject, the first facet should be the basic facet. For example, *Diagnosis of the mental degeneration of criminals*, basic facet is not stated . But by implication the basic facet is Sociology.

2. Postulate of Concreteness

The five fundamental Categories appear in the sequence PMEST only. This means they appear in the order of their decreasing concreteness. For example, Cataloguing of manuscript in University libraries in Calcutta in 1990s. Obviously, Library Science is the basic facet and other fundamental categories according to the postulate are : University libraries [P]. Manuscript [M], Cataloguing [E]. Calcutta [S], 1990s [T].

Postulate of Connecting symbol for Fundamental Category

Personality	,	(comma)
Matter	;	(Semi - colon)
Energy	:	(Colon)
Space	.	(dot)
Time	'	(Single inverted Comma)

Let us illustrate from CC6

Title : Indian University Libraries in the 1990's

Library Science	University Libraries	India	1990's
BF	P	S	T
2	34	44	N9

In CC6 the connecting symbol need not be inserted before [P] if it immediately follows BF. So class number will be 234.4' N9.

In CC7 the insertion of connecting symbol , (comma) is made obligatory even in case of first level personality. Moreover, the facet structure of different compound subjects has been changed in CC7 (Vide Chapter DR. Page 108).

NOTATION

Colon Classification adopts mixed base. The notation consists of :

1. Indo - Arabic numerals 1-9
2. Roman alphabet, both capitals and lower case, A to Z and a to z
3. Parenthesis ( )
4. Indicator digits
5. A Greek litter Δ (Delta)

The capacity of base is 60. the total number of indicator digits is .14. The total number of digits is 74.

INDICATOR DIGITS

Earlier the term was known as connecting digit. According to Ranganathan a connecting digit is 'any digit in class number prefixed to a facet number other than the basic number'. Later the term was replaced by the indicator digit. Indicator digits are divided into three groups :

Group A : Anteriorising Indicators

* Asterisk indicates agglomeration and interpolation

← Backward arrow indicates backward time range

" Double inverted comma : Common isolates [ACI]

Group B : Posteriorising Indicators

& Ampersand indicates phase relation

' Single inverted comma indicates time facet

. Dot indicates space facet

: Colon indicates energy facet

, Comma indicates personality facet

; Indicates matter facet

- Hyphen indicates speciator of kind 1

= Equal sign indicates speciator of kind 2

+ Plus sign indicates addition

→ Forward arrow indicates time range

Group C : Indicators for levels of Phase relation (to be discussed later)

When arranged in the ascending sequence of their ordinal values, all the digits used in CC7 will stand in the following sequence :

) & . ; : , - = → a to z 01 to 9 A to Z (* (asterisk), + (plus), " (inverted comma) and ← (backward arrow) have anteriorising value and therefore their values are not necessary.

EMPTY DIGIT

An empty digit is a digit which has no semantic value but does have its ordinal value. Usually the last digit of a species of digits is made an empty digit. In the sequence 1 2, 3, 4, ..., 8, 91, 92,....., 98, 991,......, 998, etc. (though the number has two digits and three digits, they are co-ordinate to digit 1 to 8, 91 to 98, etc. 9 or 99 themselves have no meaning. They are semantically empty). An empty digit becomes meaningful if it is added to some other digit.

Similarly the array A ...... Y can be lengthened with the use of Z as empty digit. So also the array a,....y can be lengthened. Thus the device provides for infinite extrapolation in any array. An empty digit has been used as a sectorising digit and in CC it is used to form sectors.

Sector Device

It is a device used for increasing the capacity of an array with the aid of an empty digit. It provides for infinite extrapolation in a given notational system. With this device we can add unlimited numbers to represent co-ordinate ideas. The range 1 to 8 of the array is denoted by sector (S - A) and so on. We can have sectors using the packet notation. The Subject Device (SD) part of a class number is enclosed in circular brackets, that is packeted. These sectors are (S - (a)), (S - (1)). (S - (A)).

Zone Analysis

The introduction of sector device led Ranganathan to develop the concept of Zone Analysis. In fact sectors have been grouped into zones. The use of different digits has given rise to the formation of zones in an array. In CC7 the following abbreviations are used to denote Zones, in which no quasi digit has more than 3 digits :

1. (Z - a) - read as "Zone a"
2. (Z - 0) - read as "Zone 0"
3. (Z - 1) - read as "Zone 1"
4. (Z - A) - read as "Zone A"
5. (Z - ()) - read as "Packeted Zone"

The Zone Analysis brings forth enormous hospitality in array. The concept of Zone Analysis proves the full necessity of mixed notation.

Emptying Digit

Any new idea may crop up and requires a position between any two existing consecutive ideas. This is known as interpolation. Ranganathan has developed the concept of 'emptying digit' to have interpolation between any two Main Subjects or any two Space Isolates falling consecutively in the already existing array. The digits T, V, X are emptying digits. An emptying digit is a digit that empties the preceding digit of its semantic value, but allows it to retain its usual ordinal value. Examples from CC7 :

L	Medicine	44	India
LX	Pharmacognosy	44T	Nepal
M	Useful Arts	44V	Ceylon
		44X	Pakistan
		45	Iran.

EMPTY - EMPTYING DIGITS

The concept of 'Empty - Emptying Digit has been postulated to allow a large number of interpolations between any two consecutive ordinal numbers in an array. In other words this device makes infinity of interpolations possible. Each of the digits U, W, and Y is postulated to be 'Empty - Emptying Digits'. Examples from CC7 :

L U 5	Public health
L U 6	Hospital
L U 7	Sanitarium
L U D	Medical technology
M	Useful arts.

TELESCOPED ARRAY

Telescoped array 'is an array of classes in a schedule of classification, made of coordinate and subordinate isolates, an viewed from the Idea Plane, but whose class numbers appear to be co - ordinate, as viewed from the Notational Plane'. CC often practices Telescoping in array. Let us consider the following classes from the Space Facet of CC7 :

1.	World	As viewed from the Idea Plane 'World' as a whole belongs to class of order 1.
4.	Asia	Continents come under order 2 since they are subdivisions of 'world'.
5.	Europe	But in the example

6. Africa	the world and the continents appear to be coordinate from the Notational Plane
7. America	
8. Australia	if they are subordinated to order 1 the other digits 4 to 9 remain vacant. Therefore, the array of order 2 has been telescoped into array of order 1. Telescoping of two consecutive arrays saves one digit in the class number. This is done to satisfy the Law of Parsimony (overall economy).

FIVE DEVICES

Ranganathan suggests five devices for formation or sharpening of foci in a facet. In fact, within a basic subject we may have to make provision for new foci from time to time. In CC this may be done in five ways. They are Chronological Device, Geographical Device, Subject Device, Alphabetical Device and Enumeration Device. Each of these devices is applicable both in the idea plane and the notational plane. The use of the first three devices shorten the length of the schedule. The advantages of these devices are that they : 1 avoid enumeration and thereby shorten the schedule; 2 give autonomy to the classifier; 3 secure automatic conformity to the canons of consistent sequence, helpful sequence, scheduled mnemonics, and hospitality in array as well as chain.

Chronological Device (CD)

It consists in using appropriate chronological number for the formation or the subdivision of isolate which is capable of chronological subdivision. Sometime we need to specify a new focus by means of its date of origin. The cases where this device may be employed are generally indicated in the schedules. For example, CC uses this device in Literature where authors are specified by this date of birth.

Geographical Device (GD)

It simply means the use of place facet other than its normal way. For example, GD is employed to individualise certain religion. In Q (Religion) Sikhism 8441 (7th edition).

Subject Device (SD)

It consists in using the appropriate class number for the formation or subdivision of a class which is capable of such formation or subdivision. Many illustrative divisions by (SD) are given in the schedules. For example, In R_4 (Ethics)$_4$ professional Ethics [Divisions by (SD)], 4(2) Librarian, 4 (L) Medical man (CC7).

Alphabetical Device (AD)

It consists in using the first or the first two or the first three, etc initial letters or proper names, trade names, etc. Schedules generally indicate where (AD) has to be applied. In case of name with two words (AD) should be applied to each component word and the two components should be connected by '+' plus sign as indicator digit. For example, Home and the World, a novel by Tagore (H + W).

Enumeration Device (ED)

The Enumeration Device in the idea plane is employed to form focal ideas in an array of a schedule by their enumeration. The sequence of focal ideas is based on seminal mnemonics. In the notational plane the numbers of the base of the notational system are used continuously or with gaps for forming isolate numbers in an array of a schedule. CC uses this device less frequently than other schemes.

COMMON ISOLATES

Common isolates are applicable to all areas of knowledge. A common isolate (CI) is an isolate idea which is denoted by the same isolate term in the verbal plane and is represented by the same isolate number in the notational plane whatever be the host subject to which it is attached. Common isolates can be categorised in three ways : (a) CI dealing with subject matter; (b) CI dealing with book numbers (Language, form of expositions, etc); and (c) CI dealing with physical forms of documents (sequence number).

Common isolates dealing with subjects are of two types

Anteriorising Common Isolates (ACI) and Posteriorising Common Isolates (PCI). PCI consist of Personality, Matter, Energy, Space and Time isolates. CC7 has provided the following scheduled of common isolates : (a) Time Isolates; (b) Space Isolates; (c) Common Energy Isolates; (d) Common Matter Property Isolates; (e) Common Personality Isolates; and (f) Anteriorising Common Isolates.

Anteriorising Common Isolates (ACI)

ACI are regarded as "approach materials". Documents such as bibliography, concordance, encyclopaedia, etc. are called approach documents. We need approach materials before taking up the study of a regular treatise or a book on a subject. They are therefore, arranged anterior to documents on the subject of concern. In other words approach materials get anterior position. They are of three types :

(a) ACI applicable before Space facet. For example, a Bibliography, c Concordance, etc.

(b) ACI applicable only after space facet. For example, r periodical administrative report, s statistics (serials).

(c) ACI applicable after Time facet. For example, t commission report, A_4 survey, etc.

CC6 does not provide any connecting symbol for their attachment to a host class. CC7 provides the indicator digit "(double inverted commas) for "Anteriorising Common Isolates. Examples, Bibliography of mathematics will be represented by B "a and not by Ba ; Encyclopedia of mathematics will be B "k and not by Bk.

It may be mentioned in passing that ACI possess their ordered facet structure.

Posteriorising Common Isolate (PCI)

PCI narrow down the extension of the subjects to which they are applied. Therefore, the subjects with these isolates get the posterior position. They are arranged after the documents on the subjects to which they are attached. Use of connecting symbols is necessary for their attachment to the class numbers. For example, 2.44, b Library profession in India.

1. **Personality common isolate** : They stand mainly for institutions. For example, Indian Mathematical Society founded in 1931 -

   B.44, g, 9N31 [g - Learned body, 9N31 - a national body is represented by 9 and N31 is 1931]

2. **Matter property common isolate** : A list of matter property common isolates is given in CC7. For example, an intrinsic value of painting - N_6; $_a7_2$ [N_6 - painting,; an indicator digit for matter, $_a7_2$ an intrinsic value]

3. **Energy Common isolate** : A list of energy common isolates appears on page 93 of CC7. For example, Observations of solar eclipse, Bx, 3; 57 : a R_2 [Bx - Astronomy, 3 - Sun, 57 - Ellipse, a R_2 - observation, : indicator digit for energy]

4. **Space Common isolate** : They are listed separately in the scheme. For example, College libraries in India - 2, J_3.44 [J_3 College libraries. (Story) indicator digit for space, 44 India].

5. **Time Common isolate** : Time isolates are listed separately in the scheme. For example, Mass communication in India in the 1990's. 4.44' N9 [Mass Communication 4, ' indicator digit for time, N9 - 1990's].

PHASE RELATIONS

In classification edition may occur between subjects (Inter - subject), between facets of subjects (Intra - facet) and between isolates of the same array, (Intra - array). Such relations are called

Phase Relations. In CC7 six kinds of phase relations are recognised. The schedule of Digits for Phase Relations runs as follows :

Kinds of Phase relation	*Inter - subject*	*Intra - facet*	*Intra - array*
General	a	j	t
Bias	b	k	u
Comparison	c	m	v
Difference	d	n	w
Tool	e	p	x
Influencing	g	r	y

The Indicator Digit for Phase Relations is '&' (Ampersand) In CC6 Indicator Digit was zero ')'.

1. **General Phase :** It denotes a complete relation between the primary and secondary phases. The sequence of phases will be the same as the sequence of component phases in the sequence of classes, isolates or arrays, as the case may be. For example, Relation between Political Science and Economics. W & aX (Intra - subject), Relation between anatomy and physiology L ; 2 & j3 (Intra - facet), Relation between rural folk and city folk Y_{31} & t5 (intra - array).
2. **Bias Phase :** In Bias Phase relation the exposition of Phase 1 is biased towards Phase 2. Phase 1 is called the biased phase, phase 2 is named the biasing phase, For example, Mathematics for Engineers B & bD (Inter - subject). Mathematics - phase 1. Anatomy for Pathologists would be L ; 2 & k 4 (intra - facet). Import duty biased towards export duty would be X72, 951 & u5 (Intra - array)
3. **Comparison Phase :** Here the subject with smaller ordinal value will be phase 1. For example, Botany compared with Zoology. I & cK (inter - subject)

   Anatomy compared with physiology L ; 2 & m^3 (intra - facet)

Comparative study of spring and autumn u_2, 761 & v^3 (Intra - array).

4. **Difference Phase :** Here the subject with earlier class number is treated as Phase 1. For example,

   Difference between Plants and Animals I & dK (Inter - subject)

   Difference between epistemology and metaphysics R_2 &$_n$3 (Intra - facet)

   Difference between undergraduate and postgraduate education T, 181 & $_w{}^2$ (Intra - array)

5. **Tool Phase :** Here the subject used as a tool is treated as phase 2.

   For example, Literature through art 0 122 & $_e$N

6. **Influencing Phase :** The influencing Phase relation denotes that the influence of Phase 2 on phase 1 is expounded. For example, Influence of Geography on Agriculture J & $_g$U (Inter - subject).

   Influence of logic on ethics R_4 &$_r$1 (Intra - facet)

   Influence of direct tax on indirect tax X 72, 01 & $_y$2 (Intra - array)

SYSTEMS AND SPECIALS

Systems and specials were enumerated with the concerned main classes into the sixth edition. In the 7th edition they have found place in the schedule of basic subjects.

1. **System :** the terms system basic subject denote a division of a main class expounded according to a school of thought. The class number is derived by the chronological device that is, the year of birth of the system. Examples :

L - K	Allopathy	K stand for 1600 to 1699 A.D.
L - L	Homeopathy	Lstands for 1700 to 1799 A.D.
X - J	Capitalism	J stands for 1500 to 1599 A.D.
X - N1	Communism	N1 stands for 1910's.

2. **Specials** : The terms 'Special basic subjects' denote a division of a main class in which the subject of study is restricted in certain special manner. The class numbers are derived by enumeration. For example,

L - 9 E	Adult medicine
L - 9 G	Male medicine
L - 9 H	Female medicine.

ALPHABETIC INDEX

The index of CC refers only to elementary terms, never to compound subjects. The relative aspect of a subject are provided only in the form of class numbers, not being named as in DDC or UDC. CC6 has provided the following four indexes : General Index; Geographical Index; two indexes to Natural groups in Botany and Zoology. Index volume for CC7 is yet to be published.

BOOK NUMBER

The classification specifies the construction of book number as part of the scheme. The following facet formula is prescribed by CC6 for the construction of book numbers (CC7 follows the same with minor modification) :

[L] {F] [Y] [SN] . [V] - [S]; [C] : [EVN] where

L = Language in which the book is written. The language Number is taken from part 2 Chapter 5 of CC6 or Chapter DG of CC7.

F = Number for the form of exposition, taken from Form schedule given in Chapter 02 of part 2 of CC6 (Chapter CC of CC7).

Y = Year of publication, taken from Time schedule.

SN = Serial Number. This is serially made to begin with 1 for the second book received in the library. In CC7 it is termed as Accession Facet.

V = Number for the volume, taken from the book itself.

S = Supplement Number, taken from the book itself.

C = Number for copy other than the first serially made as for SN.

If the BN of the first copy is N 88, the BN of second copy N 88; 1 and so on.

EVN

Evaluation. The digit 'g' is used as the evaluation 'number'. In CC7 it is denoted as 'Attachment Facet'. In case of a version followed by "y"; in case of evaluation or review : followed by "g".

It should be noted that Colon Book Number is essentially based on the year of publication of the book. The connecting digits used are : dot (.) for volume ; hyphen (-) for supplement ; semicolon (;) for copy ; and colon (:) for evaluation.

COLLECTION NUMBER

'Collection number is the mark added to the Class Number cum Book Number of a book to indicate collection containing it. In other words it denotes the collection in which it is placed in the library. For example :

Under - sized	: Underline the Book Number D $\underline{\text{N 88}}$
Over - sized	: Overline the Book Number D $\overline{\text{N 88}}$
worn - out book	: Encircle the Book Number D $\boxed{\text{N 88}}$
Rare Book	: RB ; Reading Room RR; etc,

CALL NUMBER

The Class Number, the Book Number and the Collection Number together form the Call Number. The components of a Call Number may be separated in the following ways :

When written in a horizontal straight line a double space should be left between the Class Number and Book Number. For example, B 43 N88. The Book Number may be written below the Class Number. For example,

B 43

N 88

The collection Number may be written below the Book Number in both cases.

EVALUATION

This is the great universal classification scheme to be designed by one person - mathematician - turned - librarian. The Colon Classification stands in a class of its own for coherence and system making it the easiest of the general schemes to use properly. It has constituted an almost complete break with traditional method of classifying. In fact Ranganathan's Colon Classification fully manifests the theory of facet analysis and synthesis. The systematic order and the degree of detail due to analysis and synthesis are two merits of CC. Although CC is used relatively in few libraries its underlying theory has had a major impact on all classification schemes. Revision of DDC, particularly in recant editions, reflects the influence of facet analysis and synthesis.

The revision policy of the scheme has been criticised. Major changes have been incorporated in the seventh edition for obvious reasons. The changes are so enormous that many libraries using CC may not be in a position to change over to the current edition. But still the Colon Classification will certainly make the strongest appeal to the seekers of perfection.

5

In Search of the Author

The idea of authorship indicates the concept of original contribution as well as new interpretation of existing knowledge recorded in documents. The concept of originality is the root of intellectual contribution and, so, it is ascribed to the individual or individuals as intellectual property right. This right establishes the relation and ownership of the another with the concerned documents. The authors are the intellectual contributors and such contributions are recorded and documented in any physical format for the operation of knowledge industries and benefit of user community.

In the case of single author and the creative contribution can be discreetly identified. But authorship, originality and intellectual contribution become blurred and it is very difficult to ascribe individual's intellectual responsibility in a work authored by more than one person, corporate bodies and mixed authorship. The writer of a text is precisely the author of the text, but at the same time, the editors, compilers, commentators, interpreters, continuators can also be regarded as authors for their respective intellectual contributions, however, little it may be. In case of ancient and medieval texts the same theme was created or recreated by a number of individual authors. Modern interpretations of those texts are also regarded as original contributions and the persons responsible are also authors. The inspiration of previous authors, corporate bodies as such, cannot be intellectually responsible but the persons of the corporate bodies cannot be identified as authors. The reality of the claims of original intellectual contributions in the works as authors is much more complex than it might suggest. The authorship is more complicated when published in different physical formats, such as film, audio cassette, video cassette, microform, CD-ROM.

AUTHORSHIP : THE CONCEPT

The history of library catalogue reveals that there was a gradual and uneven development of inventorial function to finding list function from the ancient period to the sixteenth century. There was no concept of authorship, an such, and the documents were listed under the name of the person or title a were convenient to the custodian of the libraries. During the sixteenth century the list of books or manuscripts became a finding list or index to literature. The works of Conrad Gesner (1545), Florianus Treflerus (1560) and Andrew Maunsell (1595) considerable emphasis was given on the value of author indexes. Their attempts were to highlight the authors' names as search points by the readers and the rules for an author catalogue germinated. During the seventeenth century emphasis was given on author ad surnames were used as entry words in the finding lists. The work of Maunsell exhibited the first attempt of a code of cataloguing rules highlighting authors' names.

At the beginning of the seventeenth century Sir Thomas Bodley, during the compilation work of the Bodleian library catalogue, emphasised the point of view of the readers and insisted upon author rather than subject headings. During this century the lists of documents were used as finding lists rather than inventories. The names of authors entered under surnames were used for main entries and search points.

The concept of authorship is deeply rooted in intellectual tradition since the ancient period both for identity of the documents and for making inventories of the documents. Titles were also main element of bibliographic identity, particularly by in the orient. In the western world the classical works were identified by their authors. Sometimes the authorship was known and sometimes unknown during the medieval period. In such cases documents were identified either by author or by title. After the invention of printing by movable types multiple copies of particular documents were available. By printing the name of the author on the title pages the concept of authorship was strengthened to establish the right of the authors on the intellectual contribution. The practice of preparing the main entries under the name of the author in library catalogues has been made in conformity to the age-old tradition. Main entries were prepared either under the author or under the title in the catalogue and in most cases the names of the authors were the search points.

The concept of authorship was confined to personal authors until the middle of the nineteen century. Corporate authorship was first identified and recognised by the British Museum Code as the entry element for bibliographic identification. Personal authors are responsible for the intellectual contribution and the intellectual responsibility can be assigned. Corporate authorship has no relationship with intellectual responsibility because a corporate body, as such, cannot think and write making intellectual contribution. The individuals associated with the production of the documents are unidentified and not known. Therefore, the main entries under corporate bodies go against the concept of intellectual responsibility. However, a corporate body with the unidentified group of individuals that comprise the body under the particular official authority, has been recognised as the heading of the main entry to be used like identification tag in all the catalogue codes except the Prussian Instruction. The reason behind this is that users are expected to search the documents under the name of the corporate bodies and not under the unknown individuals associated with such bodies because those individuals cannot be identified and they might not be associated with such corporate bodies for all the time the corporate bodies exist.

The prime importance has been given to the authors in preparation of the library catalogues for two basic reasons. The first is that the name of the author as printed on the title page and the spine is the most easily identifiable feature of a book. The catalogue entries under authors are made under their most identifiable feature. The concept of the author catalogue to provide a guide to the contents of a library is a later development. The second reason for the importance of author catalogue is that the catalogue-users are expected to search all the books written by a particular author in one place.

The definition of authorship has become extended and widened during one and half centuries because of the nature of publications and documents. Not only the corporate authorship, in case of individual authorship there may be more than one author for a particular translator, annotator, illustrator, and such other persons can claim the authorship of a book not written by such persons. The library catalogue has the role of both, as a bibliographic database as well as a bibliographic search instrument. The concept of 'intellectual responsibility' has also been widened and not just limited to the writer of the first text. In such cases besides the writer of the text, anybody can claim the authorship of a book not writing the text in original. The extent of 'intellectual responsibility' can go to any extent. The identification of authorship in so many ways and in so many documents as well as their collocation in the library catalogue can be an intriguing problem. The two criteria of author entries - identification tag, and intellectual responsibility' have caused considerable confusion in the past and also in the present in a more perplexed manner.

Author approach was specified by C.A. Cutter more than a century ago as,

1. To enable a person to find a document of which the author is known or the title is known,

2. Which works of a particular author and which editions of a particular work are in the library?

It is very difficult and sometimes impossible to collocate all the entries in the catalogue reconciling both the objectives stated above. First objective can be fulfilled by making entries strictly on the basis of the title page as in the British Museum Code. But problems arise when an author uses different forms of names in different documents, one or more pseudonyms for different works and different names. To solve these problems if the works of one author are collocated under uniform heading. Whatever it may be, it goes against the rule of specific entry for each of the works. All the users may not know the uniform heading as well as the specific headings under which he has to search. The cataloguer is presented with two options,

1. either by making the entry according to title page, or
2. a 'sought' heading for all the works of a particular author available in various alphabetic arrangement.

Cataloguers can only fully satisfy either objective 1 or objective 2, but not the both. Added entries and references can be made to allow for the objective which was not primarily fulfilled. Notwithstanding the basic conflict remains.

In the process of cataloguing the cataloguer has to determine the form of the name of the author among all the alternatives, which will be used as author heading. He has to face the problem whether he would give emphasis on objective 1 or objective 2. The first objective considers a book as an individual entity and the second objective considers a book as one of the group of books. The inherent conflict and the collocation of entries in the catalogue have become a perennial problem for cataloguing. C.A. Cutter recognised the inherent conflict and suggested some solutions, He writes,

"It must be remembered that the object is not merely to facilitate the finding of a given book by an author's name. If this were all, it might have been better to make the entry, as proposed by Mr. Crestadoro, under the part of the name mentioned in the title, which would lead to having *Bulwer* in one book, *Lytton* in another, *Bulwer - Lytton* in a third... This might have been best with [the first objective]...but we have also [the second objective]... to provide for - the finding of all the books of a given author - and this can most conveniently be done if they are all collected in one place."

Cutter, in this way resolved the conflict by making the second objective more important than the first. He recommended that there would by a uniform heading for each author. But the problem confronted by the cataloguers in all libraries for all the time cannot be uniform to choose a particular uniform heading.

The concept of corporate body as author was initiated by the British Museum Code, extended and established by Cutter's Code and recognised by the later Codes, is a logical extension of the idea that has been accepted for the cataloguing purpose to assign responsibility to the agency with author identity. The corporate body is a corporate person having the responsibility and exclusive authority with the right to act as individual person. The corporate body is responsible for the intellectual or bibliographic content of the book to be considered as author heading or the heading of the main entry for cataloguing purpose because the users are expected to search for the document under the particular corporate body. It meets Cutter's criterion of 'convenience of public'. A corporate body prepares and publishes all its official documents.

AUTHORSHIP : THE IDENTITY

The identity of authorship is a vexed problem to cataloguers and a complex search point for the users. The crisis of identity of the author of a book is confronted by two groups of people from two different angles. There is no problem if a book is written by one person and his name is printed on the title page. But the various types of authorship, assigning 'intellectual responsibility'. The 'sought' heading identifying the author, 'uniform heading' selected from among a number of headings of a particular author, 'changed' names of an author, and such other situations have made the job of the cataloguers difficult for choosing the 'real' name of the author and the select the particular form of name under which an author entry should be made. The users are confused to pinpoint the particular form of name of the author under which he has to make the search. There are many definitions of authorship but the authorship has not been defined properly to the satisfaction of both the groups of people, cataloguers and users because the name of the author is used like a 'tag', far from the intellectual responsibility.

The British Museum Code (1841) states "Subject to the condition that the information must be taken from the book itself, the heading of the Main entry is the Name of the Author, except in case of certain works published by Societies and in the instances of Special Headings cited in Rule 17; excepting also Official Publications, which are entered under the name of the authority by which they are issued..."

Charles A. Cutter in his *Rules for a Dictionary Catalog* (4th ed. 1904) defines that "Author, in the narrower sense, is the person who writes a book; in a wider sense it may be applied to him who is the cause of the book's existence by putting together the writings of several authors (usually called the editor, more properly to be called the collector). Bodies of men (societies, cities, legislative bodies, countries) are to be considered the authors of their memoirs, transactions, journals, debates, reports, etc."

According to ALA code (1949) the author is "1. The writer of a work, as distinguished from the translator, editor, etc. By extension, an artist, composer, photographer, cartographer, etc. 2. In the broader sense, the maker of the work or the person or body immediately responsible for its existence. Thus, a person who collects and puts together the writings of several authors (Compiler or editor) may be said to be the author of a collection. A corporate body may be considered the author of publications issued in its name or by its authority." However, under Rule 1 ALA (1949) expands its definition as "The author is considered to be the person or body chiefly responsible for the intellectual content of the book, literary, artistic or musical... Governments, societies, institutions, and other organizations are to be regarded as authors of the publications far for which they as corporate bodies are responsible, but the papers, addresses, etc., of their officials, members or employees as individuals. are entered under personal author, even though issued by the corporate body."

AACR (1967) defines the author as "The person or corporate body chiefly responsible for the creation of the intellectual or artistic content of a work, e.g., the writer of a book. The artist who paints a picture, the photographer who takes a photograph."

AACR 11 (1978) and AACR 11 R (1988) define the personal author only as "A personal author is the person chiefly responsible for the creation of the intellectual or artistic content of a work."

Seymour Lubetzky did not give the definition of 'author' in his CCR (1960). The statement of Principles of the International Conference on Cataloguing Principles, Paris, 1961, does not mention the definition of 'author'. Cutter's definition of authorship is firmly based on the concept of intellectual responsibility. The AA code (1908) firmly adheres to the concept of the bibliographic unit. It accepts the concept of intellectual responsibility for author heading, but does not always prove adequate for solving all problems of authorship. In this respect ALA (1949) followed the AA code (1908). AACR (1967) follows the tradition of intellectual responsibility as the primary criterion of authorship. But the concept of intellectual responsibility is considerably modified by making the title page the primary source for the heading.

Entry under author with a book in hand is by no means a tool for search by the users in the whole of the catalogue, even with the largely expanded definition of 'author'. Entry under author serves adequately for the books with single responsible authorship, personal or corporate. But in case of shared authorship multiple authorship, mixed authorship, related or dependent authorship, concealed authorship, and such other cases the title pages of books in hand create many problems of collocation of entries.

Dr. S.R. Ranganathan in his *Classified Catalogue Code with additional rules for Dictionary Catalogue Code* (5th ed.) emphasised the choice and form of author heading for the main entry or author entry. He does not accept the concept of intellectual responsibility of a document to be catalogue but advises to select the author heading according to users' choice of searching a document for all practical purposes. The Canon of Ascertainability clearly states "The Principle prescribing that the information found in the title-page of the document catalogued and its over-flow pages should determine the choice and rendering of the main entry. At the same time he states the reality that "Unfortunately, the title-page and its over-flow have not yet began to give all the data needed for making the main entry in the catalogue."

Ranganathan visualised the main entry in other words, choice and form of the author heading in various situations. He solved the problems by the Canon of Sought-Heading in particular situation. Ranganathan states "The principle that the decision whether an entry

1. With a particular type of heading, or
2. With a particular choice for that heading, or
3. With a particular rendering of that choice, or
4. A particular added entry arising out of it,

Should be based on the answer to the question : "Is reader or library staff likely to look for a book under the particular type or choice or rendering of heading or in the particular added entry".

This concept of Ranganathan qualifies his three laws of

library science that 'Books are for use', 'Every Reader its book' and 'Every Book its Reader'. Since libraries are established for the users he gave prime importance to users' approach to the library catalogue. No other catalogue code recognised this very important and vital approach except Cutter. C.A. Cutter states "The convenience of the public is always to be set before the case of the cataloguer." He asserts "But strict consistency in a rule and uniformity in its application sometimes lead to practices which clash with the public's habitual way of looking at things. When these habits are general and deeply rooted, it is unwise for the cataloguer to ignore them, even if they demand a sacrifice of system and simplicity".

LITERARY UNIT VERSUS BIBLIOGRAPHIC UNIT

There is a distinction between the book and the work in cataloguing. This distinction has tremendous impact upon author identity as to the form and choice of author heading. The distinction has whether the author heading for the main entry will be based on the concept of intellectual responsibility or title page tag. The inventory concept of cataloguing which means whether a particular book by a particular author is available in the library, assumes interest in the book or the individual volume or book in hand at the time of cataloguing. The concept of intellectual responsibility refers to all the bibliographic units of a particular literary unit in all physical formats and intellectual expression. In this situation the work is of more permanent interest and importance to the users. The conflict between these two concepts has given rise to inconsistencies within the code of rules for author cataloguing.

The distinction between a work and a book is also inherent in the identification of bibliographic unit and literary unit for the purpose of cataloguing. The literary unit assembles under one heading in the catalogue of all the entries for works by one author without considering the forms of names the author uses in the little pages of his books. The bibliographic unit refers to the collection of all entries for various versons of the same work under one uniform heading. Some users may be interested in literary unit of books and some others may be interested in bibliographic unit. The rules in the catalogue codes are not uniform for choice and form of main entry headings for all the cases either literary unit or bibliographic unit.

Such inconsistencies and confusion have been expressed with examples by James A. Tait. He states 'The bibliographic unit is generally accepted cataloguing practice because of acceptance of the work as the unit in cataloguing rather than the book. This principle is frequently ignored in AA (1908) and ALA (1949). It becomes particularly important in the case of title entry for anonymous works. Both AA (1908) and ALA (1949 have a long series of rules covering the entry of anonymous works, for example, where the first word of the title may be spelled in more than one way; translations of anonymous works; anonymous classics; works known by a standardised form of title, for example the *Bible*. The fact that AA (1908) and ALA (1949) make these elaborate provisions merely emphasises the importance of the concepts, and it is a surprising element in these two codes in view of the fact that they ignore its presence in all rules for works by named authors." Form headings may be used in the author catalogue and these support the concept of the bibliographic unit. Such usage may be made when both the author element and title element are insufficient for identification and construction of bibliographic unit. The provision of uniform headings and uniform titles has been made in Paris Principles (1961) and AACR (1967).

AUTHOR AND ACCESS POINT

The term 'access points' has been used for headings in AACR 2 which was used in all the previous catalogue codes as 'entries'. Obviously it has been done to get the benefits of technological capabilities of the computer. But the 'main entry heading' concept has been retained in AACR 2. This main entry heading or main access point is the name of the author or other-equivalent. Access points have been defined as "a name, term, code, etc. under which a bibliographic record may be searched and identified". The term 'main entry heading' comes from the text of AACR 2 and not from the glossary. The term 'author' has been replaced by 'statement of responsibility' which has been used both in the broader sense as well as in the narrower sense in comparison to the previous concepts of authorship.

'Main entry' as defined in all previous codes is used in AACR 2 as the unit record, which includes the 'main entry heading' for authors and author-equivalents as well as all other access points used in the catalogue. The AACR 2 rules for the statement of responsibility (a broader concept than authorship concepts of the previous codes) strongly suggest that the ISBD record taken by itself cannot determine the main entry heading. The cataloguer cannot construct a main entry heading from the statement of responsibility area only in all the cases. The cataloguer may have to use sources other than the prescribed sources or statement of responsibility to construct the main entry heading.

Phyllis A. Richmond in his paper *AACR 2-A Review Article* (1980) has given a logical observation. He writes "Throughout AACR 2, it is obvious that there was a struggle between the desire to word exactly from the data in the item at hand and the desire to provide authoritative data about the item even if it meant using alternative sources. This appears in the matter of using birth and death dates for authors, for providing hierarchy in some kinds of corporate authors, for distinguishing among types of documents issued by corporate bodies, for designations of pseudonyms and various kinds of names, for use in a variety of notes, and so on. An even more fundamental point of conflict comes at the very beginning with the statement which replaces the notion of a work with that of form : `It is the cardinal principle of the use of Part I that the description of a physical item should be based in the first instance on the chapter dealing with the class of materials to which that time belongs... In short the starting point for description is the physical form of the item in hand'. Resolution of such conflicts requires a general agreement on principles of cataloguing". The variety of documents as published data units in any physical form, the share of intellectual responsibility expressed or hidden, and the nature and characteristics of documents create innumerable problems both the catalogue code makers as well as the cataloguers.

The Library of Congress has observed (1978) that "Another benefit expected to follow adoption of AACR 2 concerns the user's retrieval of bibliographic information. AACR 2 has been formulated to provide headings that are more often in conformity with names as they appear in works and citations than is now the case, thereby reducing the time that users lose when they encounter cross-references rather than the catalog entries they seek. The increased convenience and time savings of accessing a database that produces a greater number of sought headings is an advantage compounded by the total use of the catalogue".

AACR 2, with the standardised bibliographic description based on ISBDs, can create searchable database as library catalogue with machine-readable bibliographic description in a particular library as well as in a networked centralised and cooperative cataloguing system with multiple search facilities. But the problem of name authority control still persists. The access points for a particular author, whether for a particular book or all the works of that particular author, and collocation of works for the purpose of access to database may not be uniformly available. There is the problem of name authority control even in online search. Automation of library catalogue can organise the catalogue from the viewpoint of cataloguers but from the search point of users there are some problems.

ALA conference on "Authority Control : The key to Tomorrow's Catalogue" held in May, 1979 at Atlantic City, N.J. discussed in detail the problems of name authority control. The comment made in the announcement was that "Authority control - one of the librarians most important bibliographical tools - is also one of the most overlooked and under worked devices in libraryland. Automation is , however, bringing it to the forefront as one of the most important cataloguing and searching tools that is required to establish and maintain order in our processing and user worlds. The closing-the-catalog-vogue, the advent of on-line terminals, COM, and other developments have brought the realization that we cannot hide incorrect entries, old-fashioned terms, and outmoded concepts in our modern, easily accessible public catalog. Authority control is a must if chaos is to be kept out of our modern bibliographical and searching systems". Authority control is a must but many problems to control the authority control both in cataloguing and in search strategy.

Computerised catalogue can be prepared in the library in two situations, 1. Stand-alone computer in the library, or 2. membership of online cooperative cataloguing network. In the first situation library catalogue can be prepared in a particular library with a computer system using appropriate library application software as housekeeping operations. In the second situation the library can be a part of the large library and information network and can get the facilities of centralised cataloguing or shared cataloguing. In both the situations effectiveness and efficiency of the library catalogue depends entirely on the competence of the cataloguers who control the preparation of access points and the descriptive part of the catalogue the computer cannot evaluate the data it receives, and will thus record, reproduce, and transmit, without question, even data which contain errors. Therefore, well-trained, efficient and experienced cataloguing specialists are required both at the local level and national level. The wisdom of the cataloguers in understanding of the nature of documents and their contents as well as proper determination of access points and collocation of headings is essential for users' access.

6

Bibliographic Record and Control

The written records of mankind were deliberately preserved and organised for the posterity. Such readable documents, inscribed, written or printed having the attribute of unchangeable and permanent impression on a particular kind of physical base made the documents transmitted through centuries. The invention of printing by movable types solved the problems of non-availability of multiple copies of a particular document. Book became the vehicle of communication, record of thought and experience, feelings and emotions, ideas and applications, knowledge and wisdom, and all intellectual activities.

The book has been performing its role and became the witness of a whole range of basic changes which were taking place from time to time. The cumulative effects of such changes led to tremendous impact over the intellectual advancement of the human society and growth and advancement of all kinds of human knowledge in all its ramifications. The new way of looking at things and situations. The new ideas, the hitherto unknown interpretations, the insight into the past and present knowledge, as well as new innovations in science and technologies are documented in bibliographic records.

Libraries, through the centuries, made attempts to prepare the lists, catalogues and indexes of such bibliographic records so that they could later be retrieved and consulted. During seventeenth century journals appeared with continuing and latest records of human thoughts. A separate type of indexing service was used to list the writings of this genre. During twentieth century the non-print media were used and stored in libraries. Separate retrieval systems and administrative agencies were created to serve the users of information in these media. The latest media are the electronic databases, online searching and networking both for bibliographic records and their indexes providing own internal potential for automated self-indexing leading to bibliographic control and access.

Information storage and retrieval techniques have become associated separately with different formats, new physical containers, subjects, and information-service agencies. The fast advancement of human knowledge, particularly in the fields of basic sciences, technology and its applications, medicine, agriculture and social sciences, as well as the innovations of new technologies have made the nature of bibliographic records and their control very much complex. Libraries have played a vital role in contemporary societies with their responsibilities for collection, storage, organisation, retrieval and dissemination of knowledge. Libraries have continued to support the whole course of human endeavour and shaping future activities.

The libraries have undergone a major change in modern period. The physical formats of the documents, nature and characteristics of bibliographic records, collection management policies, needs and requirements of the users, changed service patterns, specialised services as well as electronic storage and access to databases. The libraries have to play the role of comprehensive resource centres and the librarians have to play the role of information providers. Therefore, the libraries have to supplement the traditional carriers of information and intellectual contribution. At the same time the concept of single library services as stand alone institutions has become obsolete. The services of a library are not restricted to the resources available in that particular library. The needs and requirements of the users in present day libraries are so specific as well as sometimes so comprehensive on a particular field, that a single library, however large it may be, cannot serve the users' needs properly.

Because of the changing needs and requirements and dependence upon information and its ultimate utilisation in all life activities in modern social and intellectual environment. The information resources have become vital instruments for users' services. The bibliographic and non-bibliographic records, their organisation and control have become crucial in library management. The growth of information, information services, sources and systems, and the electronic technology used in these areas are the concern of the librarians as information scientists. But the characteristics of information, the reasons and ways users search for it are regardless of the processing technology, physical medium, and human organisation involved in its storage, organisation and dissemination cannot be attempted to cope with by the librarians. The database agencies, commercial and noncommercial organisations having specialised information management infrastructural facilities can manage and control the information resources. Librarians can only attempt to keep track of the information sources, systems and retrieval services as well as the documents as bibliographical records.

BIBLIOGRAPHIC DATA

Bibliographic data, as a whole, for a particular document and the data elements in particular are the tools for bibliographic control. The data elements are the identification units of a particular document for the purpose of cataloguing and for preparation of bibliographics. Bibliographic data elements are most significant for bibliographic record and bibliographic control. Ronald Hagler mentions the significance and utility of data elements in the following words,

"1. to identify a particular document uniquely in order to distinguish it from others (for example, a data of publication or a count of the number of pages in a printed book)

2. to show how two or more documents are associated with one another (for example, in that they have a common author or that one is a continuation or reprint of the other) and

3. to provide the basis for access points which enable a searcher to locate the record of a document in a file; these may relate to-

   (a) objective facts about the document itself (for example, its title or the fact that it constitutes the proceedings of a conference) or

   (b) the topic(s) and concept(s) treated in its intellectual content; simplistically, the subject(s) of the document."

Bibliographic data regarding three items mentioned above must be incorporated in bibliographic records both for catalogues and bibliographic tools. The primary value of the title of a document is as a description of the content of the document to the users. The title of a document in the bibliographic record is to identify the document itself under a specific tag, 'the name of a work'. Sometimes the term 'work' is ambiguous from the cataloguer's or bibliographer's point of view as well as from users' point of view. The intellectual content of a document is usually known a 'work'. Bibliographic record and control involve both the physical document with physical characteristics as well as the intellectual content it embodies or the work. These two aspects cannot be separated in a document. But the users' approach may be either of the two aspects. For these reasons the identification of a particular document, listing of documents by cataloguers or bibliographers and bibliographical searching by users become complicated. Usually the reason is that document entity (physical) gets precedence in bibliographic record because the primary function is not to interpret the document (work or intellectual entity) to users, but to provide access points to search the document in the form of one or more physical entities. Whatever term may be used to identify a document, such as item publication, edition or a work (intellectual content) the users are interested to get access it for particular purpose.

DOCUMENTS : INTERRELATIONSHIPS

The jobs of bibliographic record and control confront many complex and complicated problems because of the interrelationships among the individual documents can be endless. All the relationships of any two or more documents are not available on records, may not be identified properly or the relationships may not be anticipated. The bibliographic data on such relationships are not always found within the related documents themselves. The author of a particular document cannot imagine how many documents will be published related to that document during his lifetime and after his death by how many persons in various bibliographic formats having different authorship identity. Multiple shared authorship, multiple mixed authorship, various related and dependent and related works, various kinds of editions, compilations, translations, adapted words, and permutation and combination of intellectual responsibility as well as related documents may cause innumerable documents published and to be published in future. The identification of bibliographic record and management of bibliographic control of the documents with multifaceted relationships become practically impossible. In such cases the bibliographers have to investigate outside a concerned document in hand to ascertain all possible interrelationships.

Significant types of interrelationships may be summarised for basic bibliographic relationships. There may be many more but to begin with the identification of relationships the following points are important.

1. The physical formats of the same document may differ in following ways,

(a) Paper print, mircrocopy, CD - ROM, online access

(b) Bound with hard cover, leather binding, paperback without illustrations, students, edition, etc.

2. The bibliographic entity may differ while the intellectual content remains the same in the following ways,

   (a) the same content may be published with different titles,

   (b) the same content republished by different publishers as reprints,

   (c) previously published book with a machine - readable disk,

3. The same content published in different editions may differ, such as,

   (a) simple print edition and illustrated edition, various literary form, from drama to fiction or fiction to drama, revised text, supplementary materials, same content with editorial note, etc,

   (b) research works or essays edited keeping the original form but with prefatory notes, additional updated materials, appendices, and the like,

   (c) the text as independent publication, same text in anthologies, compilations, collected works, critical editions, facsimile edition of rare books with or without editorial note, etc,

   (d) different publications issued under a series with a composite or new title,

   (e) collection of several works of the same author published under a new title simultaneously with the individual titles,

   (f) work being a required to another previously published work by a different author, a supplement to another work or a continuation of another work with a different title,

   (g) keeping the title almost identical a work may be

published with distinctly different intellectual content not identical to original work by the author, as edited, revised or completely there - revised edition written by other persons. In such cases the texts vary very much from edition to edition. An example is given below -

The original work was 'Manual of Library Economy' by James Duff Brown, first published in 1903. The title page of the seventh edition is as follows,

James Duff Brown's
Manual
of
Library Economy
Seventh Edition
Completely rewritten
by
R. Northwood Lock FLA
Grafton and Co
London
1961

On the verso of the title page the edition statement is given as noted below -

First Edition, 1903
Second Edition, revised, 1907
Third Edition, rewritten by W.C. Berwick Sayers, 1920
Fourth Edition, revised, 1931
Fifth Edition, revised with additions, 1937
sixth Edition, rewritten, 1949, reprinted with corrections, 1950
Seventh Edition, completely rewritten by R. Northwood Lock, 1961
© Andre' Deutsch Ltd.
Dedicated to the Memory
of
James Duff Brown
(1862 - 1914)

In this work the original author was alive till the second revised edition. The third rewritten edition was the intellectual contribution of W.C. Berwick Sayers (1882 - 1960). Fourth revised edition, fifth revised edition and sixth edition which was rewritten were the intellectual contribution of W.C. Berwick Sayers. The seventh edition was completely rewritten by R. Northwood Lock but in all the editions the name of the author is James Duff Brown and the title is 'Manual of Library Economy'. The text and content of all the editions vary from each other, rewritten by two authors other than James Duff Brown but the interrelationships are very much evident.

The establishment of bibliographic relationships of documents is a complex and intriguing area for cataloguers and bibliographers because they have to inform the users about the intellectual contributions of the documents in different physical formats, variations in formats and they have to devise mechanisms to collocate all the documents showing their interrelationships and genealogical relations as information sources for getting access to the needed documents.

Bibliographic relationships are primarily shown in citations, references, bibliographies given at the end of the documents, indexes. The sources, etc, as well as in library catalogues, subject and author bibliographies in addition to documents themselves. The common areas of relationships may be revealed in the related documents, such as

(a) various editions of the same work

(b) sequels, continuations, etc

(c) items in the same series

(d) the same and similar works in various collections

(e) interdisciplinary and multidisciplinary works

(f) citation analysis

(g) bibliographic references.

The bibliographic descriptions in annotated bibliography,

data elements in library catalogues, bibliographic references, third level cataloguing of AACR 2, Cross reference citations, and the like, have their own way of showing the abovementioned and other relationships.

INTELLECTUAL RESPONSIBILITY

The AACR 2R88 uses the term "statement of responsibility" by giving less emphasis on what is known as `intellectual responsibility' because in most of the documents the intellectual content and its contributor cannot be easily identified except documents written by single authors. In machine - readable catalogues and bibliographics the physical description part has been standardised and there is no scope for annotation or critical evaluation of the intellectual content of the author or authors. It is not permitted to add such words as `by' or `and' in square brackets to a statement of responsibility if they do not appear in the work to be catalogued. However, Rule 1.1 F 8 does allow to add an explanatory word or phrase if the relationship between the title and the person or group named in the statement of responsibility, "is not clear" which means other than that of author and is not explicitly stated as such.

Despite its extensive instructions on construction headings for persons. The AACR 2 R 88 makes explicit reference neither to personal name authority control nor to authority control in general. Both terms are absent from the entire text, including the glossary. This situation makes it difficult to prepare bibliographic record and to make effective bibliographic control. AACR 2 R 88 rules 22.2 B2 and 22.2 B3 sanction the practice of dividing authors' works among two or more headings. This practice goes against the collection of all the works together under one heading. This situation denies the fact that one individual produced several different types of works under several names. Although both rules instruct cataloguers to connect the various heading with explanatory references, but users cannot always be relied upon to take proper notice of these.

Intellectual responsibility has become increasingly difficult to define as more and more works are the contributions of a number of persons interacting in varied ways, whether as individuals or as members of corporate bodies. Intellectual contribution is authoritatively established in the work of a person created as singular contributor, and unquestionably the person is the sole owner of intellectual responsibility but in case of mixed authorship, shared authorship or otherwise multiple authorship, the extent of intellectual responsibility is very difficult to ascertain and most difficult to identify.

Intellectual responsibility of the surrogates as authors other than the principal authors has been accepted in cataloguing and bibliographic entries. The terms as editor, compiler, translator, illustrator, etc. are being used to identify the persons as holder of intellectual responsibility. The persons, so designated, may perform any one or more of the functions as stated by Ronald Hagler. The functions are

"1. cause a work to come into existence by conceiving its scope, general focus, and arrangement, then convincing others to do the actual writing
2. reconstruct a deceased author's intended text by examining existing editions, manuscripts, and other evidence
3. add a commentary, glosses, footnotes, bibliography, etc. (together called critical apparatus) to an existing work by someone else
4. abridge, revise, paraphrase, bowdlerise, or other wise modify an existing work by someone else
5. select for inclusion in a new publication material which was created for other purposes by one or many persons or bodies (his activity is often called compiling, as in the case of an anthology, but it may also be called editing, as in the case of conference proceedings)"

The description on the title page of a book records the intellectual origin of the work known as a statement of responsibility. Such description may be clear and explicit or sometimes vague and ambiguous. In the latter case some interpretation is required to determine which of the named persons have acted mainly to the creation of the intellectual content of the document for mentioning in the bibliographic record.

There is a basic difference between library catalogues and bibliographies. In library catalogues various access points or catalogue entries or references are used for access to a particular document in the library created by a person or persons with a focus to intellectual responsibility of any proportion. In bibliographics, not limited to the resources of a particular library, the name of a person, corporate body or an access tag is used as access or search point without much consideration regarding the intellectual responsibility of various types of 'authors' in a particular document.

Nancy Williamson in her 'Cataloguing and Bibliography: A Comparative Study of The Relationships as seen through Their Principles and Practices (1977) writes

"In many instances it was clear that the bibliographers were not concerned with establishing intellectual responsibility for a work, but rather with identifying it and locating it. Furthermore, they assumed that a name is a better means of identification than a title ..... There was title in the sample of bibliographics which suggested that bibliographers considered title entries an improvement over author entries. In truth, there seemed to be a strong preference for the use of some other feature of the work if possible, leaving title as the last possible choice..." She further observes "In the light of the bibliographer's approach to authorship, the definition of authorship should be reexamined. In this context some thought rules toward greater use of title entry is valid. With specific reference to works prepared under editorial direction and collections prepared by a compiler, reconsideration should be given to the possibility of accepting the name of the editor or compiler named on the title page of a work as viable entry."

The difference between catalogue entry and bibliographic entry is big in the manual catalogue system but in machine - readable catalogues and databases this difference does affect much. But in bibliographic record and control the focus must be on bibliographic database and their organisation as well as searchability of access points and bibliographic collation.

BIBLIOGRAPHIC CONTROL

For the purpose of the knowledge management in libraries the basic apparatus is the bibliographic control. The operations involved in bibliographic control are distinguished from the activities of cataloguing for identifying the needs and requirements of the immediate library users and access to documents in a library. Preparation of catalogue comes under technical services and access to bibliographic data comes under users' services or information services. Bibliographic control makes a bridge between the two. It enables the people to identify the documents, existence of documents useful for their purposes and to know the nature and characteristics of each of the documents identification of a particular document as well as all the documents available on a particular topic, by a particular author or categorisation of documents for any particular purpose.

Bibliographic control is not just the preparation of list of documents or bibliographics, but it performs many functions. These are -

1. Identification of all the documents produced in any physical format,
2. Identification of the individual works contained within a document or parts of the documents as distinct bibliographic entity including articles in journals, papers published in collections, units of anthologies, conference and seminar papers as individual entity in the proceedings, etc.,
3. Providing access points for multiple access of the documents and their parts, if any, under author, title, subject

or any other access mechanism,

4. Producing and collecting of all bibliographic records prepared according to standard format of citation and collocation of documents as bibliographic instruments to help the users,
5. Providing locations of the documents, wherever they are available, to enable the users for having access to them,
6. Indicating methods of access with mention to physical format, such as book, journal, online search, CD - ROM, disk, and the like.

The operations of bibliographic control involve both the physical document and the intellectual content with the identity of intellectual responsibility, it incorporates. These two types of operations complicate the job of bibliographic control both for the bibliographers and the searchers or users. Bibliographic control is a procedure through which the searchers can have access to the documents in the form of one or more physical formats. The individual records in a bibliographic file is an organised sequence of document descriptions. All kinds of document description in machine - readable format are known as bibliographic records.

Uniformity and standardisation of bibliographic records are essential norms both for individual entry as well as bibliographic database. For adequate identification and consistency the following principles are to be followed :

1. Each bibliographic record must be unique in its identity and no two records are identical,
2. The bibliographic description of a record must be accessed by searchable access points, such as author, title, subject, series, or any other heading,
3. The bibliographic description of a document must be presented in uniform and standardised manner so that their identity and interpretation can be unambiguous.

Standardisation of bibliographic description, uniqueness in individual identity and information transfer mechanism ensure the following facilities,

1. Participant institutions can contribute to union catalogues ensuring resource sharing and cooperative cataloguing with the facility of broader bibliographic access, and
2. Such institutions can download and upload records, and interchange bibliographic data of any category and of any physical format.

Bibliographic control covers a wide range of library and information techniques and disciplines. These may include cataloguing, systematic bibliography, indexing, abstracting, citation analysis, subject access by controlled vocabulary, personal name authority control, standardisation of bibliographic format, bibliographic description, machine - readable cataloguing, indexing systems, thesaurus construction and other related areas.

7

Bibliographic Description and Access

Computer and telecommunication technologies greatly facilitate storage and access to information and documents. Computers can themselves can promote such activities through compatibility of bibliographic records and transfer of such records to be performed automatically. Bibliographic and information services are very largely involved in manipulating records representing physical items, such as books, periodicals, periodical articles, and other carriers of information in machine - readable storage and transfer systems. The standardisation and compatibility issues directly affect both the database operators as well as users of information services. Standardisation of bibliographic descriptions, identity of data elements, users, online searches storage in users' computers are the vital issues in bibliographic description and access.

During past two decades much has been achieved in standardisation and compatibility among bibliographic records as well as information transfer protocols. An international standard format for bibliographic record exchange has been devised and widely adopted. It is ISO 2709. Based on this standard, the UNISIST Reference Manual Provided a complete working manual for the international standardisation of the form and content of computer - readable bibliographic descriptions prepared by abstracting and indexing services and others. The MARC exchange format and its various applications have also been widely adopted for establishing significant level of compatibility and standardisation of exchange formats.

The contributions of IFLA for international standard bibliographic descriptions for a wide variety of materials have become vital for achieving standardisation of bibliographic formats of various documents. The International Standard Book Number (ISBN) and the International Standard Scrial Number (ISSN) facilitate unique identification of these bibliographic items and interlinking of different databases. Much work has been done for the areas of author authority - control and subject authority control. Information system designers and users can benefit from developments in hardware and software compatibilities that originate in other application areas. Standards developed for programming languages, command languages, input/output devices, storage devices, character sets, telecommunications and networking links have made a breakthrough in electronic storage and transfer of information.

Information storage and transfer systems are concerned with the processing of records representing some bibliographic item or document in various physical formats. The system to process bibliographic records with the help of electronic technologies stimulated the global activities of machine - readable storage and access to databases with standardised bibliographical description by the means of achieving international compatibility of such records so that machine - readable records can be integrated and exchanged at international level. The ultimate objective was described by D. Anderson in 'Universal Bibliographic Control : a long term policy. A Plan for action "(1974). The purpose of which is :

"... to make universally and promptly available, in a form which is internationally acceptable, basic bibliographic

data on all publications issued in all countries.

The concept of UBC (Universal Bibliographic Control) presupposes the creation of a network made up of component national parts, each of which covers a wide range of publishing and library activities, all integrated at the international level to form the total system."

A bibliographic record for a document can be subdivided into four major components. These are :

1. Description of the document or physical item itself with such elements as author, title, publisher, and other essential elements to identify a particular item,
2. Highlighting the elements from complete description of the bibliographic record, such as personal or corporate author for intellectual responsibility or title etc, as search tag, to act as access points through which the record can be searched and retrieved,
3. A unique identifier for the document, and
4. Subject heading terms representing the subject matter of a document, which might be controlled vocabulary terms or authority file based on thesaurus, or words and phrases drawn from the document itself.

In last two decades, IFLA has produced a series of "standard bibliographic description" of documents in various physical formats to cover the first component. Such bibliographic descriptions of a particular physical format specify the data elements needed to completely describe a bibliographic item, the sequence in which they should be presented, and the punctuation conventions to be used with them. The bibliographic record format for description is flexible enough to allow an individual user to select those parts of the description needed to serve a particular purpose.

The ISBDs for various physical formats have been accepted internationally as standardised bibliographic description. All these have been recognised as the basis for rules for bibliographic description in AACR 2 for English speaking countries as well as catalogue codes for some other countries. But these bibliographic descriptions deal with the content of the 'record', rather than with the representation of that content or with the content of the 'document' described. Two important steps towards Universal Bibliographic Control for the purpose of unique identification of a document were the adoption of a system for uniquely identifying publications by International Standard Book Number (ISBN) as well as International Standard Serial Number (ISSN). Since ISBNs or ISSNs are included in IFLA's standard bibliographic descriptions, these descriptions serve to identify documents uniquely as well as describing them.

The ISBDs give the bibliographic description of a document as a whole but these are not designed to contribute directly to choice of access points. The access points for a document are to be decided by the library for its users. International standardisation of this aspect is very difficult, if not impossible. The standard description of a document may highlight some words to be used as access points. D. J. Hickey has given his observation in "Bibliographic Control In Theory" (1980) as stated below :

> "Bibliographic information not included in the descriptive process can hardly be selected as the basis for an access point; thus it is important, wherever possible, for the descriptive information to be identified and recorded in a standardized way so that all significant access points will be embedded in an appropriate context and can be uniformly identified for retrieval purposes ... The ISBD... lays the groundwork for possible future agreement about the way in which access points are chosen and their form of representation in a bibliographic file."

The information storage and transfer systems are concerned with the access to a particular document as well as a group of documents or access to information for such document or documents. Therefore, various access points for different types of needs and requirement of the users should be ensured in the mechanism of information storage, organisation and search strategy.

BIBLIOGRAPHIC RECORD FORMAT

The International Meeting of Cataloguing Experts at Copenhagen in 1969 adopted the following resolution :

> "Efforts should be directed toward creating a system for the international exchange of information by which the standard bibliographic description of each publication would be established and distributed by a national agency in the country of origin... The effectiveness of the system would depend upon the maximum standardization of the form and content of the bibliographic description."

Computer application in library and information services and networkings necessitated international standardisation of bibliographic description and record. Therefore, international standards were formulated. IFLA produced a series of "standard bibliographic descriptions" to specify the data elements needed to completely describe a bibliographic item and the sequence in which they should be presented. Accordingly, IFLA published the "International Standard Bibliographic Description" for monograph ISBD (M) in 1974. The purpose was to "provide internationally accepted framework for the representation of descriptive information in bibliographic records". "International standard Bibliographic Description for Serials," ISBD (S) was published in 1977. In the same year "General International Standard Bibliographic Description," ISBD (G) was published.

These international standards and ISBDs for other types of materials, formed the basis for the rules for bibliographic description in AACR 2 and its revision. Other ISBDs have been formulated for music, for non - book materials, for maps and for antiquarian materials and an ISBD (CP) for "analyticals" (Component part of works). The ISBD texts are subject to a five - yearly review. The Society of American Archivists (SAA). The

Library of Congress, the Research Library Group jointly formulated standard data elements used in Archives, Manuscripts and Records Repositions Information Systems as the Format for Archives and Manuscript Materials in machine - readable form.

The unique identification of a document or publication become possible towards Universal Bibliographic Control by the adoption of the unique number as International Standard Book Number (ISBN) for monographs and International Standard Serial Number (ISSN) for serial publications. The ISBN number consists of four segments - the country segment, publisher segment, work segment, and check digit - each separated by a hyphen. The ISBN was introduced in 1968, so earlier works will not have such numbers. Because inclusion of the ISBN is voluntary, not every work will include one, ISSN was introduced in the following year.

Publishers use ISBN for their computerised inventory control and financial accounting systems. Therefore, the ISBN is intended to identify any form publication its publisher might invoice separately. So, a paperback, hard bound and an expensive leatherbound edition of the same publication each receives a different ISBN. The same book with two publishers' imprint has a separate ISBN relating to each publisher. Thus, there cannot be an absolute one - to - one relationship either between an ISBN and a work or between an ISBN and a library catalogue record. ISBN has ten characters.

The ISSN consists of eight characters : seven numerals followed by a check digit. An ISSN is conventionally shown as four digit segments separated by a hyphen. An ISSN uniquely identifies all issues of a serial publication while they have the same key - title. When a serial publication changes title, the issues under the new title have a new ISSN and a corresponding new key - title. International Data System of UNISIST coordinates the assignments of ISSNs and key - titles by national agencies.

INTERNATIONAL STANDARD BIBLIOGRAPHIC DESCRIPTION FOR MONOGRAPHIC PUBLICATIONS, ISBD (M)

International Standard Bibliographic Description was formulated to make available all bibliographic data of a particular document in any physical format and there are ISBDs for different types of physical formats. The bibliographic formats were designed for the purpose of :

1. Standardisation of the format of descriptive portion of the bibliographic record for all types of documents,
2. Making it easier to recognise data elements regardless of the language of their content, and
3. Making the data stored and retrievable in machine - readable formats.

Obviously, the title page of a book remains the most important source for the data required for bibliographic description. ISBD (M) recognises the title page of a book as the main source of information. Different main sources have been recognised for each physical carrier of content in which there is no title page formally or its equivalent. But the arrangement of information on the main source no longer governs either the choice of which data elements are to be included in the record or their arrangement in the record. These are governed by the standardised format. Therefore, ISBDs specify other sources of data required for standardised bibliographic description. These sources include verso of the title page, cover and external sources depending on the type of data element involved.

The scope of ISBD (M) specifies requirements for the description of printed monographic publications with the order to the elements of the description, and specifies a system of punctuation for that description. The primary purpose of the ISBD (M) is to aid the international communication of bibliographic information by making records from different sources interchangeable, assisting in the interpretation of records across language barriers and assisting in the conversion of bibliographic records to machine - readable format.

ISBD (M) specifies eight areas for bibliographic data to be presented in the sequence given below :

Area 1. Title and Statement of Responsibility Area
Area 2. Edition Area
Area 3. Material - specific Data Area
Area 4. Publication, Distribution, etc. Area
Area 5. Physical Description Area
Area 6. Series Area
Area 7. Note(s) Area
Area 8. Standard Number, etc. Area

There is enumeration of the elements in each of the above mentioned areas.

INTERNATIONAL SERIALS DATA SYSTEM (ISDS)

The International Serials Data System (ISDS) is an intergovernmental organisation established within the framework of the UNESCO - PGI programme. the aim of ISDS is to provide a reliable and uptodate machine - readable database of world serials publications covering the full range of recorded knowledge and containing essential information for the identification and bibliographic control of serials. The ISDS functions as a network of national and regional centres established in various countries and coordinated by the International Centre located in Paris. ISDS provides almost complete bibliographic control of the current serial publication of the world output.

This international serials directory provides all accurate ISSN. ISDS has sole responsibility for the assignment and control of ISSN. Records on all serials titles numbered by the ISDS network are published in the Register. Updating of the Register is ensured by the ISDS centres throughout the world. The ISDS record contains the ISSN, the Key title, other forms of title, the abbreviated key title, the imprint, the issuing body, the classification number (UDC or DDC), all types of related titles, and other information. All ISDS data elements can be used as access points to the record.

The national and regional centres register systematically all new serials and title changes which occurred. The records are forwarded to the International Centre of ISDS in machine - readable format. The records are verified, processed and added to the ISDS database. As one of the objectives of the ISDS is to have complete bibliographic control, the database also contains short records of serials of local interest or ephemeral nature which are excluded from general dissemination. Complete records of such serials are maintained at the respective national centres.

MACHINE - READABLE STORAGE AND EXCHANGE FORMAT

Machine - readable bibliographic record format for storage and exchange of bibliographic and information databases refers to the method of organising data so that each item of data can be unambiguously identified. In manual catalogues and printed bibliographies, the records and data elements are readily identified visually, by such characteristics as position, sequence and spacing. In machine readable records, there must be explicit way of determining the end of one data element and the beginning of another. In machine - readable format, the need for precision in determining the beginning and end of every data element is essential and, therefore, must be in accordance with internationally recognised codes that can indicate what kind of element or part of the element it is and how many characters it occupies.

The machine - readable record format of a particular bibliographic item, a book, serial, periodical article, etc. has three major components : These are

1. The structure of the record, which is physical representation of data on the machine - readable medium.
2. The content designators or labels, which are the means of identifying the data elements or providing additional information about each.
3. The contents of the record, which are the data elements

themselves, such as names of authors, titles, and other elements to identify a particular document.

The most important record format is MARC (Machine - Readable Cataloguing). It refers to a specific set of conventions for representing an identified ensemble of bibliographic data. Initiated by the Library of Congress MARC I evolved in 1966 as a format for a machine - readable catalogue record, an instrument in the MARC Pilot Project and the MARC Interim System that followed. In 1968 the MARC II format was put into use and the full MARC System began functioning. It was proved useful in the United States. It became a model to be followed in other countries and changed a bit to accommodate local needs.

The standardisation of LC MARC format on the basis of MARC II was the result of much initiative, planning, experiment and well thought out decisions. At that time, the British National Bibliography personnel visited the Library of Congress to investigate the possibility of a UK MARC project. The staff of the Library of Congress and the British National Bibliography worked together to make an attempt to specify a format that might be used by both the agencies. This cooperation had a far - reaching effect and both the agencies recognised the future implications of a bibliographic format that is interchangeable and of the agreed standard with a view to develop MARC projects in other countries. Both the organisations were active in their respective national standard organisations. In 1969, both the proposed American National Standards Institute (ANSI) format and the British Standards Institute (BSI) format were submitted to the International Organisation for Standardisation (ISO). The MARC projects in the United States and Britain and the proposed ANSI, BSI and ISO standards gave inspiration to many countries to plan for and implement their own MARC systems. The MARC format became the US national standard in 1971 (ANSI 239.2 - 1971).

ISO 2709

With the purpose of standardisation of machine - readable

data elements d international data exchange format ISO published its standard as International Standard ISO 2709 under the title "Documentation - Format for bibliographic information interchange on magnetic tape" in 1973, which must be used in conjunction with other ISO standards relating to character sets and tape labelling. It was the same as the American ANSI Z 39.2 and the British BS : 4748. It was designed to regulate only the essential structural features of MARC as a variable field format and was not limited to bibliographic records only. ISO 2709 - based format can be used to process any kind of information requiring variable - length fields, bibliographic and other types of information. The scope and field of applications was stated as "This International Standard specifies the requirements for a generalized exchange format which will hold records describing all forms of material capable of bibliographic description as well as related records such as authority records. It does not define the length of the content of individual records and does not assign any meaning to tags, indicators or identifiers; these specifications being the functions of an implementation format."

This international standard describes a generalised structure and a framework designed specially for communication between data processing systems. It is not for use as processing format within systems. All implementation formats follow this standard. This standard describes bibliographic record, data field, subfield identifier, indicator, directory, record label, directory map, separating character, subfield, structure, field tag and structure of communication format for bibliographic and non - bibliographic record.

UNISIST REFERENCE MANUAL

ISO 2709 and MARC format paved the way for storage and transfer of bibliographic data for various types of bibliographic documents and records, but these were not suitable for information services like abstracting and information services. There was a demand for abstracting and indexing databases in machine - readable format both for storage and transfer.

Standardisation and compatibility of information processing became essential. UNISIST undertook a project to study the feasibility of information network in science and technology areas and created the record format. The UNISIST Reference Manual for Machine - readable Bibliographic Descriptions was published by UNESCO in 1974 and the second edition was published in 1981.

It was primarily created for abstracting and indexing services, but it could be used in other applications in the field of information processing and exchange. The manual defines a carrier format structure, gives detailed specifications of the form and content of individual bibliographic data elements and defines the data element sets needed to describe particular types of documents. The Reference Manual describes an exchange format as well as with a few additions, it could be made into a processing format. The Manual for bibliographic description, was developed with the needs of indexing and abstracting services. A particular feature of the Reference Manual is its ability to handle component parts of composite documents, such as analyticals including periodical articles. It also includes rules for data elements for 'authorship' or 'intellectual responsibility' areas while there was no international agreement on these areas, to be used as an international exchange format.

The UNISIST International Centre for Bibliographic Description (UNIBID) was established in 1976 by the British Library under a contract with UNESCO to operate within the framework of UNISIST. The objectives were defined as :

1. To maintain the UNISIST Reference Manual, to issue amendments and additions, and to promote its use, especially in making provision for suitable training.
2. To provide an information service on existing systems of bibliographic description.
3. To participate in the coordination of activities, including research and development, within the field of standardizing

procedures of bibliographic description used by the information community.

4. To coopèrate with other agencies and organizations operating within the General Information Programme in general and UNISIST in particular, such as those related to the IFLA/UBC office.

UNIBID organised the International Symposium on Machine - Readable Bibliographic Exchange Formats, held in Sicily in April 1978. This symposium provided the impetus for ongoing work on a Common Communication Format (CCF). Programmes were envisaged to develop software for a comprehensive information processing package based on the Reference Manual. The following areas were identified for this purpose :

1. Database management systems
2. Data interchange
3. Functional compatibility
4. End - user Compatibility
5. Machine assistance for searching

UNIMARC

The MARC format, both in its structure and its content designators, has caused a revolution in the creation of databases worldwide. The original MARC came to be called LC MARC and later US MARC, MARC format in Britain was known as UK MAC. In Canada the format was CAN MARC. MARC format was so popular and useful that several countries of the world accepted this format with some local variations. All MARC formats were similar enough that they can be translated into one another using a simple program. It could be done in between any two countries but not internationally. Therefore, IFLA sponsored a universal MARC format for international record exchange to overcome the problems of interchange and standardisation. It was not possible to meet all the requirement of all the countries by one single bibliographic record format.

Therefore, UNIMARC has been designed as a communication and exchange format. The exchange format is a carrier of bibliographic data from one system to another. Its most important attribute is that in providing a standard method of exchanging data from one system to another. The format can satisfy the diversity of users and systems. An exchange format can reduce the conversion effort. If each database format is made compatible with the exchange format, the concerned database centres need to do is to create the conversion programme from exchange format to their internal formats. UNIMARC, based on MARC record structure, provides standardisation in content designators for all bibliographic data elements of ISBD as 'descriptive block'. It can hold data in variable length fields also with full bibliographic description, headings or access points, a set of subject data and other information as stipulated in the AACR 2. The record structure has three elements, a leader providing general information about the record, a directory as a guide to the content and the data, the content of the record.

UNIMARC format specifies the tags, indicators and subfield codes to be assigned to bibliographic records in machine - readable form and specifies also the logical and physical format in which the records and their content designators. It covers monographs, serials cartographic materials, music, sound recordings, graphic and audiovideo materials. The IFLA programme of Universal Bibliographic Control International MARC (UBCIM) continues to promote and maintain the UNIMARC format.

COMMON COMMUNICATION FORMAT (CCF)

The International Symposium sponsored by UNESCO was held in Sicily in 1978 for the development of a common communication format that would meet the needs of libraries and documentation centres of all types and to bridge differences between the library community and information service community. Technically, the CCF represents a major advance in formatting because it provides for different levels of description within the same record. CCF differs from UNIMARC by specifying no rules for description, permitting minimal records, and introducing the concept of groups of fields called record 'segments'. Through the use of segments CCF records permit specific kinds of relationships to exist between fields, groups of fields, and records.

CCF has designated only eight data elements as mandatory. Five are required chiefly for computer processing of the record, and most of these can be computer - generated. They include such elements as the unique record identifier, the name of the agency preparing the record, the date when the record was entered into a file, and so on. Another two or three elements are mandatory because they are considered necessary to identify the item uniquely. These include the language and script of the item and the title, and in case of a serial, the ISSN and key - title. All other data elements are optional.

The CCF has been designed to provide a standard format for the following purposes :

1. To permit the exchange of bibliographic records between groups of libraries and abstracting and indexing services.
2. To permit a bibliographic agency to use a single set of computer programmes to manipulate bibliographic records received from both libraries and abstracting and indexing services.
3. To serve as the basis of a format for an agency's own bibliographic database, by providing a list of useful data elements. To assist the development of individual systems, other UNESCO documentation will provide implementation notes for the CCF, and guide for AACR 2 cataloguers who use the CCF.

BIBLIOGRAPHIC ACCESS

The purpose of all the activities of bibliographic description and control is to provide the most direct access to the content of a particular document as well as a number of documents essential to the stated needs and requirement of the users. Every user wants the largest possible assemblage of potentially relevant documents and information to be available for any search. The compilers of cataloguer, bibliographies and information sources are expected to build the files in a consistent and predictable manner in a system for accessing the descriptions of single documents and groups of documents. The wise searcher learns how to use that system to find what is needed. The bibliographic files must be created as the best organised kind of information access tools.

The objective of creating the files for users' search implies a mechanism for isolating a single record or a related group of them from among many others. The mechanism involves two kinds of systems as follows :

(a) storage and arrangement of documents and information sources in a systematic way so that there can be retrieved at any point of time for any purpose, and

(b) indexing of the documents and information sources available to the users for manipulation of multiple access.

These processor consist of the following methods;

1. determination of useful access points for each document or information source from among its data elements,
2. structuring and arranging these access points in a predictable way so that the users can make a purposeful and useful search,
3. linking the access points of document or information source for multiple search, and
4. interlinking of access points for related and surroge materials.

The staff of the library or the information centre are responsible for organisation and maintenance of the above mentioned activities at input stage. The steps involved at the output side of the service are almost similar to those involved at input. The users submit requests to the library or the information centre and the staff members prepare search strategies for the requests of the users. After preparation of the search strategies, these are matched in some way against the database of document representations. Document representations that match the search strategies and satisfy the logical requirements of the search are retrieved from the database and delivered to the users.

F.W. Lancaster mentions that the major components of the service comprise six major subsystems :

"1. The document selection subsystem.
2. The description and indexing subsystem.
3. The vocabulary subsystem.
4. The searching subsystem.
5. The subsystem of interaction between the user and the system (user - system interface).
6. The matching subsystem, that is, the subsystem that actually matches document representations against request representations."

The purpose of bibliographic access is primarily the organisation of information about the documents the library or information centre collects. It is not just restricted to a particular library or information centre. The electronic storage media and communication technologies have made it possible to have global access in various formats, physical and electronic.

8

INTERNATIONAL SWITCHING LANGUAGE

For many years members of the scientific community have been feeling after powerful tools for arrangement and retrieval of subject information. Classification has been gaining new momentum since World War II, partly through the potentialities of the computer and partly through interests of philosophers, logicians, historians of science, psychologists, semioticians and scientist - taxonomists. However slight be the achievement of the Royal Society and Scientific Information Conference in 1948, its intention was significant. In fact, it marked the beginning of a new era and concentrated on the concern of the scientific community to cope with the ever increasing flood of scientific and technical publication. There was a thrill of suggestions in the Washington conference in 1958. In spite of the significant role of the computer, developments tended to be along rather conventional lines. A new vista opened up during the 1960's. In developed countries the intention and achievement almost went hand in hand. They were on the whole managing to keep the problems in the handling of information under control. But the third World countries were increasingly at a disadvantage in not having the same access to the free flow of scientific information as the developed world. In this context a joint control committee was set up by UNESCO and ICSU in 1967 to carry out a feasibility study of a World Science Information System, to be called UNISIST. A detailed report of the committee was largely approved at an international conference in October 1971.

The UNESCO programme was aimed at the development of a network of information systems. In the UNISIST Study Report (UNESCO, 1971) the purport of classification systems and thesauri in individual information systems was discussed, and the different uses that could be made of them were indicated. Special emphasis was given to those topics in sections dealing with problems of disciplined - and mission - oriented centres, role of scientists in document and data analysis, organisational issues pertaining to content analysis, indexing with broad categories, compatibility of indexing vocabularies, and language barriers and metalanguages.

It was also suggested that a standard list of broad subject headings might prove useful to locate and transfer large blocks of information. To facilitate document and information exchange between different provinces of scientific documentation (regional, linguistic, sectoral), a world - wide scheme of subject categorizations was deemed necessary. In addition to a standard list of subject headings intended for 'shallow indexing' as opposed to the deeper sort of content analysis it was also felt that more research was necessary to develop a common formal framework for analysing convertibility and organising adhoc intermediate languages, with regard to both to semantic and to syntactical components. Thus a proposal came for setting up a permanent organization.

Wysocki presented a summary of what should be expected of a Broad System of Ordering at the FID conference in Budapest in September 1972 and the FID was entrusted with the task of developing such a system. It may be mentioned in passing that prior to a contract with UNESCO on the elaboration of such a Broad System the FID/CCC had been investigating whether the UDC could be transformed into a 'roof classification' for other classification schemes or become a 'switching language' for the transfer of 'large blocks of information' or whether a Standard Reference Code (SRC) could be developed. But before the completion of this investigation a new combined group was formed, following the Budapest conference. This group included representatives both from the FID/CCC and FID/CR.

In May 1975 this group presented to this Advisory Board of UNISIST at its meeting in Paris, a scheme to be called the Broad System Ordering (BSO). Thus a paper presented on behalf of UNESCO at the FID meeting bore its first visible fruit in 1978 in the form of published 'Broad System of Ordering : Schedule and Index,"

The work has been delegated to three - member committee consisting of Eric Coates, Geofrey Lloyed and Dusan Simandl.

BSO is a knowledge classification which attempts to reflect a modern consensual world outlook and because it is essentially concept - oriented rather than word - oriented, its captions are supplemented by definition notes whenever the scope and meaning of the caption is not clear from its context in the systematic schedules. The system gives solutions to many dilemmas met by searchers looking for "composite" subjects which can be represented in language only by phrases. Familiarisation with the system is made easy by the fact that its arrangement is governed by a repeated and widely applied underlying pattern which enhances its overall simplicity.

As an example of displayed knowledge organisation employing concept indexing and structured according to modern integrative level theory and twentieth century faceted classification principles pioneered by S.R. Ranganathan, BSO maps and disentagles knowledge on to a consistent and relatively simple repetitive pattern of arrangement for an Internet search methods and offers a subject contextual reference framework against which to plot a comprehensive and systematic search strategy. It is particularly useful in classifying decision - making in searching for subjects which can be named only by phrases rather than single words.

DEFINITION AND SCOPE

The scheme has been devised to function as

(a) a tool for interconnection of information systems, services and centres

(b) a tool for tagging (i.e. shallow indexing)

(c) a referral tool for identification and location of all kinds of information sources and services.

In theory the switching operation requires a neutral code system in which concepts are represented. In practice, however, such a switching system can be set up and sustained by linking local indexing concept representations with neutral language representations of the equivalent concepts. This is achieved through the constructions of table of concordances. If the neutral language can be presented in a systematised form, with ordered collection of conceptually related subjects, it would be easier to form these equivalence - based linkages.

The proposed switching language for UNISIST was rightly described as a broad classification. But at the outset there were considerable difficulties in arriving at an operationally satisfactory and practicable definition of what was to be understood by "broad'. On the one hand the scheme was not be too detailed, which on the plea of `broad' might have been overlooked. Finally, the criterion adopted for what was to be included in the scheme was dependent on the extent to which organisational activity and institutionalisation were revealed in relation to the subject field or area of study. Thus there was an inquiry about the existence of an `organised information source' in relation to the subject. Organised information was detailed as the following :

(a) an organisation supporting or sponsoring the regular issue of specialist information,

(b) an abstracting or indexing service,

(c) an information collection (as a library or a data bank) and

(d) a department of university teaching.

Thus the criterion for cut - off actual in BSO was in a form of 'institutional warrant'. It may be noted that the category (d) was later dropped.

MAIN CLASSES

The basic order of main classes resembles closely that of Bibliographic Classification (BC), identifying the following main areas into which main classes can be categorised.

Second Outline of BSO

088	Phenomena and Entities from a multo - non - disciplinary point of view.
100	Knowledge generally
200	Science and Technology (Together)
300	Life Sciences
359	Applications of Life Sciences
460	Education
470	Human needs
500	Humanities and Social Studies
600	Technology
710	Construction Technology
740	Transport Technology and Services
760	Military Science and Technology
780	Mining
800	Process Industries
860	Metal Technology
910	Language and Literature
940	Arts
970	Religion and Atheism
992	Esoteric practices and movements.

FACET STRUCTURES

Though the facet structure is not explicitly set out in the schedules the BSO is , in fact, a faceted classification. In the majority of cases the citation order within subject fields is regularly the reverse of the sequence of the separate elements as found in the schedules. Thus implication of this for schedule sequence is that within each subject field, the further detail is laid out in the schedule in sequence corresponding to an underlying series of facets and the pattern is recurred as we pass from one major domain to another, for example, Natural sciences to Life Sciences, Life science to Human sciences, and so on.

The basic facet pattern embodied in particular subject fields is as follows :

1. Tools or equipment for carrying out operations,
2. Operations (i.e. purposive activities by people),
3. Processes, interactions,
4. Parts, sub - systems, objects of action or study,
5. Objects of action or study, products, or total systems.

In addition to the above facet structures there are common Time and Place facets. For the use in classing organisations and information sources by BSO, an optional facet is also provided to designate the type of organisation for information sources. Thus the scheme has three general facets roughly corresponding to form auxiliaries in other schemes.

NOTATION

The scheme features an entirely new system of notation based on Indo - Arabic numerals. The numerals are supplemented by two punctuation, signs - the hyphen and the comma and occasionally Roman alphabet is used where only individualisation but not grouping is required. In ordinal values the punctuation signs precede numerals and numerals precede the alphabets.

All codes begin with a number of the millesimal array 000 to 999. Further subjects may be interposed between any two subjects represented by adding to the first of the two consecutive milesimal numbers a comma followed by a two - digit code belonging to the centesimal array 00 to 99. In similar fashion further subjects may be interposed between consecutive numbers of centesimal array by adding a comma followed by two digits from a further 00 to 99 array.

RELATIONSHIPS WITHIN A SUBJECT FIELD

The BSO uses paradigmatic and syntagmatic relationships in its hierarchies and for subject composition. Paradigmatic relationships are included in the scheme. As noted earlier a standard schedule order is maintained throughout the scheme. Following the principle of inversion, the citation order in those subjects where synthesis is permissible is the reverse of this. The notation for primary topics consists of three digits for main headings, followed by a comma and two more digits for subdivision :

716	Building construction and services
,10, 30	Building materials
,30	Building construction work
,37	Timber construction
,40	Parts of buildings
,45	Walls
,50	Engineering services and installations
,52	Heating
,70	Finishing and decorating.

Where no instruction is given for notational syntheses, combination within the same subject field is achieved by the use of , 0 , as a linking symbol.

RELATIONSHIPS BETWEEN SUBJECT AREAS AND GROUPS

When the methods of one field are applied to the objects of another field, complex subjects can be expressed by combining two notations, separated by hyphen and the citation order is governed by the following relational formula :

"Cite first : the notation for the element denoting application area, mission, purpose, end - product or whole system : more generally the subject which "receives" an action or effect or is seen according to a particular viewpoint, or has a property attributed to it."

"Cite second : The notation for the element denoting aspect, approach, action applied, agent : more generally the subject element which" contributes' an aspect, approach or action."

For example, the citation order for Environmental aspects of building construction, is Building Construction (716) followed by Environment (390), giving the composite notation 716-390.

Similarly, Chemistry in glass technology is 856-230 and Medical Jurisprudence is 420-560.

INDEX

The index has definitely enhanced the usefulness of the scheme. But this has been criticised in connection with the inadequate size of its entry vocabulary. It contains about twenty five per cent more entries than the schedules, which indicate that synonyms are not granted generous treatment. The index exhibits cross - references and see references. Some *Cross - references* are undoubtedly helpful, but some *see - references* may cause frustration. Entries are more specific than the heading they lead to. The index entry is indicated by a '0' preceding it.

CONCLUSIONS

The overall order of main subject fields offers an interesting structure because it is quite different from that in most other schemes. In fact, it has resulted in some coveted collocations, but also in one or two undesirable separations. The most prominent, perhaps, is the placement of philosophy as the first discipline to be treated while Religion is the last. But there are several instances of welcome arrangements. It is helpful to have subjects such as communication and management at the early part of the schedule. The Physical Sciences stand near the beginning and modern areas of study such as plasma and fluid physics and polymer chemistry are paid proper attention. But closely related applications such as Materials and Energy are treated with Technology. Geography fares well here, being placed among Earth Sciences, immediately following Astronomy. The Environment has achieved a disciplinary status through institutional warrant, which in term, has brought Human needs class earlier to offer a useful umbrella for topics such as housing, clothing, etc.

The placement of History under the combined heading Humanities and Social Sciences evades the issue of whether or not it is a Social Science. After all, the scheme presents a reasonable and up-to-date conspectus of knowledge. It is modern in its flexible notation, moderate synthetic properties and careful structure and faceting. The succession of topics reflects the theory of integrative level as explored by the CRG (Classification Research Group). Careful attention is paid to the placement of technologies with respect to sciences on which they depend.

The scheme with detail is suitable for indexing secondary information sources rather than documents. But there is no analysis of the particular problems of indexing secondary sources or organisation over and above the pressing problem of determining the proper level of depth and detail for the scheme.

A.C. Foskett points out that the scheme suffers from two weaknesses. The low intensity of indexing, though a minor defect, necessitates improvement. The second defect is definitely fundamental. An established organisation is a vital requisite to maintain the vigour of any classification scheme. But the BSO had been developed and managed by a team of three stalwarts.

The FID relinquished responsibility for the scheme in 1990, and copyright is in the hand of the BSO Panel. Although the BSO was not designed for classification of books in libraries, it could very will be employed for broad goal as an international switching language.

From a subjective point of view, we would be happy to see some success for the scheme as a bridge between systems or an umbrella for a variouś specialised schemes, both because there is a need for such functions and because the time and talent behind it have led to an end product which is simple, yet intellectually impressive.

9

THESAURUS : THE SEARCH TOOL

A thesaurus is a tool for vocabulary control. By guiding indexers and searchers about which terms to use, it can help to improve the quality of retrieval. In fact, thesauri are commonly used in information storage and retrieval; words or phrases are attributed to each document according to its content, and enquiries which might be answered by one or more documents in the whole collection are similarly given descriptive words: where thee is a sufficient degree of match, the identities of the documents are detected.

Usually, the thesaurus is designed for indexing and searching in a specific subject area. Examples of subject areas covered by thesauri are education, metallurgy, and art and architecture.

WHAT IS IN A THESAURUS ?

A thesaurus gives several types of information to indexers and searchers.

Preferred terms

Obviously, the thesaurus has to indicate which terms indexers and searchers are allowed to use. These terms are called preferred terms.

This is a major part of vocabulary control-restricting the

vocabulary so that it is easier to predict what words might have been used to index a concept.

Non-preferred terms

In addition to preferred terms, a thesaurus also needs to indicate some terms that indexers and searchers are not to use. These terms are called non-preferred terms.

It should be possible to look up a non-preferred term and see what preferred term would be used instead. This will save time and make it less likely that the best preferred term will be missed.

A thesaurus also usually allows you to look up a preferred term and see its non-preferred terms. This can give us a better idea of what the term is supposed to mean.

Semantic Relations

As well as linking preferred terms with non-preferred terms, a thesaurus also shows links are usually for semantic relations. Like a link between a preferred term and a non-preferred term, one of these semantic links can help to direct us to the right term and make the meaning of a term clearer.

APPLICATION

A good thesaurus should make it clear what a term is meant to cover. It can accomplish this to some extent by showing non-preferred terms and semantic relations. Other ways of guiding in using a thesaurus include introductory matter and scope notes. A scope note often takes the form of a definition of the term. Ensuring that terms are used consistently with the same meaning is another major aspect of vocabulary control.

Usually, a thesaurus lists all its preferred terms explicitly. Such thesauri are enumerative. Some thesauri indicate some preferred terms indirectly; instead of listing all the preferred terms, they give rules for creating them out of components. Such thesauri are at least partly synthetic.

CONSTRUCTION

Gerard Salton in 1968 "Automatic Information Organisation and Retrieval" (McGraw-Hill, 1968) listed up five principles of thesaurus construction. These are as follows:

1. Raw concepts should not be included in the thesaurus as they could not be expected to produce many matches between documents and search requests.
2. Very common high-frequency terms should be excluded from the thesaurus since they produce too many matches for effective control.
3. Nonsignificant words should be studied carefully before they are included in the list of words to be eliminated.
4. Ambiguous terms should be included only for the seases that are likely to be present in the document collections to be treated.
5. Each concept class should include only terms of roughly equivalent frequency so that the matching characteristics are approximately the same for each term within a category.

MODIFYING AND INVENTING TERMS

Standardising the Form of Words

Words collected should already be nouns or noun phrases. Here we present some further guidelines for the forms that term should take in the final thesaurus.

Guidelines	*Examples*
Plural for things that can be counted	TUBES
Singular for "mass" nouns	WOOD
Singular for process,	REFRIGERATION
properties and conditions	WEIGHT
	POVERTY
Not inverted	RADAR ANTENNAS
	(rather than "ANTENNAS, RADAR")
Excluding prepositions	CARBOHYDRATE METABOLISM

	(rather than "METABOLISM OF CARBOHYDRATES")
Excluding punctuation marks diacritics, special characters, and abbreviations	COOPERATIVE PROGRAMS (rather than "Co-operative programs") MUSICAL NOTES (rather than "(Musical) Notes" or "MUS.Notes".

TERMS WITH MORE THAN ONE MEANING

A homograph is an expression that has the same spelling as another expression, but a different meaning. A thesaurus needs to distinguish between homographs. A unique term may be created out of a homograph by adding a parenthetical qualifier: for example,

PORT (WINE)

It may be noted that including parentheses is contrary to the guideline given above; namely, to avoid punctuation. A unique may also be created out of a homograph by adding another word without punctuation, for example, "PORT WINE".

INTRODUCING NEW TERMS

In addition to terms collected from various sources, we may often need to introduce new terms of our own. For example,

1. broad concept terms
2. structural terms
3. Terms for nontextual material

Broad concept terms

Terms that represent broad concepts may be introduced because they are useful in broad searchers. For example, "TRAFFIC STATIONS", because it can be used to replace a search for "AIR PORTS OR BUS TERMINALS OR TRAIN STATIONS OR......

Structural Terms

Terms may also be introduced because they help to clarify

the structure of semantic relations. For example, "EMPLOYMENT OF SPECIFIC GROUPS" to clarify the relationship between "EMPLOYMENT" and "YOUTH EMPLOYMENT".

Terms for nontextual material

If we construct a thesaurus for indexing material which is not in the form of text, we have fewer sources for terms. We have to find ourselves inventing our own terms more. For example,

A picture shows things that are not referred to in the caption, including a bottle. After examining the picture, we might decide to add "BOTTLES" to our list of terms.

Preferred terms and non-preferred terms

Equivalent terms

After collecting terms for thesaurus we need to decide which are equivalent terms. For purposes of indexing and searching, a set of equivalent terms will all be treated as though they meant the same thing and will be represented by a single preferred term.

Spelling and synonyms

Sometimes, equivalent terms really do mean the same thing. so, it obviously makes sense to use a single preferred term to represent that one meaning.

1. A word may have more than one spelling; for example, "AESTHETICS" and "ESTHETICS."
2. Two different words may have essentially the same meaning, for example, "AUTOMATION" and "MECHANIZATION".

Quasi-Synonyms

Sometimes, equivalent terms mean different things in ordinary language. For indexing and retrieval, it is better to group the different meanings together. Such equivalent terms are called quasi-synonyms.

Terms with overlapping meanings are sometimes treated as equivalent. For example, "GENIUSES" and "PRODIGIES" might be treated s equivalent, even though the two terms mean different things.

A term whose scope is included in that of another term is sometimes treated as equivalent. For example "STEEL" might be treated as equivalent to "METAL" if it is not important to distinguish items on steel from items on other metals.

Excluding concepts with Scope Notes

A scope note may indicate a concept that is excluded from the scope of the term.

This may be done to show that the term has a narrower meaning than some users of the thesaurus might have in mind; for example

BEARS

SN does not include Pandas

It may also be done to draw attention to an excluded meaning of an ambiguous term; for example,

PARTIES

SN Political parties only. Do not use for social gatherings

References to other terms in Scope Notes

Some scope notes refer to other terms, especially to indicate how to deal with a concept that is excluded, for example,

LICENSING

SN Excludes aspects covered by the terms 'School Accreditation' and 'Teacher Accentuation'.

Additional Instructions in Scope Notes

A scope note may give additional instructions to indexers.

For example, it may remind indexers of other types of terms that they should assign:

HOSPITALIZATION

SN Assign also terms for the conditions for which patients were hospitalized, if applicable.

Instructions for Synthesis

In a synthetic thesaurus, instructions for synthesis may appear in scope notes; for example,

HISTORY

SN. Append also as a subdivision after terms Designating disciplines, activities, living things, etc. For example, 'intercropping-history', 'Goats-history'.

SCOPE NOTES

The most common type of guide to applying terms in a thesaurus is the *scope note*. A scope note is normally preceded by the notation SN

Scope notes take a variety of forms

Definitions in Scope Notes

A scope note may be a definition, for example

SPACE ERROR

SN Tendency to be biased by the spatial position of stimulating in relation to the observer.

Form of Definitions in Scope Notes

A definition in a scope note should apply to the *noun form*, not to a related verb or adjective. For example, this scope not for "INDEXING".

SN To assigning of natural language terms to documents.

Content definitions in Scope Notes

A thesaurus term should have a single meaning. Any definitions in the term's scope note should reflect that meaning.

For example, this scope note for "ACCENT"

SN	Stress placed on a syllable; variation in pronunciation due to linguistic background is incorrect because it confuses two different meanings of the term.

Including Concepts with Scope Notes

A scope note may indicate a concept that is included in the scope of the term; for example,

MECHANIZED INFORMATION RETRIEVAL

SN	Included Pre-Computer methods, such as Punched Card Systems.

Thesaurus Displays

For any thesaurus display, you may need to make several decisions. These decisions are likely to include the following:

1. Which types of terms will have entries
2. how to indicate special types of terms
3. what types of links will be shown to other terms
4. how many levels of lining will be shown
5. how to indicate link types
6. where the linked terms are placed

   (a) relative to the entry term

   (b) relatative to each other.

1. A thesaurus display might have entries only for *preferred thesaurus*; for example

Ex	Convicts
Eye	Examinations
Eye	Patches

Eye Glasses

Eyes

Folder

At least one of the displays, however, should provide entries for *non-preferred terms* as well, to allow users to browse through these for the correct preferred terms:

Extremism

Ex Convicts

Ex Military Personnel

Eye Catchers

Eye Examinations

Eye Patches

Eye Glasses

Eyes

Fables

Fabric Design Drawings

HOW TO INDICATE SPECIAL TYPES OF TERMS

We can put all the non-preferred terms in italics.

Of course, users should be able to tell that a term is a non-prefered term if it has a *USE* reference after it.

TYPES OF LINKS TO OTHER TERMS

Thesaurus display should cover all the term links that are important to people who will use the thesaurus

EXTREMISM

USE RADICALISM

Ex-MILITARY PERSONNEL

USE VETERANS

HOW MANY LEVELS OF LINKING WILL BE SHOWN

The display could indicate more than one level of *broader term* :

MONOCLES
BT EYEGLASSES
.BT OPTICAL DEVICES
.. BT EQUIPMENT

MULTILINGUAL THESAURI

Multilingual subject searching has no easy and obvious solution. An ideal solution to the complex problem of multilingual thesaurus construction would be the establishment of a language independent knowledge base, which would form a conceptual structure common to all access languages.

Three aspects are essential for good modern thesauri : Firstly, they should be multilingual to support access to information resources not published in one's native language, and in order to facilitate cross-cultural communication in an increasingly global information society. Secondly they should be semantically structured rather than alphabetically. This is partly to allow equal representation of all languages and partly because semantic structures make the conceptual context of each terms and its translations more explicit than randomly sorted lists. Thirdly, they should assist user comprehension and hence recall and precision in information retrieval by offering definitions, scope notes and even short encyclopedic articles.

THE NEED

While modern information and communication technology facilitates global data transfer, it does not thereby facilitate global communication. Currently, both the Internet and international businesses largely use English for international communication, which poses problems of cross-cultural communication for both native and no-native speakers of English. Furthermore, English may soon cease to dominate global communication. Instead language groups from Asia Pacific and Latin American are predicted to dominate the Internet. Multilingual thesauri will be required to support communication between these language groups as well as between them and currently dominating Western European languages. Unfortunately, many so-called multilingual thesauri for subject access on the Internet or in library OPACs are in fact monolingual thesauri in conjunction or multilingual dictionaries. These forms of multilingual information retrieval systems fail frequently, as can be demonstrated by a close inspection of LISA (Library and Information Science Abstracts). The LISA thesaurus contains only a minority of foreign entry terms although it contains abstracts and full texts from more than sixty-eight countries. Because all abstracts are translated into English, this leads to grossly inconsistent search results when there are no exact equivalents across languages.

THE IMPORTANCE OF EXPLICIT CONCEPTUAL STRUCTURES

By providing facets or other semantic structures, a thesaurus aids users in their understanding of how terms are related to each other by underlying conceptual relations. This has two purposes. firstly, it improves understanding of the meaning of a term within its subject area, and can thus be used for didactic purposes (introducing students to the subject matter of the thesaurus). Secondly, it can enhance query formulation in information retrieval systems. Because users find it easier to recognise and select query terms or concepts than to formulate themselves, explicit query expansion such as offered by a semantically structured thesaurus can be successfully used to trigger the memory of searchers looking for particular items (thus making use of the semantic priming effect).

For a multilingual thesaurus, there are three ways of implementing facets or other semantic structures. Firstly, we can create a conceptual structure that is common to all languages to be included, an option recommended by international guidelines. Alternatively, we can adopt the structure suggested by one of the languages in the thesaurus for all languages, which is the more practical approach, but which favours one language and hence control over the others. We can choose a third way whereby we can retain the conceptual structures suggested by the use of terminology in each language within five broad categories. The advantage of this approach is that linguistic and cultural differences can be fully displayed. For only faceted thesauri provide the flexibility of simultaneously presenting several possibly contradictory viewpoints.

CONCLUSION

A thesaurus is obviously a key tool in the subject analysis, indexing and retrieval of information. Classification schemes are valuable in allowing certain sorts of searches, and structuring information in a way that shows relationships and stimulates new links whilst at the same time free from the problems of using real words, but the problems and difficulties of identifying such relationships and structuring them through hierarchical, two-dimensional system of a classification scheme may be difficult or even impossible. A thesaurus is a retrieval vocabulary which can be used for both indexing and searching in number of different systems.

The layout of a thesaurus is very much a matter of personal preference. Manual production with typing always raises the problem of updating and insertion of new terms, which of course is easily overcome with the advent of word-processing packages with the complete thesauruses held on floppy disk. This allows regular modification to the vocabulary, with printouts taking place when the number of new terms suggests that another edition is required.

10

Classification and Indexing : Correlation

There must be a good deal of classification in any form of subject indexing. In fact, the only difference between a classified and alphabetical subject catalogue is the method of arrangement. The classified order takes the full advantage of classification to show the major relationships of subjects by juxtaposition and sequence. The alphabetical catalogue displays these relationships by cross-references but they are to be derived from a classification system. Similarly the various classes denoted by subject headings are a product of classification.

The Indexing is not only the process of making the entries of an index, it is something more. Organising the entries in a file in a predetermined order and supplementing the entries with all sorts of cross references that is, organising a searchable file, is the sole purpose of indexing. A passing reference may be made to Swift's Battle of the Books written in 1697, which attacked alphabetical indexing of books with metaphors of entering a gentleman's house by the back door, putting salt on sparrows' tails to catch them, and tickling fish. As the style grows in inwardness, the process becomes simultaneously synthetic and syndetic. While scanning the documents for preparation of index efforts are made to include all possible approach points of users and exclude all possibilities that the users may consider trivials. While some are selected others are rejected as entries in the index.

INDEXING PROCESS

Selected entries in the index are grouped or arranged in an order. Simultaneously identifiers are interlinked. which facilitates search of the users. In this process of indexing essential operations are - scanning the documents, analysing the contents of the documents according to predetermined criteria, tagging individual items with appropriate identifiers and adding locative information to each identifier for the indication of its location in the store.

Indexing is completely neither an art nor a science but is a combination of both. Indexing as an art anticipates the use of sense and taste, as a science appreciates the use of rules and patterns. But these rules are empirical and do not lead us to universally accepted results as should be in science. Thus strictly speaking indexing is not a science. Similarly, it forfeits its claim as a true art as it prohibits the projection of individuality and the contribution of creative ideas during the process.

DEWEY'S VIEW

When Dewey (in the first paragraph) in the Preface to his classification of 1876, spoke of " the following classification and index", while stating later on that this "system was devised for cataloguing and indexing purposes, then he surely meant by "indexing" the establishment of indexes. Since then the term "indexing" has come to be applied in a wider sense, even to the point of including the connotation of 'Classifying' or 'Classing', [Dewey 18, Glossary] but in the DDC terminology the former distinction is still kept alive.

CLASSING Vs INDEXING

The difference between classing and indexing is one of direction, and one that ought to be kept up in order to identify a very visible trend in the subject analysis of documents of today, what accounts for this difference ? If classing is defined as

'Classification System', then in such operation the concepts of new realities are related back to the concepts existing already in an established classification system, thus relating new knowledge to existing knowledge.

The term 'indexing' is used in at least three different ways:

(a) As synonymous with the organisation of knowledge in libraries. In this sense it includes author and title indexing and description of documents as well as all subject work.

(b) As the act of recording the contents of a collection, in constrast to the act of searching the collection for required information or documents.

(c) In its narrowest sense as providing an alphabetical key to a systematic order.

'Indexing' may be defined as 'indicating new knowledge/information of documents by pertinent terms or phrases', with the general trend today being toward phrases as the more adequate formulation of the information in question. Thus new information is indicated independently from existing information, that is, without stressing the necessity of a relation to pre-established classificatory structures. The relationship to previous knowledge rests entirely on the expressions used by an author or indexer.

CONCLUSION

There are clearly advantages and disadvantages to both methods and so far it has been a question of individual preference of people whether they would choose the one method or the other for their subject analysis. In the past few years, however, it has been found that advantages of both methods could or should purposely be combined.

It has been recognised that one needs a classification system for ordering of document representation and an indexing method for a better description of minute items of document contents. Thus a multi - level subject analysis has been advocated and realised.

A similar procedure has long been employed by all those abstracting services which arrange their abstracts according to groupings found useful in their respective fields, and which index their items for better lingual access to the details of a document. The groupings are usually not based on existing classification systems, either because of the bad reputations of these systems, especially in the application to special subject-fields, or because the use of a universal system would not make sense for the arrangement of a narrow field and its fringe subjects scattered all over such a universal system.

11

Intricacies in Indexing Systems: Implications for Organising the Internet

The past hundred years have seen the development of numerous systems for the structured representation of knowledge and information, including hierarchical classification systems with notation as well as alphabetical indexing systems with sophisticated features for the representation of term relationships.

DETAILED CLASSIFICATION SYSTEMS

At the end of the nineteenth century, the Universal Decimal Classification (UDC) was developed for the detailed specification of information contained in parts of books and serials. It built upon the Dewey Decimal Classification. DDC was designed for the arrangement of books on library shelves and thus was not specific enough for the representation of the topics of chapters and articles. The designers of UDC refined the Dewey classification and developed symbols for the representation of relationships between subjects.

Ranganathan developed the Colon Classification in India in the 1930s. He believed in the importance of ultimate specificity in the representation of the subjects of documents. His scheme works in the representation of the subjects of documents. His scheme is characterised by its many synthetic features : the classification schedule provides the building blocks, and the classifier puts the elements together. Ranganathan is also credited with the invention of chain indexing, an economical system of providing access to the terms in the string. Because the method is based on the structure of the classification scheme and on the terminology found in the schedules, it is speedy and semi-mechanical operation. Moreover, the successive subject headings are derived by deleting components one by one.

J.E.L. Farradane (Analysis and organization of knowledge for retrieval. Aslib Proceedings, 1970, 22, 607-616) developed a set of nine symbols to represent relationships between concepts. An example of the application of his system is the string "Sugar Cane/ : Sugar, Raw/ ; Filterability/- Measuring/; Filter". Farradane's relational indexing has been the subject of scholarly research, but was not properly implemented. PRECIS, the Preserved Context Index System was developed by Derek Austin under the influence of Noam Chomsky's work on transformational grammar. It was implemented by several organisations in Canada and England, but has been largely abandoned or simplified by these organisations.

Some had proposed PRECIS as an alternative to Library of Congress Subject Headings (LCSH), but this was never a real possibility. Many libraries used LCSH, and a good many machine-readable cataloguing records contained those headings. In fact, the synthesis of subdivisions with headings in LCSH has been found to be too complicated, and the Library of Congress has embarked on a programme of Subdivision Simplification : more combinations of terms will be established editorially at LC, and less original synthesis will have to be done by cataloguers.

SETTING ASIDE COMPLEX SYSTEMS

The bibliographic classification systems have a better theoretical basis than the widely adopted Library of Congress Classification Scheme. The draft proposal for LCC subclass ZA, information Resources, provides evidence for this : under "Information Superhighway," class numbers are enumerated for the forms Periodicals, Congresses, Dictionaries, Directories, etc. These same forms are enumerated with different notations under other topics within the draft schedule. The synthesis of form divisions was a feature if the Dewey Decimal Classification early on; just about all subsequent bibliographic classification schemes have increased the amount of synthesis relative to enumeration. Synthetic features result in a more compact classification schedule, give a mnemonic character to a scheme, and most importantly, allow the classifier to represent specifically the holdings of a local collection.

Alphabetical indexing systems with syntactic enhancements allow for more sophisticated retrieval than (a) the largely precoordinate Library of Congress Subject Headings or (b) simple post coordination of descriptors derived from thesauri. The role indicators are designed to eliminate the false drops which result from simple combination of terms.

IGNORING COMPLEX SYSTEMS

Sophisticated classification and indexing systems require a substantial training period as well as time-consuming human analysis. Management is reluctant to pay for this.

Rigid hierarchical classification schemes cannot keep up with scientific advances. Sections of the widely-used schemes - notably Dewey - are restructured periodically, but there are always protests from the library community when the revisions necessitate reclassification of large parts of a collection. People classify things in different ways. The systems replete with options - such as Bliss - have not been widely adopted, perhaps for the economic reason : a professional librarian has to select an option and document it locally.

The claims of Farradane, Austin, and other information scientists to have identified all possible relationships are inconsistent with the linguistic literature, in which new syntactic structures are constantly being identified. An indexing system with only seven or nine relationships indicators is sure to bread down when new constructs are encountered.

We live in a society in which people want information quickly; they do not want to study the structure of an indexing system or the notation of a classification scheme. Complex information systems require human intermediaries, and the management is reluctant to hire them. There is also considerable evidence that people are reluctant to consult intermediaries; they want to be able to search by themselves.

INDEXING THE INTERNET

Many of the systems currently used for indexing the Internet employ simple automatic indexing algorithms. They extract words from titles or full text, sometimes adding weights to words in significant positions. Users of electronic databases are increasingly encountering the problem of excessive frequency of search terms. Researchers have shown the automatic ranking algorithms used to deal with this problem perform inconsistently.

Some librarians have advocated the application of the Dewey Decimal Classification to organise the massive number of electronic documents on the Internet. In our views, the DDC is not an appropriate scheme for organising electronic documents because its primary facet is discipline, not concrete topic. Since DDC was designed to organise whole books, if selected to index the Internet, it would have to be refined to accommodate documents. Such refinement has already been done - in the form of UDC - but the problems with the notation, currency, and management of that scheme should also be taken into consideration. We consult the Internet for the latest information; they cannot wait for an international committee to decide in which class a new topic should by placed.

CONCLUSIONS

The ultimate representation of the thought content of a document, which was espoused by Ranganathan, represents optimization in classification and indexing. Human beings may not require this. Pointing the user to a manageable chunk of text or number of documents that can be scanned in a reasonable amount of time for the desired fact or information would constitute satisfying in the field of content analysis. There is considerable evidence that users do not want intermediary to retrieve only the single most specific document on a topic. Users want to select from a group of document and make their own relevance judgments.

The type of index structure that reflects the philosophy of satisfying is the back -of -the - book index. It has a simple structure : direct access to natural - language terms is provided by the alphabetical arrangement, obviating both the extra book - up and the interpretation of symbols that classification requires. In book indexes, aspects of topics are represented via natural language subheadings. These are not standardized terms, but coined modifications, formulated by a human indexer to reflect the text being analyzed. Natural language prepositions and conjunctions are used to indicate relationships between topics. Unlike most classification notations, book index structure is infinitely hospitable that is, a new topic can always be interpolated.

What is being proposed here is book index structure, not the exhaustivity of a typical back - of - the book index. On the internet, the structure should be applied at the document or series level, not to the individual "information nugget". Subject headings summarises the content of documents, while book indexes provide access to the detailed information. An integrated exhaustive index to the entire Internet is clearly impracticable, but an index on the summary level is feasible Merged exhaustive indexes can be created for particular fields.

The specific topics of Internet documents need to be represented and ideally controlled by a thesaurus. The aspects of those topics must also be represented in natural language. An index to the Internet could be like the index to a continuously revised encyclopedia : book - index - like entries in an open system. Book index structure involves human content analysis, but not the development of artificial notation. The intelligence required is the recognition of concepts, along with the ability to represent information in terms likely to be sought by end - users. Book indexes are generally compiled by a single person, but an index to Internet resources will have to be a team effort. Indexes by multiple authors need a controlled vocabulary, and this requires centralised management. A thesaurus for the Internet should, of course, be maintained electronically, with on - screen approval of candidate terms.

Indexing is a value - added process. A good index saves the time of the user, and hence is worth paying for the ray of light in this chaotic environment is that schools of library and information science are increasingly advertising for faculty members who specialise in the organisation of information. It is recognised that the decentralised nature of the Internet requires original solutions to the problems of access : no single organisation is providing all the requisite cataloguing and indexing data for the wide variety of media available electronically. It is hoped that the systems for organising information which were developed in the last century will not be ignored, that their design flows will not be replicated and that our increasing knowledge of human factors will be incorporated into systems for indexing.

12

INTERNET AND ONLINE SEARCH

The Internet is the largest, widest and most complex computer network or networking of worldwide networks, a conglomeration of networks in the world providing access to immensely extensive wealth of databases and services. It is wonderful for bibliographic and information services but, at the same time access to specific information can be very difficult and frustrating. The user may know they have access to information and services they need, but may not know how to find them. The popular belief is that it is vast, wonderful and panacea for all information trouble. We are living in the 'information era' as popularly known, having information super highways in the internet and marked by Alvin Tofler as the third wave after the 'Agricultural wave and the 'Industrial wave' in the whole history of making. During information era 'knowledge' with reign supreme and it will result in paradigm changes in every sphere of knowledge and industry.

At the early phase Internet as known now a days, was not conceived as information superhighway or networking of computer networks to swim in the cyberspace. In the beginning a research group was created for the scientific and technological innovations to support the Allied battle strategies during world war IT to the geopolitical pressures of the Cold War and for preparation against an apprehension of nuclear holocaust, which never happened. The stage was set for the supportive research environment and key technical development of operation Research. The US department of Defence took the initiative to provide a stable and fast method of electronic communication for military and government agencies. The three US military services contracted out operation research work to universities and non profit organisations.

Advanced Research Projects Agency (ARPA) of US government became the patron of computer research. The agency funded research into numerous aspects of hardware and software development, including graphics, simulations, head-mounted displays. Parallel processing and networking, Research in artificial intelligence began in 1960s. The computer scientist Alan Perlis said, "that the purpose of the military is to support ARPA, and the purpose of ARPA is to support research". By the end of 1969 the ARPA net was in operation as the first long-distance packet-switching network. Vinton Cerf, a computer scientist and Robert Kahn, an MIT mathematics professor developed a set of software "protocols" to enable different types of computers to exchange packets, despite varying packet sizes and computer speeds. The result was TCP/IP (Transmission Control Protocol/ Internet Protocol). It was released in 1973. The former converts messages into packet streams and reassemble them and the latter transports the packets across different nodes, even different types of networks. With the beginning in the hands of two persons thousands of people contributed to the operation of this network. Thus, ARPAnet was to help scientists and researchers share precious computing resources.

The main source of traffic on the network became the e-mail. The researchers used the network for personal communications and information sharing. TCP/IP mode possible the text-based network communication system including electronic mail, discussion lists, file indexing, and hyper-text. But e-mail became the most widely used service, most convenient and most functional in the network. By the late 1970's, computer networks other than ARPAnet had began using its network protocol, TCP/IP. Use of the standard and reliable communication by treating each computer on the network as an equal, without depending on a particular computer or portion of the network for its operation made the network operational with independent computer installation.

By the early-1980s TCP/IP was linking ARPAnet to other networks, including the NSFnet of the National Science Foundation, another federal agency, and Usenet. The result was first called ARPA-hypernet and then simply Internet. By 1983, the military portion of ARPAnet, which was mainly created for US defence purposes, had broken off and became MILNET. Loosing MILNET, ARPANET was associated with other networks with TCP/IP protocol and individual researchers. ARPAnet was shut down in 1990, and NSFnet went offline. This conglomeration of networks became known as the Internet, now in private hands. This history of Internet is the story of electronic and technological researches of government, universities, industry, corporations and tens of thousands of individuals working in full and sincere cooperation together. Ithiel de Sola Pool of MIT called it "The largest machine that man has ever constructed."

The origin, history and development of Internet make it clear that the network was conceived and sponsored by US military and government agencies to provide a stable and fast system of communication network to be able to survive a nuclear war which would never be easily accessible to people at large. The networks was never designed to be used in the public domain. The array of difficult interfaces of Internet stems from its roots as a military strategic communication. The "protocols", interfaces and search tools created by the scientists and technologists associated with the communication network, dissociation of MILNET from ARPANET, going away from the online network by NSFnet caused Internet a free public network without any control of any kind of authority whatsoever. Any individual and any group of persons took the control of Internet as a public domain.

During the early phase more than one computer formed a local area networks (LANs) and with LANs the computer joined in much larger wide area networks (WANs), and in this process Internet became actually a worldwide network of other WANs, LANs, and a large number of individual systems. Internet began as a research tools and over years the features and facilities most widely used on Internet have been research-specific, allowing for the searching of computer files by users of remote computers, or allowing for the transfer of files between computers in the network. Primarily the use was not meant for the end-users. These traditional capabilities creating opportunities for exploring research facilities became meaningful and critical to librarians to serve the end-users with immediate transfer or copying of information, that would take days or weeks to obtain in hard copy.

Traditional capabilities include hardware interconnectivity, network compatibility, database of files and file transfer, network carrier and other communication capabilities. Hardware and network compatibility became possible through the networking protocol TCP/IP (Transmission Control Protocol/Internet Protocol). Telnet Protocol gave the ability to access any system connected to the network., It is a simple protocol for passing terminal specific codes as data between user node and server (remote) nodes on the network. Telnet protocol had the standardisation to communicate between various systems and it was used to support both terminal-to- terminal and application-to-application traffic between systems. A subset of the telnet protocol formed the basis for the file transfer protocol and mail transfer protocol.

Because of the decentralised nature of the Internet and its services, practically no one, either individual or organisation, is responsible for making the network search easy for the clientele.

The Internet is essentially an anarchy which depends on cooperation among its users. The Internet has become colossal in size and therefore, locating and searching of information have become very difficult. But a number of technologists and several institutions have created and developed a number of search tools to get access to Internet resources. The basic search tools are mentioned here.

FILE TRANSFER PROTOCOL (FTP)

The first and most basic type of Internet file access is through file transfer protocol (FTP). All the systems connected to Internet support it. Through this protocol the files containing information can be found on a remote system. If a user of a particular computer wants a copy of a data file available on a remote site he would use ftp to get it on his own computer screen, FTP facilitates transfers of files of all types, from software application to text. It is capable of operating in two different modes. The standard mode (ASCII) allows for the transfer of text files, such as textual documents, pages of printed or nonprinted reading materials, reports, letters, etc. The binary mode allows for the transfer of all other types, such as graphics, images, audiovisual materials, etc.

Most attractive feature of ftp is that the user interface implementation was made fairly uniform across all types of systems. It provides users with an important way to accomplish transfer of information and files throughout the Internet. But the search process within the vast resources of Internet is to some extent complex, and it requires technically experienced library staff. The basic requirement is Internet access through international telecom carrier of the country. During past years services like anonymous FTP became widespread, which allows any one to gain access to and transfer files without obtaining prior permission form the database owner. Some sites offer services such as online access to library catalogue. The user has to know in advance the location of the service and how to gain access to it. FTP is needed to get information at certain sites with gopher and Web servers, particularly databases required in research libraries. FTP facilitates access to specific file or programme.

E-MAIL

The software for E-mail was invented in 1972 and first e-mail messages were sent across ARPAnet in the year. At first scientists used e-mail to collaborate on search projects, particularly defence information. Therefore, there were some rules to obey. ARPA limited the use of the network to official business. Later, mailing-list software permitted large groups of people to discuss common interests, making e-mail a mass medium as well as a point-to-point one.

The best known and the most used of all Internet applications, e-mail is a highly popular method of communication between users at remote sites. Internet mail was made possible through the utilisation of simple mail transfer protocol (SMTP), which made standardisation in the transmission of messages between computer of dissimilar type. Thus, e-mail became the main source of traffic on Internet. Although, basically invented for sharing computing resources and research communication, mostly e-mail was used for personal communications and information sharing.

End-user mail application programmes provide the interface to enable a user to prepare and send mail, to identify recipients, and to view or save incoming messages. During several years after its introduction, the crude and minimal facilities of e-mail were developed by sophisticated software. The communication facilities became highly capable for handling embedded multimedia objects through the use of the multi-purpose Internet mail extensions (MIME) standard. By using the MIME-compliant mail agents, graphic and sound objects could be included in transmissions of electronic mail.

International communication network as information carrier, ftp, and e-mail provided meaningful and extensive access to the vast information resources available on Internet. The capabilities of information transfer, remote access facilities, obtaining copies of relevant information located at near or more distant sites, made possible to offer widespread access to information resources for serious researchers. But access to specific information or concerned databases and their use relied heavily on a level of relative competence in searching systems and search tools as well as on a knowledge of locations where on the Internet critical information is stored.

ARCHIE

By the late 1980s, such a vast and wide spectrum of information was available on the Internet that it was difficult and, sometimes impossible, to find what the users wanted and to get access even in case of experienced Internet users. Therefore, Internet search tools were created to facilitate organise and manage information according to users' specific requirements. Archie was one of the first tools developed by the scientists at McGill University. Archie made it possible to catalogue files available via anonymous FTP services. This search tool made it easier to find information on the Internet by searching through many different file groups for text strings that user specified.

Archie made it easier to find a file by using the basic FTP services. it provided lists of publicly available services and allowed users to search through the lists for sites that could best serve their needs. At the same, the service helped the users connect to the sites. The users need a working understanding of UNIX, the most common operating system on the Internet. They should also understand how to use the basic FTP-related services. Archie is the file search utility in Internet search. Archie facilitates access to updated lists of files available for FTP transfer. Archie servers are often found on Gopher servers as Gopher items and can be used to search FTP and Archie databases by keyword to find files containing specific information.

GOPHER AND SEARCH TOOLS

Gopher was the major Internet interface at the early phase for providing higher level of services. It was developed at the University of Minnesota in 1991 after the name of its mascot. Gopher provides a text menu interface to a variety of Internet services. Gopher enabled users to navigate the Internet using only the cursor and "Return" key on their keyboards. Users could access information without having to worry about Unix commands, where the information was located, or the underlying protocols that were used to transfer the information. Veronica and Jughead were developed as Internet search tools for further aid to users in finding information in Gopherspace.

Gopher servers guide the users to other Gophers to get access to specific information through searching. Gopher works best when the user has vast some idea where the information is stored. Archie, Veronica and Jughead were developed to make lists of the resources of the Internet. Archie keeps an updated list of file available for ftp transfer, and Archie servers are often found on gopher servers as gopher item and can be used to search ftp or Archie databases by key word to find files containing specific information.

The users can log on to Gopher servers and browse files stored there by subject. Veronica is used to search Gopher servers around the world. Gopher is best to use for searching information on a broad theme. FTP is better for a specific file or programme and at the sometime Gopher facilitates use of ftp as well. While the database of Archie contains a list of ftp-available files, Veronica maintains a list of Gopher items. A search of Veronica's database provides not just files, but directories, as well, also lists of remote log in opportunities. Veronica has the capability to create a menu of Gopher-accessible desired items, so that, through a Veronica search, a user can create a personalised items of contents. Jughead maintains database of an organisation's own resources as opposed to Veronica's archiving of the whole Internet Gopherspace.

Gopher replaced and enhanced new search tool for the general Internet users and made resource-finding accessible which was restricted to limited number of users having computer expertise. With the advent of Gopher, the case of finding information caught up to the case of manipulating information. The application of Gopher gained wide acceptance among the Internets general users. It became recognised as a technological breakthrough in basic Internet protocol. The design of Gopher was based on the ftp model with the addition of a improved user interface. It provided directories as descriptive menus and allowed users to display or retrieve the hidden information menu items, without ever needing to know the Internet address of the required resource or the method used to retrieve it.

The search method was not that a Gopher client 'asked' the remote Gopher server for a menu of information files it could offer the user. The server 'answered' the request by sending the client a menu of files, as well as a hidden packet of information for each menu item presented. The hidden information contained all the required technical information to enable the client to send a properly formatted request for information represented by the menu items. The hidden item information would include the address of the server with the information, directory path on which the information could be found, the name of the file containing the information, the type of information contained in the file, and the identification of the port with which to contact the remote server.

Gopher facilitated to popularise the client/server computer search model both by academics and computer specialists as an efficient model for the deployment of expensive computing resources. The reason for the development and efficiency was that the client or the computer on the receiving end where a user requests information, performs some of the information processing functions rather than being merely a 'dumb' terminal, as in traditional host-based computing. This reduces the workload on the server, or the computer that 'serves' the requested information from remote location.

In this client/server model it is important to note that once the server handed the client the 'requested' menu, there is no reason to maintain contact or connection between the server and the client. The connection is dropped because the hidden information transferred to the client for each menu item contains all the data necessary for the client to independently make a new connection and issue another unique request to any Gopher system in the network. Meanwhile the server becomes free to answer connections from other Gopher clients. Gopher also implemented the concept of book marks, which enable the user to save the location and hidden information of frequently visited or particularly interesting sites for simple and immediate return without having to renegotiate a search for the desired Gopher menu.

WORLD WIDE WEB (WWW)

While using the Internet search tools, if Gopher is used it is like wandering through library stack. If Archie, Veronica and Jughead are used, it is like searching through a card catalogue. They catalogue the resources of the Internet. All these search tools are menu-oriented tools for access to information but these were limited to serving strictly textual information. Then the need was felt and recognised for access to broader types of information, such as images and sound having visual description. The scientists and researchers continued the search for a "Killer Application" for the Internet, which would enable serving and viewing of data in all formats.

The most important and influential network interface protocol was developed at CERN, the European high-energy physics laboratory in Geneva, Switzerland. The protocol and server software was named World Wide Web (WWW) and started using in 1991. It was a step beyond Gopher by being a hypertext tool. On the WWW, any part of a document can be linked to any part of any other document conforming to the hypertext protocol including graphics, sound and video. As a result user can have access more easily to Internet resources for all types of information. One of the basic interfaces to the WWW is Lynx, a text-based browser that lets users navigate the Web by typing in digits that correspond to hypertext links.

Mosaic developed by NCSA (National Centre for Supercomputing Applications), University of Illinois, is the most popular interface to the Web today. This system released in 1993 is a graphical browser that will seen under most types of windowing systems. It uses a point and click interface for accessing information. The users can simply click with a mouse on an interesting topic, and automatically be provided with information about that topic. This hypertext-based model allows cross-reference between related resources. Web browsers (clients) also allow multimedia information to be readily displayed for the user, often with the aid of helper programmes. The Web can act as a read/write resources, because it can collect information from the user in addition to delivering information to the user.

When the librarian or patron selects information to be displayed (called a "page" on the Web), the Web client issues a standard Uniform Resource Locator (URL) request for the page of interest. Web browsers can typically issue URL requests asking for information in one of several formats hypertext format: telnet format, ftp format, file format and even gopher format, among others. Although orginally intended as a distributed network of computers, internet is viewed as a distributed space of information. Rather than transferring files between computers, a user navigates an information space of distributed items of information. The users concentrate on the logical structure of the inter connection of information and data items rather than on the underlying physical structure of computer and communication systems.

Formation of the Internet relied critically on standard network protocols and simple universal services. Similarly, new protocols and services have evolved to support this new logical structure of interconnected information spread across the worldwide network, a global hypermedia system. The world wide web is a set of protocols that allow for the location of any document on Internet through a naming system based on Universal Resource Locators (URLs) and describe a way of placing links using URLs within text documents, called Hypertext Markup language (HTML) as well as specify a way to request and send a document over the network, the Hypertext transfer Protocol (HTTP). With these standard protocols in place, one can set up a server and construct hypertext documents with links in them that point to the documents on the server. Selecting the link from within the display of a document sends a request to the server, which in response sends the document back. The retrieved document might have links in it and to documents on another server, and thus, a user might browse through an extensive corpus of material distributed around the global network simply by following the hyperlinks from one point of interest to another.

In World Wide Web a retrieved document may be an index of information and thus be searchable by specification of a query string. The results of a query against an index can be automatically composed into an HTML document with short summaries on the returned items containing embedded links that can be followed to retrieve the complete documents. Directed navigation from one document to another, an information space is created and such situation support search strategy. World Wide Web, thus, combines two underlying functions of browsing information spaces, 1. The presentation of information, and 2. the method of choosing which information to browse the next. The combination of this easy method of browsing and a growing base of information to browse on Internet set the stage for an explosive growth in WWW usage. The conceptual frame work of the WWW project has sought to encompass all existing methods of network protocols for information navigation and retrieval.

With all these protocols combined and the gateways were

provided in early WWW communication software. Therefore, WWW browsers were able to communicate with all of these information sources and present them as a unified information space to the users. The WWW became a superset of all of the available networked information services : File Transfer Protocols (FTP), Archie, Gopher and WWW itself. Thus, the WWW users were provided with a single entry point to resources of Internet as well as critical resources of the Internet. More databases were provided with more information resources anticipating more and varied types of users searching information more easily. Such situation in a continuing process led to the exponential growth of World Wide Web.

At the early phase WWW systems were line-mode browsers, which presented the hyperlinks as numbered choices in a menu that users could choose from. Mosaic system of NCSA introduced the placement of images on the hypertext page, thus creating multimedia hypertext or "hypermedia" documents which could contain pictures and graphical icons. Both the picture and icons could also be linked by clicking them to another hyper documents, further information or expanded image. The graphical user interfaces were developed on Next and X windows system machines, which displayed the hypertext in a window with the links in colour or underlined, allowing the user to move through hyperspace by clicking on links with a mouse. The users of Internet was greatly expanded by the introduction of such graphically based hypertext browsers across the three most popular computer operating system platforms : Apple Macintosh, Microsoft windows, and the X windows system.

WWW functionality was increased by further development of NCSA Mosaic system. The ability to display "forms" like those on a database request. While the user filled in the 'forms' as a complex request, he was guided to specified information from a hypertext document and, thus, could get access to complicated searches of indexed information and databases. The method is filling in the "forms" by typing in the open fields, clicking on the button choices, or choosing a menu item to build up a complex query, which are then sent to the requesting search engine and resolved, and the data are sent back to the user. The combination of forms in HTML documents, HTTP for transport, and "gateways" to other information servers made far customised network information search systems, available through the standard Mosaic interface. The client-server architecture of the system facilitates developer construct fixtures that run on the server side, integrating information sources like relational databases with structured query language queries into the hypermedia information environment. This open information systems allow for the easy integration of existing information sources and that can be extended and expanded by users in ways which was not anticipated by the original developers.

Wide Area Information System (WAIS) was developed by a company called Thinking Machines. With WAIS servers one can search document databases. It is a keyboard searching method. When the entry word or topic is typed, a WAIS server scans Internet libraries. It returns a master index providing links to all the sites related to the request. The index is weighted, indentifying which links are most closely related to the topic.

There are WAIS programmes that work independently of the WWW. The programmes can be searched through special gateway software available on many Web pages for access to Powerful WAIS Search within Mosaic. If there is a WAIS search tool in a document, this will refer to label like "WAIS SEARCH". When a topic is selected it can be available through keying. But WAIS has not been popular after the introduction of hypermedia.

TELNET is a utility which allows to log-on another system and use various services available on the host. One can TELNET into huge databases to do research or even TELNET into libraries around the world to check if they have a certain book required by the user. TELNET also offers an easy entry into the Gopherspace and the world wide Web for those users who may otherwise have access to these tools. TELNET allows to log-on to remote computers and run programmes from them.

ONLINE SEARCH

Internet search is online search having access to Internet *but not the only* way of online search. Online search can be performed within the campus or locality through local area network (LAN), metropolitan network within a city, wide area network (WAN) within a region, and national networks within a country. Catalogue of a particular library can be searched online through online public access catalogue (OPAC). Any online networked search can be integrated with other library and information network. Modern technologies have transformed library catalogues from simple resource directories to comprehensive information systems having facility for access to the information resources of the libraries of the world as well as global databases delivered directly to the end-users at their computers.

Developing and organising collections have become less important than facilitating access to information and information resources, regardless of where they are located. Information handling and organisation with the delivery technologies have spawned a robust and lively information market and the emergence of commercial suppliers of information services that support the library and information services. These service facilities are currently most evident in academic, research and special libraries. Libraries have become the information providers.

Electronic information technologies are diminishing the central role of traditional libraries. Online union catalogues and their associated communication networks allow ready access to the collective holdings of numerous libraries. They ensure the interlibrary loan requests are transmitted expeditiously only to libraries known to hold the items sought.

Access to other library collections is not just convenience, it is a matter of urgent necessity. The amount of information produced each year and the documents published as well as the costs to acquire and organise them, no individual library can satisfy with their own resources to a fraction of their users' needs. For this situation, remotely accessible online union catalogues and electronic interlibrary loan systems have become indispensable tools for librarians. The ever-increasing information databases and full-text databases are the richest resources in the information world. Such information and electronic documents can be readily analysed, rearranged and incorporated into other documents. Electronic technologies have put into the hands of librarians and information specialists tools that permit them to participate as important members of research and education teams.

The largest online search service provider was DIALOG Information Services, Inc. 3460 Hillview Avenue, Palo Alto, California, USA, with the trade mark DIALOG, a subsidiary of Knight Rider Company. Early 1995 DIALOG changed its name and merged its identity with the parent company's name. It has become Knight-Ridder Information Inc. (KRI). A branch of this company is now in India. DIALOG retrieval service has been serving users since 1972. With over 500 databases from broad scope of disciplines, it has become the largest information provider to all categories of users. The information collection contain millions of documents drawn from more sources than any other online service. The broad spectrum of subject areas includes scientific, technical, agricultural, medical sciences, humanities, social sciences, technology, patent, trademark, industry, finance and business, demographic data, statistics, newspapers, etc. Both information databases and full-text databases are available.

DIALOG offers two search options to access information : menus and commands. DIALOG menus search is ideal for those new to online searching - or for searching databases that are used infrequently. DIALOG commands provide the fastest and most precise way to search for information. The powerful and flexible search system allows instant retrieval of information the users need.

For online searching of DIALOG databases the following search tools can be used according to the requirement of the users. Subject Guide - The introductory section provides a broad subject grouping of DIALOG databases. More specific subject categories can be viewed in the DIALINDEX 1 one search section. In finding the right databases for the required information, special database collections or categories have been predefined by subject coverage. One has to just select the subject category of his choice and can begin searching.

Databases by File Number - This handy list presents a listing of DIALOG databases organised by file number or acronym.

Database Descriptions - These are organised alphabetically by database name with brief description of the wealth of information to be found in any one source. The user must consult the key on page 17 before reading the database descriptions.

DIALMAIL - It is the electronic mail service from DIALOG that allows to communicate with Dialog staff, information providers, and other DIALOG users. DIAL MAIL also provides immediate delivery of prints via electronic mail box.

There are many more services on specific areas and on specific requests for tailor - made, complete packages as well as unlimited searching. For online connectivity to DIALOG, the user needs a computer or terminal, a modem, communication software, a phone line and own DIALOG password. From user's place to remote DIALOG connectivity is made through international telecommunication network like VSNL. To obtain a password to any of DIALOG's services the user must fill in and send the appropriate DIALOG customer agrument form indicating the specific service or services. After paying the

DIALOG subscription the user is entitled to get a telecommunication access number and the password. The user has to pay a modest annual service fee and then he has to pay only for the time he is searching and only for the specific information the user will search.

13

CD-ROM Databases

The enormous storage capability of CD-ROM technology in small containers of disks has made the storage medium very attractive. This technology has made it possible to store enormous data in an unbelievable little space for any purpose, alphabets, digits, image, colour, audio, graphics, multimedia, and the like. During the early phase of CD-ROM technology, as early as mid-1980's, bibliographic databases were stored. Now a major CD-ROM market is held by bibliographic and nonbibliographic databases for library and information areas. During last two decades a large number of CD-ROM manufacturers have produced enormous organised databases for access to information and full-texts in all branches of human knowledge and these are ongoing projects by large database producers.

The data stored on such disks can be retrieved, displayed, manipulated and printed in many ways but the users cannot alter the data on the disks. New updates are periodically added to the already existing core of data, with each new disk replacing each previous disk. In addition to its huge storage capability, there are several other features of CD-ROM that make it especially useful for libraries and information centres. The data on CD-ROM are permanently and physically encoded and cannot therefore, be lost by power cuts or surges. The physical elements of the disk containers and the 'print' on them is almost permanent and cannot be damaged ordinarily in adverse atmospheric and handing conditions. These disks cannot be affected by magnetic or microwave scanning. Another advantage of CD-ROM is that users can spend as much time as they like in searching the databases without the fear of escalation of cost for the time consumed as in case of online search.

CD-ROMs are read by laser, and there is no contact or wear when the disks are in use. Frequent use of the same CD-ROM, does not affect the usability of or readability of the disk. The only irritant is dust which may stand between the disk and the laser beam, and, thus, the search and display may be affected by lack of visibility. Although CD-ROMs are durable some precautions should taken for better service. Every CD-ROM disk should be kept within a caddy to keep the dust away. Piling of CD-ROMs one over the other while storing must be avoided to preserve the disks in good working condition.

There are different ways to search in a CD-ROM database. In most cases the databases are searched in a dialogue mode by using a retrieval language created by the producer of databases. With this method every CD-ROM database would have its own retrieval language for searching. For those users searching in different databases it may be a bit difficult, since they would have to switch from one command language to the other. Another search system is hypertext system to search information on a CD-ROM. Hypertext systems are particularly appropriate for heavily cross-referenced material. Reference buttons may be inserted automatically to highlight cross-references to other material within the same document, particularly in case of a full-text database or to highlight references to other documents. If such material is available on the CD-ROM system, then the user may, by selecting a highlighted reference, automatically enlarge the material that is currently on the screen, with the referenced documents. Another easier way is to search in the database with a menu-driven user interface. Most of the CD-ROM databases are searchable in this method. Now the search has become easy and user-friendly.

Every CD-ROM database producer and publisher has developed flexible and powerful software products for searching databases on CD-ROM. Database-specific Guides are also available which give details such as field names for each database and a Tutorial. The Tutorial is a detailed explanation of how to use the information retrieval system for CD-ROM searching for first-time users.

There is a large number of big corporate bodies having well-organised updated databases covering specialised branches of human knowledge both for online search and CD-ROM products. Libraries and information centres can get the services of both types of products if interconnected to global network. Otherwise, CD-ROM Products are very useful and sometimes as good as online search as these are updated very frequently and in many cases databases for online search and CD-ROM search are almost identical. There are some information producers dealing with CD-ROM products and services only. Both bibliographic and nonbibliographic databases are available in CD-ROM. Several CD-ROM producers and their products are given below, which are information resources and services in libraries and information centres.

KR INFORMATION ONDISC

KR Information OnDisc, formerly known as DIALOG OnDIsc is responsible for CD-ROM products and services of the corporate house of Knight-Ridder Information, Inc. USA. It is a collection of databases on CD-ROM including key resources in the areas of science and technology, humanities, social sciences, education, health and biomedicine, law and government, finance and business, as well as full-text newspapers. KR Information OnDisc databases feature search software that can be used by both novice and professional information searchers.

The KR Information OnDisc collection of CD-ROM

products is based on popular and useful DIALOG databases. Each disc holds the equivalent of over 275000 pages of information. These products are easy to use and have two ways to search : An easy menu mode for novice searchers and the regular command language access for experienced searchers. Whenever needed the searcher can go online to KR Information Online for the most current and comprehensive information on the subject required. But CD-ROM searching is unlimited at an affordable price. KR Information OnDisc offers unlimited researching at fixed, yearly rates. A variety of KR Information OnDisc yearly lease options can be selected for particular needs.

A wide and complete range of databases with continuing updating on various specialised subject areas is available with OnDisc CD-ROM products. These are based on specialised databases of DIALOG. The information is always available at a fixed cost, so more people can share it and more people can gain access to the power of information. These CD-ROM products come on one or more discs with retrieval software, documentation, and user support. While updated and current information is available, update discs are sent to the customer. As the family of discs grow, the databases will be available in a consistent format. CD-ROM information can be searched much more often at no extra cost.

KR Information OnDisc encompasses all the contents offered by DIALOG, DataStar, and KR Information OnDisc to provide with integrated information solutions with in-depth collection of content, comprehensive and updated. A new product range, KR ProBase was designed to be used by information professionals. It offers information professionals all the sophisticated functionality of the DataStar system as well as all the databases with an easy to use, full-colour Windows-based application. KR Source One provides engineering documents as worldwide document delivery provider. To make CD-ROM searching easier and faster, two largest and most popular databases, Ei Compendex Plus and MEDLINE are now available in 'site enhanced' versions that allow to search across multiple discs as if they were one.

In the areas of environmental sciences and pollution control, KR Information OnDisc products have comprehensive updated databases. Ei Energy and Environment Disc and Ei ChemDisc are two engineering subsets of Ei Compendex Plus. The wealth of critical information and international databases is accessible through these CD-ROM sets. These products record the experiments and activities of different countries. More than 70000 articles are added annually to these CD-ROMs concerning new developments in the field of environmental pollution.

By an agreement with Derwent Information Limited, KR Information OnDisc is producing comprehensive databases on Power Engineering and Petroleum. These also cover Patent Technology monitoring in the petroleum and power engineering-related industries. With Windows-based versions the CD-ROM database is available with images from the Derwent World Patents Index database covering patents from 1989 to the present. There are databases on Petroleum Abstracts, DOE Energy Science and Technology, Ei Energy and Environment, and Nuclear Science Abstracts products Derwent's information products provide a comprehensive picture of technological innovations worldwide - essential information for today's business and research professionals.

Ei ChemDisc databases are worldwide coverage of chemical engineering journals and published conference proceedings. Over one million records include bibliographic data and abstracts, covering chemical operations, processes, products and agents; with emphasis on technical challenges of process control, measurement, and analysis in every environment, beginning from 1984.

Ei Compendex Plus records abstracts from every engineering discipline, including bio-engineering, chemical, civil, electronics, computer, communication, mechanical, automotive, materials, nuclear, and aerospace engineering, and many others. It is worldwide coverage of more than 4500 journals, conference proceedings, and selected government reports beginning from 1989 onwards.

Ei EEDisc covers abstracts from worldwide computer, electronic, and electrical engineering literature. More than one million records cover computer science, information science control magnetics, communications, electronics, lasers, acoustics and instrumentation, beginning from 1983 onwards.

Ei Energy and Environment Disc databases include worldwide literature on energy and the environment, consisting of air and water pollution, waste treatment, geology and geophysics, fossil fuels, power plants, nuclear technology, thermodynamics, refrigeration and cryogenics, and hydroelectric power from 1984 to present.

Environmental chemistry, Health and Safty databases provide comprehensive scientific and technical information on the environment including information on chemicals deemed to cause actual and potential problems to humans or the environment beginning from 1980 to present.

ERIC databases cover a broad spectrum of educational subjects, including adult and vocational education, counselling, educational management, reading and communication skills, curricula for handicapped and gifted children, testing and evaluation methods. These include bibliographic references and abstracts from more than 800 educational journals and thousands of research reports beginning from 1966.

The National Library of Medicine's MEDLINE database is the premier source of biomedical literature including research, clinical practice, administration, policy issues and health care services. The database combines the Index Medicus, Index to Dental Literature, and International Nursing Index to cover vertually every area of biomedicine. It includes thoroughly indexed information on toxicology, nutrition, pharmacology, medicine, veterinary medicine, psychiatry, medical engineering, pathology, experimental medicine, microbiology, psychology, parasitology, and many other allied and related subject areas. MEDLINE provides indexes and abstracts for articles from over 3600 US and international journals in 70 countries. The database uses the NLM MeSH indexing system and tree structures, allowing the users to display major subject headings and related subheadings at a glance as well as the MeSH thesaurus is available for locating all related terms. Coverage begins from 1966.

METADEX Materials Collection : Metals, Polymers, ceramics combines three well known databases - METADEX, Materials Business File and Engineered Materials Abstracts. These databases provide comprehensive coverage of worldwide materials information literature on science and practice of metallurgy, polymers, ceramics, plastics and composite materials; related materials science and engineering as they relate to these substances; the Technical and commercial developments in materials science, steel and nonferrous metals. The coverage includes information on processes and process development, products and manufacturing, fuel, energy usage, and raw materials; engineering, applications; management and economics; environmental issues and world industry information. Informative abstracts are included for most records. Databases begin from 1985.

OnDisc NTIS provides information about US government-sponsored research and development projects, engineering reports and analyses from 300 government agencies, contractors, and grantees, including NASA, DOD, DOE, and Department of Commerce. Abstracts and text cover a wide range of subjects including aeronautics, civil engineering, natural resources, physics, agriculture and food, behaviour and society, building business and economics, chemistry, energy, health planning, administration and management, and many more. Reference numbers are supplied for each abstract to facilitate retrieval of the full report from the appropriate agencies.

OnDisc Polymer Encyclopedia contain the complete text of the 19-volume Encyclopedia of Polymer Science and Technology. This standard reference work provides comprehensive coverage of polymer science and engineering, including materials, methods and the latest advances in macromolecular science. Specific areas of coverage include natural and synthetic polymeric materials; molecular, physical mechanical and biological properties; morphology and compatibility of polymers; physical processes; synthesis and reactions; robotics, engineering and processing; test methods; composites; CAD/CAM. Special emphasis is given on process and production oriented data.

KR Information OnDisc provides a long range of databases, comprehensive and updated on a broad spectrum of subject areas, specific, interdisciplinary and multidisciplinary, in CD-ROM format. Some of these are Paper, printing and Packaging Database, Petroleum Abstracts, DOE Energy Science and Technology, Nuclear Science Abstracts. Ei Manufacturing, Ei MechDisc, TOXLINE, Chemical Engineering and Biotechnology Abstracts, British Education Index, Philosopher's Index.

The Institute for Scientific Information (ISI), Philadelphia

ISI began in 1957 by offering information services covering the scientific journal literature. Since then the services have expanded to include bibliographic tools covering the journal, book, and proceedings literature in the sciences, social sciences, and the arts and humanities. ISI is among the world's largest commercial producers of information services covering the professional literature. As a leader in the information industry, ISI meets the growing needs of the users worldwide for efficient use of the scientific, technical, and scholarly literature. ISI database now encompasses over 10000 journals and multi-authored books in the sciences, social sciences, and arts and humanities each year. The Science Citation Index, Compact Disc edition is a less expensive storage medium in the libraries for multiple search of a large number or users. In retrospective searching ISI indexes are very useful because they present a variety of unique solutions to information retrieval through innovative indexing techniques, notably citation indexing and research front specialty indexing.

Literature search in science and other branches of knowledge has changed dramatically with the application of citation indexing in 1960. Citation indexing, which reveals pertinent relationships between published articles has been accepted by scientists, researchers, and librarians all over the world as relational information sources. The Science Citation Index is the most significant scientific literature recognised as an indispensable multidisciplinary reference tool. Science Citation Index Compact Disc edition has employed new Technologies to develop better products, efficient and effective tools to leading the way in the information age.

The SCI-CDE is a multidisciplinary index to the scientific journal literature, presented in a format that combines the flexibility of citation indexing with the power and capability of optical publishing technology. The compact disc format makes a number of "value-added" features possible, such as built-in "help" functions that enable searchers to master the product with little or no training, and the related records function, which automatically expands search strategies with just a few keystrokes.

An annual subscription to the SCI-CDE(Science Citation Index Compact Disc Edition) includes four quarterly cumulative issues, each consisting of two CD-ROM discs : The Title Access Disc and the Citation Access Disc. Current-year subscribers and back-year subscribers also receive a floppy diskette containing the SCI-CDE Search and Retrieval Software,. a User's Guide, and five Quick Reference Guides. One year's subscription for SCI-CDE makes available the most important scientific and technical literature published around the world containing hundreds of thousands of source items and several millions cited references.

The SCI CD Edition provides with a variety of options throughout the searching process. One can formulate a search strategy, selecting items to define the search browsing through "dictionaries" of

Cited authors	title words	author addresses
Cited works	author names	journal titles
Cited patents		

and at the same time one can move between dictionaries to choose qualifying search terms. One can also bypass the dictionaries by directly keying in specific search strategy.

The depth and breadth of searching can be adjusted by using Boolean logic and truncation within and across dictionaries. To save time, search statements created during the current session can be reused, as well as the search terms saved from other sessions can also be reused. Results of search may be printed individually or in sets. Customised set of records can be created by browsing search results, and during the process duplicate records will be eliminated automatically. Thus, the customised set will exist for reviewing, refining, or printing or saving in ASC II format. The CD Edition can be used with minimal training and with some experience one can perform complex searches of the scientific literature. One can have access to the CD database, freely adapting to personal search styles and expertise.

While the researcher has identified some useful papers, with the SCI-CD Edition, he can quickly and easily find other relevant material through the unique " related records" feature. This retrieves related articles by using the links created by authors when their bibliographies have references in common. After locating a record, the researcher will find that a number of related records is listed. Once each related record is retrieved, the total number of shared references is shown. These shared references are the key to establishing a relationship between the articles.

The researcher can expand this feature to extend the search, systematically following a trail of related records infinitely through the references they share. This capacity to identify related records and continue a search through unlimited levels, is certain to add new power and perspective to the search strategy. Even though the two articles may have no title words in common, the SCI CD Edition can still establish a subject relationship using the shared references. For example, there are references in Record A as well as references in Record B and apparently there are no relationships for the references. In the total record structure of Record A if there is a reference of a particular author available in Record B, the whole set will be automatically searched and correlated with the information of Record A. This interconnectivity of search terms of various Records is knows as "Shared References".

The Science Citation Index compact Disc Edition annual subscription includes.

* Two self-contained and independently searchable compact discs, each with its own unique entry points and features.

Disc A	Disc B
Title words	Cited author names
Citing author names	Cited works
Author addresses	Citing author names
Related records	Full bibliographies
Source journal codes	All bibliographic
Language of record	records for update
Update period indicator	period
All bibliographic records for	
the update period	

Other features are :

* Quarterly cumulative updates, with the same coverage as the Science Citation Index
* Search and retrieval software, with context-sensitive help
* User instruction manual

* Annual archival cumulation

Science Citation Index is used by librarians, information scientists, researchers, educators, R and D organisations, and students as the large scale reference for multidisciplinary searching of the scientific and technical literature. It is an invaluable aid for :

* following the works of a particular author.
* measuring the frequency and citation impact of faculty publishing,
* determining who is citing their own or their colleagues' works,
* tracking the research of a particular organisation or institution,
* locating more recent findings on earlier reported research,
* finding timely, relevant articles on virtually any scientific subject.

The Citation Index has the unique feature that enables to locate recent articles which cite, or reference, earlier published works. This index retrieves information through four access points - cited references, title word, author, and author affiliation. It indexes every article and significant item, including letters, notes, corrections and editorials, in every publication it covers. Each year, the SCI indexes over 600000 new source items and over 9000000 cited references. The in-depth coverage and complete information provided by SCI make it valuable for verifying the existence of scientific articles and the accuracy of their bibliographic descriptions.

The SCI is an integrated literature search system consisting of four separate but related indexes :

Citation Index

Source Index

Permuterm Subject Index

Corporate Index

Depending on the search problem and the information already available on the topic, any one of the four indexes can be most effective starting point. Once data are retrieved on some relevant articles, such as authors, reference citations, title words, etc. , that information can be used to enter the same index or one of the other indexes to continue the search.

The SCI is an integrated Literature search system consisting of four separate but related indexes. These are : Citation Index, Source Index, Permuterm Index and Corporate Index.

The most important and unique feature is Citation Index. It is based on the proven concept that recent papers that cite earlier documents share a subject relationship with those earlier works. Similarly, when two or more recent works cite an earlier document, they share a subject relationship with each other. The earlier document becomes, in effect, an indexing term leading to recent papers about the same subject area. With citation indexing, authors actually index their own works through their selection of subject-related references. This eliminates the problems created by fast-changing and ambiguous scientific terminology, and leads to articles that otherwise would not appear relevant to search subjects.

The Citation Index alphabetically lists the names of all first authors whose works were cited during the period covered and informs when and where those works were originally published. Only the Citation Index enables to perform search tasks not possible with conventional indexes, such as :

* retrieving information on new rather than previously published works,
* tracking citations of specific works or authors,
* conducting in-depth searches,
* identifying currently active areas of research,
* locating cited patents and cited anonymous items.

When the searcher knows the name of the author or title of paper, book, or other document relevant to his search subject, the Citation Index is the best tool to begin a search.

The Source Index is an alphabetically arranged author index to more than 600000 items annually indexed in the Science Citation Index. These items include articles, letters, editorials, reports, corrections, technical notes, obituaries, and other important items of information. For each, the Source Index provides complete bibliographic information, including full first-author address when provided by the journal. The information in the Source Index can be used for the following purposes :

* access further information about items located in other SCI indexes,
* contact authors for article reprints or for further information,
* track the works of specific authors published during the period covered,
* locate full bibliographic information on co-authors through a special feature which cross-references co-authors' names to their associated first authors,
* retrieve anonymously authored papers through the publications in which they appeared.

The Source Index is best used when the searcher knows the name of an author who publishes materials important to his field of interest. It enables to check quickly if that author has published anything during the period covered by the index. Source Index can be used to find more information on items found in other SCI indexes.

The Permuterm Subject Index is an alphabetically arranged to all of the significant words and word pairs used in the titles of the articles indexed in the Science Citation Index. These title words include the most current terminology used in all subject areas, instead of pre-determined subject headings which are often out-of-date. This subject index helps and guides :

* to retrieve information on articles in relevant subject area even if only one or two words are known to the searcher,
* to identify authors publishing in relevant subject area
* to locate articles on other subject areas related to a search topic.

When the searcher does not know the author or relevant papers on a subject, the Permuterm Subject Index is the best tool to begin the search. He can look up a word or phrase commonly used in the titles of articles related to his search subject, the PSI refers to the names of the authors who have used these words in their article titles. The names of the authors, then, can be searched in the Source Index to obtain full bibliographic descriptions of the articles.

The Corporate Index is a guide to get access to published authors and their works by their corporate or academic affiliation. This index also guides to track the research done by particular organisations or institutions, by listing all works published by affiliated authors during the period covered. The Corporate Index is divided into two sections, allowing to search subjects by organisation or by geographical area. With the information gained through the Corporate Index, the searcher can go to the Source Index to investigate the articles published by each author.

The Science Citation Index eliminates the needs to acquire and search separate discipline-oriented indexes. Its multidisciplinary coverage is capable to retrieve articles from all disciplines related to field of interest. In one convenient resource the SCI covers more than 100 disciplines in the following areas :

Agriculture and Biology

Behavioral Science

Earth Science

Environmental Science

Engineering

Mathematics and Computer Science

Medical and Life Sciences

Physical and Chemical Sciences

Technology and Applied Sciences

The CompuMath Citation Index provides access to key journals in computer science, mathematics, and related disciplines. It contains complete coverage of over 400 of the world's leading journals in core fields as well as selective coverage of relevant papers from an additional 6000 science, social sciences, and arts and humanities journals. One can search across disciplinary boundaries quickly and easily. It contains a special feature - Research Front Specialty Searching. This search Technique facilitates to pinpoint and retrieve papers in precisely defined areas of scientific research. Every search retrieves a bibliography of current papers citing the core literature of the specialty. Research Front Specialty Searching enables to locate pertinent source papers even when their titles do not explicitly indicate their relevance to the search. Major areas of coverage are :

Computer Application

Computer Sciences

Control Theory and Cybernetics

Information Science

Library Science

Mathematical Methods

Mathematics-Applied, General, Pure

Operations Research and Management Sciences

Statistics and Probability

Systems Sciences.

CompuMath Citation Index can be searched by :

Author Index

Title Word Index

Authors' Affiliation Index

Citation Index

Research Front Specialty Index

Annual coverage is more than 47000 source items and over 520000 cited references.

The ISI Atlas of Science is series of review journals that explores the present and future directions of research in science, medicine, and technology. The Atlas combines the power of computerised citation analysis with the expert interpretation of leading researchers to guide the searchers through the landscape of science, helping the searcher understand what is happening in science research today, as well as where it might lead tomorrow. The Atlas is available in various sections on different broad areas.

The Index to Scientific Book Contents and Index to Scientific and Technical Proceedings are unique, multidisciplinary tools indexing multi-authored scientific books and scientific proceedings titles, as well as the individual chapters or papers contained in them. With these references, the searcher can locate hard-to-find book and proceedings references quickly.

The contents of Index to Scientific Book Content can be searched by

(a) Contents of Books Index

(b) Author/Edition Index

(c) Title Word Index

(d) Corporate Index, and

(e) Category Index.

The contents of Index to Scientific and Technical Proceedings can be searched by (a) Author/Editor Index (b) Title Word Index (c) Sponsor Index (d) Meeting Location Index (e) Category Index (f) Corporate Index, and (g) Contents of Proceedings Index.

Social Sciences Citation Index is an essential research tool providing multidisciplinary coverage not available anywhere else.

It covers more than 50 areas of interest in the social sciences with all the articles relevant to search topic appearing in journals that do not seem to be directly related to an area of interest. It provides coverage of every substantive item from 1400 of the world's leading social sciences journals, plus material relevant to the social sciences from over 3100 science journals. The subject coverage include Anthropology and Archaeology, Area and Ethnic Group Studies, Business and Finance, Communications, Computer Applications and Cybernetics, Criminology and Penology, Demography, Educational Research, Economics, Geography, Hygiene and Public health, Information and Library Sciences, International Relations, Law, Management and Marketing, Policy Studies, Political Science, Psychology and Psychiatry, Sociology, Urban Planning and Development.

Arts and Humanities Citation Index gives complete coverage of 1300 of the world's leading arts and humanities journals, plus relevant material from 5000 social and natural sciences journals. A searcher can make valuable connections between original works of art and the articles that review or reference them between the area of interest and related disciplines. To make searches more effective, there are " implicit" citations made by a team of subject specialists whenever creative works are the subjects of articles but are not formally cited. This method is very effective to retrieve materials that would otherwise be inaccessible. Materials like paintings, musical compositions, literary works, films, and records, as well as dance, music, and theatrical performances.

The areas of subject coverage are Archaeology, Architecture, Art, Classics, Dance, Film, TV and Radio, Folklore, History, Language, Linguistics, Literature, Music, Philosophy, Theatre, Theology, Religious Studies, and the like.

OCLC SEARCH CD 450 SYSTEM

Online Computer Library Centre (OCLC) is the largest electronic online database with commitment to cataloguing, resource sharing, and technical services for more than two decades. It provides complete and comprehensive access to the 18-million record, ever growing, as union catalogue and other databases. The compact disc product of OCLC has catalogue and other databases. The compact disc product of OCLC has become the largest library database for librarians and end-users as well. The compact disc product has been named Search CD 450 system. It combines the unique resources of OCLC online union catalogue with the power, cost-effectiveness, and convenience of CD-ROM. Search CD 450 products are available all over the world.

As a non-profit organisation, OCLC remains committed to increasing the availability of information to libraries and information centres in the most cost-effective manner. OCLC has made collaboration with government agencies, scholarly associations, publishers, and other organisations to provide with additional and innovative reference and information products. OCLC online union catalogue, a massive collection of information that spans 4000 years of recorded knowledge, is adding 2 million more every year. This massive body of recorded information is available with power, storage capacity and convenience of CD-ROM is a remarkably efficient and affordable reference tool.

The Search CD 450 is a complete desktop reference library of bibliographic databases on compact disc. In a matter of minutes, a user can retrieve and review hundreds of records in a broad range of bibliographic formats. Search CD 450 is offered in series under broad subject heads. At the first stage three series are available - Education, Science and Technology, and Agriculture. Each database is equipped with :

* Sophisticated search software combined with current and retrospective files of essential, authoritative databases plus complementary subject databases from the Online Union Catalogue.

* A comprehensive Users' Guide that provides information on search strategies.

* A system Guide that shows how to install the system and customise it for the library's needs.
* ten copies of handy Pocket Reference that provides quick answers if a problem arises.

By using Search CD 450 system the library can :

* gain unlimited local access to essential databases previously available only online.
* gain unlimited local access to unique databases compiled from the OCLC Online Union Catalogue.
* Reduce search costs and eliminate time-based telecommunication charges.
* let patrons conduct their own searches with minimum assistance, practically without the help of library staff while oriented.

Search CD 450 system is easy enough for any beginner to use. Yet it is sophisticated enough to accommodate the complex search strategies demanded by experienced researchers. The reasons are noted below :

* The system's menus, prompts, and search techniques are clear and easy-to follow, with user options on screen as function key values.
* The search history saves upto 999 searches that can be displayed at any time. In addition to that, saved searches can be used with multiple databases.
* Such flexible search options as right truncation, range searching, and retrieval by controlled vocabulary may also be used.

The System Administration Module (SAM) allows to customise help screens and display formats to accommodate users' requirements. The learning for operating is easier and repeated instruction by library staff does not require several selected databases in CD-ROM are given below :

ERIC

Established by the US government, ERIC acquires, indexes and distributes the most important and comprehensive collection of education materials available today. The Search CD 450 Education Series consists of three valuable databases on five discs with in-depth information on the entire field of education.

ERIC's current files contain citations to education data compiled from 1982 to the present and consist of two separate files on one disc:

* Current Index to Journals in Education (CIJE) lists over 100000 citations and abstracts for articles in over 750 education-related journals.
* Resources in Education (RIE) contains more than 79000 annotated citations to technical and research reports, conference papers, government documents and other unique materials.

Both files allow the user to access information on thousands of subjects. ERIC users can easily locate information in the database using controlled vocabulary from the Thesaurus of ERIC Descriptions or free text terms.

ERIC-Retrospective Files provide comprehensive retrospective files for access to additional information on published and unpublished documents pertaining to education. The files are subjects of the ERIC databases.

Resources in Education consists of several discs and includes nearly 500000 citations to educational materials, including technical and research reports, conference papers. Government documents. Position papers, Historical materials, curriculum materials, Teacher guides, and theses and dissertations. Current Index to Journals in Education is on two discs that indexes over 750 education journals . Subjects covered are the same as the ERIC current files.

Education Library has been compiled from the OCLC Online Union Catalogue, the Education Library database lists over 450000 bibliographic records for materials pertaining to education. Bibliographic records in the Education Library database cover a wide range of sources, from pre-1900 records to more recent twentieth-century materials. Among the many resources cited are - books and journals, newspapers, audiovisual materials, recordings, videocassettes, archival materials, manuscripts, filmstrips, microforms and slides.

Users have a range of search options to choose from when looking for materials. In addition to author, subject, title, and key-word searching, records may be searched by publication type, geographic area, language variations in title, and more. This is a useful tool for a variety of reference activities, including collection development, bibliography compilation, author/title verification, and much more.

Search CD 450 Agriculture Series provides users with most recent information on a wide variety of resources on agriculture and related sciences. Disc one includes two current files, AGRICOLA and CRIS.

The AGRICOLA database is a compilation of materials collected by the National Agricultural Library and cooperating institutions. It consists of journal articles, and selected book chapters from over 5000 serials and books. A few of the thousands of subjects covered include : general agriculture, post control, veterinary medicine, aquaculture, chemistry, food science, agricultural engineering, agribusiness, forestry, pollution, law, economics, entromology, plant diseases, energy as related to agriculture, rural sociology, and the like.

The CRIS database is produced by the Cooperative Research Services of the US Department of Agriculture Cooperative Research Services. CRIS cites abstracts and progress reports for current research in agriculture and related sciences.

All relevant fields in the AGRICOLA database are indexed, allowing users to access records with a variety of search strategies. Abstracts, bibliographies, statistics, catalogues and other content types are identified as such in AGRICOLA records and can be used as search terms. AGRICOLA and CRIS provide with best resources for information on both completed and in-progress agricultural research. AGRICOLA has also its Retrospective Files.

Agriculture Library, an OCLC database contains, on one disc, over 300000 bibliographic records and management, field crops, forestry policy, animal breeds and breeding, wildlife management, soil conservation, horticulture, parks and public reservations, dairying and dairy products, rural sociology, and the like. Bibliographic records in the Agriculture Library database refer to books, journals, theses, microforms, film strips, videocassettes, recording, and more.

Search CD 450 Science and Technology Series provides with a vast collection of data covering a wide range of topics in science and technology. From the comprehensive science subsets of the Online Union Catalogue of OCLC to the two million titles of the National Technical Information Service (NTIS) database, this series gives access to records on academic, government, and private sources of scientific information. This series contains citations to information in a wide variety of media, including books, serials, videocassettes, sound recording, software, microforms, audiovideo materials, filmstrips, etc. All relevant fields in the databases are indexed so that users can access information with a variety of search strategies. In addition to author, title, subject and key-word searching, users can search by various classification numbers, title variations, and geographic area, among others. In addition, such content types as abstracts, government documents, surveys, handbooks, and more can be used as search parameters.

Search CD 450 Computer Library is an indispensable source of information on every aspect of computers. This CD lists over 300000 records that cover the subject from the earliest days computer development to the microchip revolution that made supercomputers possible. Government, academic and private industry sources are all utilised to provide with the most comprehensive body of information available on the computer industry.

Search CD 450 Environment Library is the unique database which provides with a reliable source of data on an increasingly important topic. This database contains over 400000 records that touch upon every facet of this complex and fascinating subject. Any kind of information on the effects of pollutants on the food chain, the extinction of animals and birds, depletion of the Ozone layer, or any of hundreds of other topics are available in this database.

Search CD 450 Energy Library database provides with information on all the energy resources like oil, nuclear, coal, solar, etc. that one cannot find anywhere else. From federal studies on the feasibility of solar poser to the future of nuclear energy consumption and development of new energy resources - all these are available in this database. The CD lists over 300000 records on hundreds of energy - related topics. It is the most complete resource of its kind.

BLDSC

The British Library Document Supply Centre (BLDSC) had the CD-ROM product known as Inside Information. Now the product is known as Inside Sciences and Inside Social Sciences and Humanities as separate CD-ROM products. These CD databases contain details of articles from the contents pages of more than 12000 of the most frequently requested journals held at the centre.

SILVERPLATTER CD-ROM PRODUCTS

MEDLINE on SilverPlatter is the entire MEDLINE database of the US National Library of Medicine from 1966 to present on compact disc. It contains bibliographic citations and abstracts of biomedical literature, and includes all foreign languages, all data elements, and fully indexed.

CANCER-CD contains references, abstracts and

commentaries of the world's literature in Cancer and related subjects from Elsevier Science Publishers, Year Book Medical Publishers, and the complete CANCERLIT file from the National Cancer Institute in conjunction with the US National Library of Medicine. SilverPlatter has merged duplicate citations into one record while preserving information that is unique to each Information Provider. Coverage is from 1985 to present.

CHEM-BANK is a collection on CD format of three major databanks of potentially hazardous chemicals : Registry of Toxic Effects of Chemical Substances (RTECS) from the US National Institute for Occupational Safty and Health; Oil and Hazardous Materials-Technical Assistance Data system (OHMTADS) from the US Environmental Protection Agency; and Chanical Hazard Response Information System (CHRIS) from the US Department of Transportation (Coast Guard).

OSH-ROM is a collection of occupational health and safety information. It contains three complete bibliographic databases : NIOSHTIC, database of the National Institute for Occupational Safety Health (USA), HSELINE, database of the International Safety Executive (UK), and CISDOC, database of the International Labour Organisation (UN). Collectively these databases contain over 300000 citations taken from over 500 journals and 100000 monographs and technical reports.

PsycLIT contains journal citations with abstracts in psychology and behavioural sciences from the PsycINFO department of the American Psychological Association. Coverage is from 1974 to present.

Sociofile is an index to and abstracts of the world's journals in sociology as complied by Sociological Abstracts. It contains abstracts of journal articles published in Sociological Abstracts since 1974 and the enhanced bibliographic citations for dissertations in sociology and related disciplines that have been added to the database since 1986.

LISA contains abstracts of the world's Literature in Library science, information science, and related disciplines as compiled by the Library Association Publishing Ltd. It covers the complete database from 1969.

POPLINE is a bibliographic database containing more than 150000 citations on population, family planning and related health care, law and policy issues. The database reaches as far back as 1886 and includes citations and abstracts to journal articles, monographs, technical reports, and unpublished works. POPLINE is maintained by the Population Information Programme at John Hopkins University, USA.

TOXLINE is a collection of toxicological information from the US National Library of medicine, containing references to published materials and research in progress in the areas of adverse drug reactions, air pollution, carcinogenesis via chemicals, drug toxicity, food contamination, occupational hazards, pesticides and herbicides, toxicological analysis, water treatment, and more.

UMI DATABASES ONDISC

The UMI CD-ROM products are ABI/INFORM, Dissertation Abstracts, Newspaper Abstracts, Periodical Abstracts and Resource /One. These are fully integrated and complementary resource for access to a broad range of sources, yet each database is also an independent reference, targeted to specific user needs. The basic record format is common to all UMI databases.

ABI/INFORM CD-ROM version provides bibliographic citations and 150-word abstracts for articles from more than 800 business and management periodicals. Dissertation Abstracts provides indexing to nearly one million doctoral dissertations and masters theses from almost 500 North American and 50 British universities. Two archival discs contain citations, in many cases, abstracts to some of the world's most valuable original research accepted for advanced degrees from 1861 to 1984. Current discs include citations and 350-word abstracts.

Newspaper abstracts indexes a number of reputed news papers of North America, with abstracts of about 25 words. Periodical Abstracts contains virtually cover-to-cover indexing of 300 current general-interest periodicals, beginning with January 1988 issues, with abstracts is about 25 words. The most frequently used titles are cited, and all Readers' Guide titles plus over a hundred more with periodical Abstracts, users can research current topics in consumer affairs, the arts, policies, science, and other subject areas of general concern. Resource/One, the information access tool, is ideal from small libraries. All UMI Ondisc databases are supported by full text services.

Faxon Informatics Pvt. Ltd, Bangalore represents the following CD-ROM database producers in India.

ADONIS BV, The Netherlands

Bowker Saur, UK

British Library Document Supply Centre, UK

Derwent Information Ltd., UK

Knight-Ridder Information Inc., USA

Meridian Data Inc., USA

OCLC Inc., USA

SilverPlatter Information Inc., USA

UMI Inc., USA

Faxon Informatics can collect any CD-ROM database to be supplied to the libraries and information centres. They offer CD-ROM networking systems and solutions as well as CD-ROM-based document management systems.

14

BIBLIOGRAPHIC UTILITIES

THE GENESIS

The role and functions of the library have changed greatly over the decades, and the pace of change has picked up rapidly with the increased use of information and communication technologies. The role of the library has also been expanded vastly. Individual library catalogues are no longer enough for searching the information and documents. Library collections have expanded beyond the printed word and these included materials in various media and different physical formats. The library users expect access to electronic resource bases and to the Internet. The more we expect from libraries, even more we expect from the the librarians.

In such situation the librarian's advantage is that he does not have to do all the library services by himself. There are many institutional, organisational and commercial databases available on some terms. Each of these database holders or vendors uses a sophisticated database management system which is the key to the services it can offer having common standard of file maintenance, search strategies, menu and/or command language and available output formats. If the same database is available from two or more vendors, there may be some differences in how it can be searched on displayed, but the differences may not be significant in searching by the user. In addition to his own library catalogue and resource bases he can avail of the facility of access to external databases.

There is a large number of vendors all over the world and there are certain incompatibilities among their services, libraries can use front-end or gateway system, an intermediate communications and interface link between a searcher on the one hand and a number of vendors on the other. A gateway provides such services as a specially created unified command language, single billing and service for trouble shooting. There are vendors who represent more than one or a number of resource database organisations.

Because of the point to point communication network between the user and the remote databases, the search is done online. In 1985, the first products of the CD-ROM bibliographic revolution were the databases on compact disk. The database management software provided on the disk was a variant of that used in online access databases remained proprietary and largely secret. Although the searching process is totally interactive, the files on a disk are a batch product and must be updated regularly with new updated cumulation. Several resource database organisations, offering both online and CD-ROM products of the same databases can provide services by switching from the CD-ROM product to the Database proprietor's ownership databases for online search while online search link is in operation for more current information than on the CD-ROM disk.

During early years of 1970's while online interactive computer system was introduced, the start-up cost of computer application in libraries including hardware, software, and staff training was very high and discouraging. The uncertainty as to the benefits of computer application, non-availability of appropriate application software, initial investment of a large sum, lack of adequate communication technology and psycho-sociological factors were not very encouraging for computer application in individual libraries. The desktop micro computers did not have the capacity for handling full bibliographic records in the quantities required. Main frame computers were too expensive even for larger libraries.

The crucial problem was library application software that had to be written from search and adapted from programmes not originally intended for bibliographic database and access to that. Those who wanted to create and develop application software found that competent programmers were only few and that software creation and development was a major and never-ending process as well as very expensive which was beyond the capability of any individual library. Particularly in the area of cataloguing the expenditure was colosal because all the libraries had to catalogue the same book in the repetitive manner and the expenditure was unproductive. With computer application having online facilities the cataloguing cost could have been shared and thus, a large sum of money could be saved by all the libraries in a co-operative library system through shared cataloguing. In their early stages a number of libraries in a region made a group for shared and cooperative cataloguing by working together to share the cost of cataloguing as well as the exorbitant cost of development of appropriate application software.

Such groups of libraries working together to share the cost of both cataloguing and automation by sharing the expenditure towards development of appropriate library application software and its consecutive versions, networking software and protocols, creation of bibliographic databases with exchange formats, were known at the early stage as "consortium". Such consortiums were later known as networks, particularly bibliographic and information networks. Each of these consortiums or networks remained very different form one another in what they required of, and what they did for, their members. This happened because each network had its own softwares for bibliographic record and exchange, own network protocols, own exchange format, and own administrative and operational model.

At the early phase the consortiums or cooperative networks were planned, designed and operational depending on the network membership of particular region. The network structures were based on usually the following types.

* Libraries of similar types like Research Libraries Group (RLG).
* Libraries of different kinds in a particular geographical area or region, for example. NELINET, the New England Library Network.
* Libraries which required particular function or service for hardware and software consultancy.

The primary objective of most early networks was the creation and maintenance of computerised union catalogue basically for the following purposes.

1. To support inter library loan services, and
2. Shared cataloguing on cooperative basis in some sort of standardised format mostly to share the exorbitant and repetitive cataloguing costs and other management expenses.

To achieve the primary objective all the libraries got the union catalogue, larger database and a database management system required for the member libraries. The system was known as cataloguing support system. It was the beginning of the standardised catalogue format for uniformity of output format and standardised exchange format within the network system. This system eradicated the necessary and inherently evil problem of cataloguing backlogs of the member libraries.

THE TERM

The term 'Bibliographic Utilities' refers to a group of larger bibliographic database organisation interconnected by bibliographic network that maintain databases of cataloguing records and offer bibliographic services related to the sharing of these records to subscribing libraries. The major bibliographic utilities offer software for local record creation, downloading and editing, and authority control services. The central database of bibliographic utilities organisation is the centralised holding information of all the member libraries that have added the specific items to their collection. Accordingly, bibliographic utilities offer services that facilitate interlibrary loan requests and general information searching.

Consortia for shared cataloguing were at first regionally based around North America during the 1970's. Four of these grew well beyond their original scope and are now commonly called the 'bibliographic utilities' to distinguish them from other types of cooperative interlibrary organisations. A cooperative database is also necessarily a union catalogue. researchable as units regardless of how its file structure distinguishes the records of each individual member library. Usually the records of individual Libraries are kept in a separate file; another permits only one record per item but it contains information on which libraries have that item.

The bibliographic utilities are technically very similar to the database vendors available all over the world, each with its own database software, the key to its potential services. Practically, the contents of the vendors, databases differ from the bibliographic utilities databases. Both the groups have become more and more similar to each other in the services they offer, but their differing histories, originating factors, administrative structure, financial control give each a different niche to fill.

The commercial database vendors maintains a huge database and update it making exorbitantly high expenditure for hardware, software, product and service development, networking cost, staff for sales and management, publicity, user-training, etc. All these are justified by the services they offer and the profits they get as commercial organisations. But in case of bibliographic utilities the dimension is different. Bibliographic utilities survive on their own members/users who create the database, use it, and share the cost. Another important difference is that commercial database vendors are independently owned and operated. But bibliographic utilities are almost member owned and usually non-profit organisation. The primary objectives are cooperation, cost sharing, shared cataloguing, union catalogue facility, resource sharing among the members. It no longer member-owned, still to a considerable degree influenced by member demands, which are expressed through active users' groups.

Following are the four bibliographic utilities organisations:

Online Computer Library Centre (OCLC)

Research Libraries Information Network (RLIN)

Western Library Network (WLN)

University of Toronto Library Automation Systems (UTLAS)

OCLC

Online computer Library Centre (OCLC), formerly known as Ohio College Library Centre was founded in 1967 by University Presidents to share library resources and reduce Library costs. OCLC introduced online cataloguing system as early as 1971 for libraries and now it is used by libraries around the world. The inter Library loan service was introduced in 1979 and since then has been used for 107 million loans among 6,600 libraries around the world.

OCLC is a nonprofit membership organisation serving more than 40,000 Libraries in 76 countries around the world. The public purpose is to further access to the world's information and to reduce library costs by offering services for libraries and their users. OCLC membership is a unique cooperative venture giving global access to all the services and database including World Cat. OCLC membership comprises the world's largest Library consortium. OCLC is governed by its members. OCLC's governance structure consist of General Members, the Users Council, and the Board of Trusters.

At the centre of OCLC services is the World Cat services, which is the most consulted database in education and research.

The database holds over 46 million cataloguing records created by libraries around the world, with a new record added every 15 seconds. The database spans over 4,000 years of recorded knowledge with 400 languages represented. OCLC member libraries contribute to World Cat.

OCLC libraries also offer the OCLC First Search service, which delivers online reference information through a rich collection of databases with links to online full text, electronic journals, web resources, library holdings, interlibrary loan and document delivery. It provides information on Electronic collections Online service, Site Search software, and Contents Alert service.

The OCLC MARC Record Service (MARS) is a complete, comprehensive database preparation and authority control service that provides high-quality, accurate, standardised bibliographic and authority data functions for libraries and research institutions. This service provides authority control, customised record processing, bibliographic record updating, smart barcode number generation, manual review, ongoing authority updating and notification services, new bibliographic record processing and TOC MARC Enrichment. MARS accommodates the needs of every type of library, from large research institutions to smaller public and research libraries.

Office of Research of OCLC continues to expand knowledge that advances the goal of its commitment to improving access to the world's information resources, whatever their form, subject, substance, language, or location. Through the integrated employment of the computer, library, and information sciences in research activities such as, performing experiments, building prototypes, advancing standards, undertaking studies, and participating in research collaborations, the Office of Research makes continuing improvement and progress.

The OCLC office of Research is a leading centre devoted exclusively to the challenges facing libraries in a rapidly changing information technology environment. Since its origin in 1978, the office has investigated trends in technology and library practice to identify technical advances that will enhance the value of library services and improve the productivity of librarians and library users. Among the areas of study are natural language processing, information retrieval, internet metadata standards, knowledge management, interface design, and classification theory and practice. In all the areas of knowledge-based content integration and technological advances for datastorage and transfer, OCLS has comprehensive control over knowledge management both for the librarians as well as end-users.

The future programmes of OCLC are to transform World Cat from a bibliographic database and online union catalogue to a globally networked information resource of text, graphics, sound and motion. This enhanced version of World Cat will include a shared knowledge base supported by a set of integrated, Web-based tools and services that facilitate contribution, discovery, exchange, delivery, and preservation of knowledge objects and shared expertise of participating institutions.

The present OCLC library cooperative of more than 40,000 institutions in 76 countries will be truly global, digital community. This will involve developing new Web-based services, implementing a new technological platform, and, most important, reaffirming a commitment to library cooperation. Libraries have used OCLC shared cataloguing to create World Cat, which today is the world's foremost bibliographic database. OCLC will extend this cooperative framework to include new participants, new types of metadata, and new automated tools to capture, organise and deliver metadata. In addition to libraries, OCLC will seek the input of metadata from museums, archives, professional societies, publishers and others, including authors. Each of these providers will use and share metadata that includes descriptions, holdings, reviews and previews as well as links to content.

OCLC is preparing Archiving and Content Management system, which will lead to preservation, digitisation and archiving services to help libraries increase access to their unique collections as well as pass them on the future generations. OCLC will establish a digital repository for electronic materials from library collections, government agencies and other sources of electronic content. Based on cooperation, this repository will accommodate changes in technologies and formats and provide access to electronic content using industry standards, both now and in the future.

Through new and enhanced services from OCLC, libraries will become a ubiquitous presence on the Web, viewed as a preferred and authoritative source of information. Libraries will customise their users' interface to World Cat, with links to reviews, full text, images, and other files in addition to bibliographic information. These services will help build the library brand on the Web. End-users will move easily between the library and the Web. OCLC will also facilitate establishing an expert library cooperative in which libraries pool expertise and resources to provide around-the-clock, around-the-world reference support for people looking for information on the Web. New or enhanced OCLC services will help libraries integrate selection, circulation, interlibrary loan and direct-buy options in order to provide information to people when and where they need it in a form they want. End-users will have access to the collections of many libraries as well as easy order and delivery options via the Web.

RLIN

The Research Libraries Group (RLG) was established in 1974 by Harvard, Yale, Columbia universities and the New York Public Library. RLG acquired the BALLOTS bibliographic data system of Stanford University and started its own bibliographic utilities known as the Research Libraries Information Network (RLIN) in 1978.

The prime reason for the establishment of the Research Libraries Information Network (RLIN) was the need of researchers for specialised research materials which could not be provided by a general database, even as large as that of OCLC. The mission-oriented, project-oriented and specialised needs of researchers could not be served by research institution alone. It was not also possible to have access to the vast, complicated and multilingual research collections without any large specialised database.

With only 159 resource sharing members, RLIN database has a record count at some 63 million, and a database focused on scholarly materials. But because RLIN allows for multiple item entries and higher quality cataloguing, this database is enriched by more than 170 million catalogue records. RLIN supports a more extensive list of non-Roman scripts, and holds records in over 365 languages (Roman and non-Roman scripts). Any research institution in the world can apply for membership and RLIN offers two rates for libraries with more and less than 5000 users. But the standard for acceptance and the financial costs of membership keep both RLG members and their records in RLIN somewhat contained.

The Research Libraries Information Network (RLIN) is now an internationally available bibliographic information system used with RLG's Library resources. For many years, research libraries, archival repositories, and special Libraries have used RLIN for cataloguing and authority work, archives and manuscript processing, and interlibrary loan.

For RLIN's cataloguing , archival control, and interlibrary loan functions RLIN Terminal for Windows software and an internet connection are needed. This software and connection also support searching in Arabic, Chinese, Cyrillic, Hibrew, Japanese, and Korean.

The resources of Research Library Group (RLG) are a set of online catalogues that offer reference libraries, archivists, catalogues, bibliographers, scholars and other researchers million of records describing materials created around the world. RLG

Union catalogue is a treasure house database of bibliographic descriptions. As a resource pool of specialised subject areas it grows daily through contribution from a range of institutions and cooperative cataloguing projects.

The RLG's union catalogue database structure supports a complete record of each item catalogued. These records include institutional holdings, notes on contents, notable illustrations, author annotations, the availability of microform service copies, as well as the existence of an electronic version of the materials.

The RLG union catalogue comprises eight bibliographic files. RLG's EUREKA search system presents them as one file, as well as the RLIN technical processing interface presents them separately.

Through a Z 39.50 connection to RLG's server, they can be searched as one or as eight as follows;

* Archival and Mixed Collections: Descriptions of Literary and historical documents, public records, and other primary source materials, in various formats, these records analyse collections, parts of collections, and single items by personal name, organisation, subject, and format; also included in Archival resources.
* Books: records for printed items catalogued individually, including microform reproductions.
* Maps: records for printed and manuscript maps and globes.
* Computer Files: records for machine-readable data files, including literary text's statistical files, and computer programmes.
* Recordings: record for musical and nonmusical sound or historical recordings, including speeches, oral histories, and interviews.
* Scores: records for manuscript and printed music.
* Serials: records for items with a recovering pattern of publication (newspaper, journals).

* Visual Materials: records for photographs, motion pictures, and graphics, including drawings, blue prints, and posters.

In addition to the above database search, RLG database contains three unique specific areas for specific search access.

ENGLISH SHORT TITLE CATALOGUE (ESTC)

The English Short Title Catalogue is an invaluable research tool for scholars interested in British based literature and culture. ESTC describes publications printed in Great Britain or its colonies from 1473 to 1800, as well as materials printed in English anywhere in the world during that period. The British Library and the North American Centre for ESTC continue to add and update records as libraries report their holdings. The ESTC online database can be searched not only be personal name and author, but by publisher and by place or date of publication.

HAND PRESS BOOK DATABASE

The Hand Press Book Database is a unique and growing catalogue of European printing from the 15th century to the 1830's. It is specially valuable for research in intellectual history, as well as in the history of printing and the history of the book. The Hand Press Book Database comprises records from the members of CERL, the Consortium of European Research Libraries.

SCIPIO: ART AND RARE BOOK SALES CATALOGUE

SCIPIO is the only existing online union catalogue of auction catalogues. These records describe art and rare book auction sales catalogues from all major North American and European auction houses as well as important private sales dating from the late 16th century to currently scheduled auctions that have not yet been held. Records contain information on dates and places of sale, catalogue title, the auction house, sellers, institutional holdings, and other information.

Bibliographic search is done by ZEPHYR, which provides a Z39.50 server for RLG's databases that can be accessed by any

Z39.50 client. Zephy lets users of other online systems search RLIN bibliographic, the ESTC English Short Title Catalogue, and CitaDel files using the same commands they use to search their own local catalogues or bibliographic utilities, and to display information from these files. Configuration information for Zephyr can be found on the Web.

WLN

Washington Library Network (WLN) was first operated by Washington State Library with its jurisdiction within the state. It was relatively a small library network. But the software development for its regional database which was developed since the late 1960's made the WLN software a very important one. The computerised bibliographic database was established in 1972 with the cooperation of the Washington Libraries. The online system was introduced in 1975.

More than 80 larger Libraries or library systems in the six states became online participants in the Washington Library Network. It included various types of libraries, state, academic, public, *etc*. As the area of operation was extended beyond Washington state to six adjacent states, it was renamed as Western Library Network keeping the same acronym, WLN.

WLN provides a broad range of innovative, high quality technical and database services to public libraries, university, college, corporate, legal, medical, and other libraries throughout North America and abroad. WLN's union catalogue contains over 15 million bibliographic records and over 30 million local library holdings.

With effect from Ist January, 1999, WLN, a non profit corporation serving over 600 libraries in The pacific Northwest region of the USA and Canada, merged with OCLC, having its Headquarters in Lacey, Washington. OCLC and WLN believe the synergy created by this merger will allow the organisation to more effectively meet a wide range of information needs for libraries and the end-users. Working together, OCLC and WLN eliminate duplicate services, introduce new and better products at lower costs for member libraries.

The WLN office has been renamed the OCLC/WLN Pacific Northwest Service Centre. It is providing support and training to WLN users in Alaska, Idaho, Montana, Oregon, Washington and British Columbia. The OCLC/WLN Pacific Northwest Service Centre is providing support and training to former WLN users.

The President and Chief Executive Office of OCLC, Jay Jordan made the statement welcoming the merger that "We believe this merger will benefit member libraries of both organizations. WLN Libraries will gain OCLC's digital, global community for cataloging, resource sharing and reference services, and OCLC member libraries will benefit from the inclusion of libraries in the Pacific Northwest tin the OCLC network OCLC brings strong financial, technical, marketing and networking resources to WLN's expertise in authority control and collection analysis. Working together, WLN and OCLC will eliminate duplicate services, introduce new and better products, and lower costs for member libraries".

The three bibliographic utilities organisations, OCLC, RLIN and WLN were established as nonprofit organisation supported and governed by the member libraries. There were no commercial considerations, whether for the use of databases or for technological innovations in bibliographic services.

UTLAS

The University of Toronto Library Automation systems (UTLAS) in Canada was a regional library network created on commercial basis. The UTLAS network was diverse in the types of libraries–academic, public government, special, etc. It had no relationship with the University of Toronto, Canada. It made an integrated approach to library automation based on the distributed processing network. During early 1980's the users of UTLAS had access to a database of over 6 million records growing at the rate of over 2.5 million records per year. The database included source files from the Library of Congress. The National Library of Canada, the Bibliotheque Nationale du Quebec, and the records of the National Library of Medicine. Bibliographic records were available for monographs, serials, audiovisual materials, music, maps manuscripts. UTLAS changed its name to Utlas International.

In addition to the national source files, there are users-created files. The Catalogue Support System of UTLAS (CATSS) supported both external databases and member-created databases. It is the largest bibliographic utility of predominantly Canadian Library membership. At a later phase ISM Library Information Services bought the service/database, and now Auto-Graphics, Inc., a California-based company own the product through its Toronto subsidiary, A-R Canada, Ltd.

A-G Canada has more than 25 million unique item records in its bibliographic database. A-G Canada offers access to its bibliographic and authority files through its own web browser software, Impact/MARC it. Like RLIN, the A-G Canada databases accept duplicate item records from different member libraries, but whereas RLIN clusters the records to facilitate searching, A-G Canada stores duplicate records in separate files. A-G Canada claims to be the second largest bibliographic utility in North America, but because it is a for-profit organisation, with a full line of ILS products and utility services.

The CATSS database is a source of bibliographic and authority data for over 600 institutions, members of consortia, and government agencies, representing over 2500 Libraries World Wide. The database contains more than 57 million libraries and authority records. The exponential growth of the Internet and the World Wide Web provide the content-rich access to information. Over one million people use this database per day. User-friendly interfaces with powerful search capabilities put global resources at the fingertips of end-users. It also provides access to third-party subscription databases and supplementary database resources.

15

GATEWAY TO KNOWLEDGE

Application of new technologies in library services, increasing multidisciplinary research, exponential growth in quantity and variety of documents and information needed for research, accelerating costs and finite resources in libraries and the complexities of navigating ever-expanding system of research sources have compelled the research libraries to prepare strategic plans for most effective user services. The changing role of research libraries in supporting research and learning in the information age has to be reviewed with new plans and programmes. Because of the interdisciplinary studies and access to specific information for specific purpose the ways of knowing must be transformed to use electronic information effectively in a variety of formats and on networks.

The library should not replace the print collection in hard copies. These are the documentary resources of the past building the research collection. The purpose of the gateway to knowledge is to provide the services that will enable the users at all levels to locate and use these resources effectively The gateway is the point of access and a source of services and support needed by the users of various categories to locate and use the information the users need in the form in which they need it. The idea of gateway is to utilise the electronic information technology.

Billy E. Frye observes (1997) "the metaphor of the library as the gateway to knowledge is very apt because it emphasizes one of the traditional functions of the library - access to information. In the context of electronic technologies, the gateway concept causes us to suspend our usual notions of boundaries, whether library walls or book covers. More than that, it offers the portent - indeed, in considerable degree the actuality - that the melding of information with the powers of electronic technologies will bring about basic changes in he ways we teach and learn, the sorts of research questions we ask, and the ways we synthesize knowledge." It has become imperative to look beyond the present situation to new approaches of access to information.

Gateway to knowledge is an approach to inevitable change of the old ideas of using the library and thinking the new ideas of library use. Technology provides the tools for increasing access to and sharing information. But technology, in itself, will not yield any result unless the institutions and the people concerned take it by heart as an essential tool for achieving best result. It is also essential to create collaborative organisational structures that would enable institutions and their libraries to share resources of their own and beyond.

The reality of library situation and the paradox of utilising electronic technology in the libraries have been very significantly given in the observation of James Govan, former librarian of the University of North Carolina. He states "The different and intriguing quality of this concept is that it acknowledges the fundamental shift in learning and investigation that information technology has introduced. This [digital] technology has the potential of liberating the academic library to become the proactive instrument in education and scholarship that it has struggled to become with printed tools. But so far no one has focused on the issues involved, the approaches to be used, or the structural changes required. No one has examined, in a formal setting, the kinds and organization of personnel; combining systems and library skills, to lead students and researchers to exploit this dual worlds of information. No one has investigated systematically the interaction of printed and electronic collections or identified the gaps in the infrastructure that prevent these collections from becoming an organic, unified tool. No one has delineated the kinds of instruction necessary to equip apprentice investigators to approach, engage, and advance this new information structure. Partial and uncoordinated efforts have been made .... but no effort that directly addresses [these] issues."

The electronic information and communication technologies are there for application in libraries and these are becoming less expensive and more powerful. Libraries can avail of the full power of these facilities for library management, resource sharing and remote access beyond geographical barriers, cooperative collection development and access to global databases. The technologies are near at hand, but the deficiencies are in the libraries and their management in planning, organisation, motivation, attitude, achieving goals and commitment to transform the enormous power of digital technology in library environment for the benefit of the users and society at large. This is the most unfortunate situation in libraries. The concept of gateway to knowledge envisages the planned and effective application of digital technology in libraries for the benefit of the users needing information and acquiring knowledge.

GATEWAY : THE PROCESS

The term, gateway is a metaphor for access to the totality of human knowledge and evokes the image of crossing the threshold to enter into the ever-expanding world of information and knowledge. The library, with its well-articulated resources as well as digital information and knowledge sources, is the means to provide optimum services to users and learners. The gateway emphasises both electronically stored databases as well as traditional print databases in hardcopy format. Gateway is considered as a portal to an ever-expanding universe of knowledge available in networked information system and accessible from virtually any location.

The gateway to knowledge can function properly in a decentralised and distributed library system. In case of academic libraries it may be campus libraries, subject libraries, faculty libraries, and the like. All the libraries must be interconnected by local library network and all these units must have access to internet and other international networks. The concept of gateway has four basic elements. These are :

1. Gateway to knowledge must have electronic access to ever-expanding knowledge resource sin all formats that are essential for research.
2. Gateway consists of various digital information and document supply services which will support access to these resources and will make the study and research most effective and comprehensive.
3. Gateway in each unit should have flexible physical space and adequate infrastructural facilities that support individual learning, group study, demonstration facilities as well as expansion facilities in response to future changes in technology and needs of the users.
4. Gateway interconnected in a large institution must work as a single organisation with coordinated gateway functions and services throughout the individual gateways.

The gateway is the digital means to access to information and knowledge sources that are needed, whatever may be the format, genre, or location. Information and communication technologies are creating suitable library environment. The users get the library resources. In addition to that the uses can get access to the internet-based e-mail for resources in remote locations, local area network or metropolitan area network for domestic resources. Library users can take help from electronic bulletin boards, computer conferences, and listserves for scholarly communication. They can browse electronically for materials from other libraries, as well as can search and retrieve the texts of journal articles, and other information sources. Traditional libraries separate library resources according to their formats-books and journals, print and non-print, cartographic and graphic, audio an audiovisual. The digital technology bring together all the formats in electronic media, and these are interactive.

The gateway provide services that enable the users and researchers, in particular, to locate and to get access to resources in the mot effective way. Gateway increases library support for study and learning to become self-sufficient in locating and using the resources made tailored to their needs and requirements. The gateway coordinates different library services and functions in a consistent and predictable manner. The goal is to make use of various systems and methods for efficient and effective library service.

The gateway is a place for individual and group study and a centre for interactive learning using digital resources and networks. The concept of gateway within a library having a dedicated and flexible space supports the concept of traditional library, but gateway space coordinates all the digital information services and digital learning resources. So, it is a combination of traditional library concept with computer and communication technologies. As the electronic information system is a pervasive feature of learning, the users can prepare themselves to use the system throughout their lines as an essential element of their education. This system is very effective both for group study and individual learning. The gateway facilities can support a growing number of electronic multimedia databases including hypertexts and hypermedia. This can support integrated programmes into particular subject area or particular project.

The gateway itself is the organisation within an institution or the library by coordinating all the distributed units located at different places, and by providing all the information sources and knowledge resources to all the distributed units. The coordination of services and programmes is identified with the gateway. The goals of the gateway are convenience, efficiency, timeliness and unification of services and programmes. The gateway services reduce duplication, encourage subject-based and programme-based research facilities as well a clearing support. The gateway is responsive to the changing informational needs of the users. The gateway sets a process that aims for service flexibility, premium services to users, access to global information at any point or unit and maintenance of library system devoted to excellence in library service.

GATEWAY : THE CONCEPT

The gateway library for knowledge management will be an integral part of the information and database management in the global network environment that is far more complex that the 1990s. If such environment is properly created in a library system, the gateway library will be a qualitative improvement over the existing situation of access to information and organisation of knowledge. The gateway library will provide identifying, linking and management of information leading to knowledge management that are not possible with the largest databases all over the world and most efficient global networking, because knowledge is very much a personal attainment of the individual and the specificity and gradation of attainment vary individual to individual.

The concept of the gateway library can be transformed into operational system by rethinking of existing library and information systems that are very much general in nature giving emphasis on the needs and requirement of the people at large. The specificity of individual and personal needs and requirement at various stages are not given that much importance. For these reasons, distinctions should be drawn between information and tools for managing it, between access to databases and right search engines for personal needs as well as between users service in general in a library and integrated and multifaceted personal search having proper access to information and back up documents in any format.

Electronic technologies are delivering new capabilities with multimedia and hypertext access for multisensory transmission of knowledge. The gateway library can have the critical element of success on the assumption that how it organise information and integrate various media and sources of information for personal need at a particular point of time. The distributed system of gateway library will electronically connect users into a world wide information resource from a particular point to every individual according to his need and suitability of information. Even the resource-poor libraries having the information infrastructure can have access to the best libraries of the world as well as largest global databases. It can encourage interlibrary loan services, getting electronic copies of documents for researchers as well as it can integrate information of local area libraries, university departments, research institution, R & D organisations, archives, personal libraries, individual scholars or any source for which no bibliographic control is available.

The concept of gateway library is not applicable to small and medium size library working within a building. It is meant for multi-campus library or a single campus with many departmental or subject libraries having separate buildings for specified user groups for various programmes. The concept of gateway library is best suited for distributed library and information resources on specialised subject areas having multidisciplinary user needs. There will be no centralised database creation, single resource centre under one roof, no single form of computing service or no monopolistic provider of most services. Providing services will be distributed throughout the distributed units of the library, whether multi-campus or single campus. Each unit library will grow according to its requirements, client groups, service specialisation, disciplines. These will be integratedly correlated by networking for coordinated and integrated service to all the users of the institution.

The gateway library will not be in itself a collection of resources. It may hold few resources but will provide access to books, journals, cartographic and graphic materials, audiovisual, multimedia, CD-ROM and global database resources. It will be built by the librarians at their own unit through training and continuing education for updated specialised expertise.

Gateway Libraries are not just collection of library materials and information sources. What is required is the creation of effective gateways to knowledge. The idea is organising the collection and information resources for enhancing the learning levels of any individual in the areas he needs. This is not the task of technologists, computer experts or network specialists. They can create the infrastructure, technologically efficient, to create and transfer data. But they cannot create the knowledge, the intellectual attainment of individuals. The librarians know the individual needs of an user at a particular point of time and can guide the users to the specific document of information source for the personalised requirements to attain the knowledge. Technology is the means, not the end. The end is providing the knowledge resource to individual users seeking knowledge.

GATEWAY : THE PROVIDER

The gateway library mainly relates to the research library, where scholars are provided with the recorded knowledge of human society. The traditional paradigm for achieving this is to get access to all printed and nonprinted recorded knowledge in various formats and containers. Scholars and librarians have attempted to organise and provide access to such records for thousands of years by holding the documents in libraries and by preparing the records of such documents in the forms of indexes, catalogues, bibliographies, and the like.

Computer application in the libraries as well as the new electronic technologies have facilitated the work of preparation for the records of the documents. In addition to that information sources have been created, organised and have become accessible both in quantity and in classified order. Such facilities have widened the availability of enormous quantum of information organised in systematic order. Thus, the information of the documents is at the finger tips. The latest technologies have made it possible easy access to information sources, the documents themselves are available in electronic format. The scholarly information resources as well as the original documents created by the authors are available in the library from any part of the world. This has created the new paradigm in the research and academic libraries in particular.

The new paradigm consists of new genres of information and each genre requires specialised expertise to select items of information. These include application software, network protocols, search strategies, search engines, bibliographic files, identification of databases, correlative searches, full-text documents, hypertexts, multimedia, and the like. All these services are available in libraries, and gateway libraries can best utilise these services. The electronic library also can have access to the resources of Internet. Now all these services are user-friendly.

The scholars sitting at individual gateway or workstation can have access to information, databases and the full-text literature regardless of their locations of resource. The information resources are varied, easily accessible, usable for specific purpose and comparable as required. The electronic workstation performs the search functions well and effective and telecommunication technology can efficiently support the transfer of information. For the rest, the traditional library documents continue to be most significant medium.

The librarians of gateway library know what is available on the specific needs of the scholar and can connect easily to any resource base. The front door of the electronic library is the gateway which will provide the catalogues of resources, and will connect the scholar to the resource bases worldwide. The gateway provides a single, convenient and specific entry point to a carefully selected resource base of information available in multiple formats. The Uniform Resource Locater (URL) is a very helpful tool for searching.

The research and higher academic libraries are the primary resource base for the scholars with their large, specialised and scholarly collections. The research libraries and academic libraries cannot contain all scholarly publications, but the gateway library holds tools that enable the scholars to identify, access and select specific information from the universe of all possible information. The gateway library presupposes a partnership between scholars and librarians to preserve the essential volumes of the scholarly community.

No research library or academic library can be more than a microcosm of the corpus of human knowledge in any specific field. The ever-expanding document resource and specialisation of knowledge as well as multidisciplinary research make the access to resource a very complex job. Particularly the electronic databases create the problems of finding the right information, getting the right source, determining the quality and authenticity of resource base and access to knowledge source.

Piter Lyman observes (1997) that gateway library with its collections and technological infrastructure will provide the following services:

"*Access to information and knowledge will be provided in the format appropriate to its content*. The question is no longer whether to purchase information but how to select the format in which the information is most useful. Census data was historically printed but is virtually useless in print format today; researchers need to use it collected in a form that can be subjected to computerized statistical analysis. Other examples are more ambiguous and require a decision about how information is going to be used : should art history images be collected as color prints, as slides, or as digital images that can be distributed on the network and analyzed by computer ?

Users will learn how to select the information they need to conduct research. Digital information resources require technical skill to access and to use. The gateway library must acquire appropriate technologies and be prepared to teach scholars and students how to use them.

Information will be provided in a form customized to meet the reader's needs. Scholars and students will need to make copies of digital information in the format in which it will be most useful. This will require selecting the right information, having the right to include it in one's own works (although copyright policy will regulate this in new ways on the network), and printing, e-mailing it, or copying it by diskette.

The basic reason for creating gateway library is that no library collection can be complete and that researchers and scholars must have access to information from anywhere in the world. The gateway library is just an access point to the information resources and knowledge bases available globally. The gateway library must train users to make their own judgement to select, evaluate and use information and knowledge base in the formats they need. The gateway library is the right place for individual users for personal knowledge, and at the same time it should be designed for collaborative research and group learning.

GATEWAY : THE MISSION

Gateway library is not a different kind of library or a new kind of library. Gateway library or gateway is a branch or branches of a large research or academic library. In other words, gateway is the focal point for research services integratedly organised for scholars and learners of high academic standard. A large-sized research and academic library can create many gateways for highly specialised services for specific subject areas or interdisciplinary and multidisciplinary subject areas. The mission of gateway is not the centralised users services but is created for distributed specialised services at many points or branches. The idea of gateway is to offer document and information services to specialised user groups for enhanced learning and acquiring further knowledge.

The attributes of the gateway, as different from existing

library and information services, are identified in three areas noted below.

1. The gateway is a teaching library to help specialised user groups at different academic levels learn how to identify the information they need from the ever-growing mass of information and cultural evidences in electronic and other forms.
2. The gateway is a centre for learning how to assess and evaluate information for turning it into knowledge. As an access centre for learning, the gateway encourages and invites discussion and interactions among learners and researchers in small groups as a part of ongoing process of discovering new knowledge base.
3. Gateway must not be a tool for only access to information. The librarians must have the role of becoming editors and selectors for filtering information to help learners select the specifically required information they need from the plethora of information available all over the world.

The prime function of the gateway is teaching to the users at various levels. The learners and faculty come to library for assistance to enter into the multi-faceted world of information and databases. The electronic information resources seem to generate more demand for instructional support. The librarians are to see the kind of teaching and instruction as central to the mission of gateway. The library must take leading role in teaching. It is a fact that electronic information significantly changes the learners perceptions and users of information. The gateway library should supplement traditional library reading and study spaces with flexible areas for interaction among learners and researchers in the electronic library environment.

The principal focus of librarians is the access to information. The principal problem of the users, however, is too much information. Information is expanding faster than any one can predict. The sheer volume of information threatens to over whelm whatever might be useful. The problem for the librarians is to create the tools that will enable users to identify and locate the information they need and deliver it in the format they require.

There is being addition to each area of knowledge as well as knowledge is changing. The individual researcher is unlikely to have an overview of the entire knowledge area. The gateway librarians will have to provide the overview by mapping the changing world of information and navigational tools that will enable a researcher to identify, evaluate and collocate information for a particular purpose. The knowledge base must be deepened by librarians by filtering information for the researchers. Gateway needs to develop expert systems that incorporate the changing nature of inquiry for the related sources of information.

The gateway is responsive to information technology and to the influence of digital information on teaching and learning. The exponential growth in the quantity and variety of information compete the librarians to become increasingly specialised. They must be specialised to manage the enormous volume of sources needed for research, changing nature of inquiry, and continued development of information technology. They must have specialised knowledge on the environment, comparative literary and historical studies that cut across disciplines. For this reason, they require a greater depth of knowledge about sources and how they are used in research and learning. The gateway library that emphasises teaching, learning, research and specialised search strategies and search tools require a radically different structural organisation.

The gateway library should be structured as a part of the international research community. The future of successful research will require cooperative arrangements for preserving the varied evidentiary sources and records. Gateway libraries should be prepared to face the situation ahead.

BIBLIOGRAPHY

1. Anglo - American Cataloguing Rules, British Text, 1967
2. Angle - American Cataloguing Rules, 2nd ed, London, LA, 1978
3. Bakewell, K.G.B. : A Manual of Cataloguing Practice, Oxford, 1972
4. Chakrabarti, B. Library Classification theory, Calcutta World Press, 1994
5. Chan, Lois Mai and Mitchell, Joan S. : Dewey Decimal Classification Edition 21 and international perspectives, Forest Press, 1996
6. Cutter, C.A. : Rules for a dictionary catalogue. 4th ed., 1904
7. Dhyani, P : 'Colon Classification - Edition 7 - An appraisal.' *International Classification* 1988, 15 (1), 13-16
8. Downing, M.H. and Downing, D.H. : Introduction to Cataloguing and Classification. 6th ed. MeFarland and Co. 1992
9. Horner, John : Cataloguing. London, AAl, 1970
10. Hunter, Eric. J. : Computerised Cataloguing. London, Clive Bingley, 1983
11. Hunter, Eric. J and Bakewell, K.G.B. : Cataloguing, London, Clive Bingley, 1971
12. Metarazzo, James M and Connolly, Suzanne D. Ed. : Knowledge and special libraries. Butterworth - Heinemann, 1999
13. Quigg, Patrick : Theory of Cataloguing. London, Clive Binglay, 1971

14. Ranganathan, S.R. : Prolegomena to library classification. 2rd ed Bombay, Asia Publishing house, 1967

15. Rowley, Jennifer F : Organizing Knowledge : an introduction to information retrieval. Ashgate, 1992

16. Shera, J.H. and Egar, M.E. : The Classified Catalog. Chicago, 1956

17. Svenonius. E. : 'Unanswered questions in the design of controlled vocabularies.' JASIS 1986, 37, 330 - 40

18. Tait, James A : Authors and Titles. London, Clive Bingley, 1969

19. Tait, James A and Anderson, Douglas : Descriptive Cataloguing, London, Clive Bingley, 1971

INDEX

D

E

F

G

H

I

J

K

L